Anabaptism
Revisited

Anabaptism
Revisited

Essays on
Anabaptist/Mennonite studies
in honor of C. J. Dyck

Walter Klaassen, Editor

HERALD PRESS
Scottdale, Pennsylvania
Waterloo, Ontario

Library of Congress Cataloging-in-Publication Data
Anabaptism revisited : essays on Anabaptist/Mennonite studies in honor
   of C. J. Dyck / Walter Klaassen, editor.
      p. cm.
   Includes bibliographical references.
   ISBN 0-8361-3577-6 (alk. paper)
   1. Anabaptists. 2. Mennonites. I. Dyck, Cornelius J.
II. Klaassen, Walter, 1926-
BX4931.2.A49   1992   91-29009
284'.3—dc20   CIP

The paper used in this publication is recycled and meets the minimum
requirements of American National Standard for Information
Sciences—Permanence Paper for Printed Library Materials, ANSI Z39.48-1984.

TABLE OF CONTENTS

PART II: MENNONITES TODAY

ACKNOWLEDGMENTS

I am pleased to acknowledge the very important part played by the Institute of Mennonite Studies in preparing this volume for publication. Willard M. Swartley and Richard A. Kauffman, directors, negotiated its publication by Herald Press, Elizabeth Yoder and Mary Ellen Martin did the copy editing and proofreading respectively, and Wilma Cender and Kevin Miller prepared the copy for printing.

My thanks go also to Loren Johns and Michael King, book editors at Herald Press, who so graciously agreed to publish this volume. I thank H. J. Goertz for permission to publish "The Rise of the Baptism of Adult Believers in Swiss Anabaptism," which first appeared in German in *Mennonitische Geschichtsblätter* 46 (1989).

Special thanks go to Robert Kreider, with whom I first worked to plan this *Festschrift*.

--Walter Klaassen, Editor

PREFACE

It is a special privilege for me to offer this collection of essays to Professor Cornelius J. Dyck on the occasion of his retirement from formal teaching at Mennonite Biblical Seminary and Associated Mennonite Biblical Seminaries, Elkhart, Indiana.

I have known C. J. since, sometime in the early 1940s, he and I rode together on horseback to a community pasture west of the North Saskatchewan River across from the town of Laird, to round up a herd of young horses and bring them back home for the winter. Our families were neighbors, and their mutual sojourn in the Trakt Colony near the Volga provided for that close link so often found among Mennonites.

I was excited and proud to be associated with him when the heady news of his dramatic work in rescuing refugees in Berlin in 1945 came back to Laird, but I did not meet him again until the winter of 1961 at the Mennonite Biblical Seminary in Elkhart. Since then our paths have crossed regularly as colleagues in the fraternity of Anabaptist scholarship. I have spent many comfortable and pleasant hours enjoying the hospitality of C. J. and his wife, Wilma, and have worked with him particularly in the publication of Anabaptist sources in English translation, The Classics of the Radical Reformation.

All of us who have written have done so out of respect for C. J. and also out of a sense of gratitude for the leading role he took over the years in the promotion of Mennonite and Anabaptist research, especially through publication. He devoted himself so totally to his work that he could never get around to some beckoning research and writing projects of his own. The integrity and devotion with which he worked for his students, his seminary colleagues, his church, and the international scholarly community continue to be an inspiration and also an admonition to all associated with him.

Perhaps now that he has been set free from the demands of daily teaching and committee meetings, he will at least have the leisure and strength to do what so often he postponed on behalf of others.

We trust, C. J., that the essays offered here in appreciation will bring you pleasure and that the volume will continue to be a reminder to you of the high esteem in which you are held by all of us.

--Walter Klaassen
on behalf of the contributors

PART 1: SIXTEENTH- AND SEVENTEENTH-CENTURY STUDIES

CHAPTER 1

The Melchiorites and the Ziegenhain Order of Discipline, 1538-39

Werner O. Packull

The Anabaptist influence on the *Ziegenhain Order of Discipline* (Zuchtordnung) and on Martin Bucer has been a matter of scholarly debate for some time. Christian Hege,[1] George Williams,[2] Franklin Littell,[3] Kenneth Davis[4] all argued in various degrees for an Anabaptist influence on Bucer and on the *Ziegenhain Order of Discipline* (hereafter *Order of Discipline*). The assertions of a strong influence by the Anabaptists on the *Order of Discipline* and indirectly on the entire Reformed tradition have been challenged, however, by the findings of James Spalding and John Stalnaker. In a recent essay Spalding noted that the "three-mark doctrine" was already present in Bucer's *Von der waren Seelsorge*, written and published before the Marburg Disputation, which had preceded the Synod of Ziegenhain, where the *Order of Discipline* was agreed upon. Then, in an exercise that creates havoc with traditional distinctives between Lutherans and Reformed, Spalding traced the first clear enunciation of the third-mark concept to the writings of Erasmus Sarcerius, a good Lutheran with no apparent exposure to Anabaptism.[5]

Stalnaker's challenge came from another side. Surveying the interaction between the Anabaptists and magisterial reformers in Hesse through the spectacles of a political realist, Stalnaker minimized the Anabaptist influence on either Bucer or the *Order of Discipline*.[6] He saw the apparent concessions to Anabaptism as a "piece of brilliant diplomacy" in an ongoing effort to expand central authority and social control.

In light of the above claims and counterclaims, this paper proposes to reexamine a possible Anabaptist influence on the *Order of Discipline*. The Anabaptists most directly involved were the Melchiorites led by Peter Tasch. The role of key players such as Bucer and Tasch, it will be argued, must be understood against the larger background of both the changing fortunes of the Melchiorite movement and the peculiar situation in Hesse.

I. The Background to Hessian Melchioritism

In order to understand the key events of 1538 it will be necessary to give a brief background of Hessian Anabaptism, especially in its Melchiorite expression.[7] Previous scholarship has not always separated the various forms of Anabaptism found in Hesse.[8] Four different orientations may be distinguished: (1) the rural followers of Melchior Rinck, concentrated in eastern Hesse; (2) the more urban Melchiorites, concentrated in western Hesse; (3) Anabaptists attracted by the Hutterites; and (4) "Swiss" Anabaptists. While it is true that these groups overlapped and were interrelated, they also represented distinctly different orientations. Anabaptism, inspired by the two Melchiors, initially took a popular orientation. This was not the case for the Hutterites or Swiss followers. If a common denominator existed, it must be sought in anti-clericalism. As Stalnaker rightly noted, the Anabaptists drew on a reservoir of resentment that manifested itself in "vitriolic contempt" and "fiercely hostile" attitudes toward the clergy.[9] The clergy were held to be "immoral, false prophets, Pharisees, hypocrites and tearing wolves." Anabaptists considered it particularly offensive that the Reformed ministers continued to live unreformed lives, to condone and participate in unjust economic practices such as usury.[10]

The Hessian magistrates became increasingly alarmed to find that, although original Anabaptism feeding on the aftermath of 1525 declined, Melchiorite activity, seemingly inspired by Münster, increased. As early as October 25, 1534, Landgrave Philip of Hesse feared that "many of the common people in the surrounding larger and lesser towns were inclined to the same insurrection."[11] Münster replaced Müntzer as a cause of concern. The flow of Anabaptist refugees into Hessian territory after the collapse of Münster did nothing to allay these fears. The authorities failed to appreciate that most of the fugitives represented a chastened Melchioritism anxious to shed any connections with Münster.

In May 1536 about thirty Melchiorites were taken by surprise near Gemünden (a.d. Wohra) in Hesse. Among the prisoners were Georg Schnabel, Hermann Bastian, Leonhard Fälber, and Peter Lose.[12] Schnabel, one of the indigenous leaders, was a repeat offender who, according to the *Regulations* of 1531,[13] had exhausted all legal process. He had been ordered to leave the territory three years earlier,[14] but felt no particular compunction to do so. When arrested in May 1536, he told Governor Jörg von Kolmatsch "that even if he promised, swore and provided guarantors, he would not keep it."[15] Such disregard of law and authority could not be ignored. The landgrave, who in principle refused the death penalty for religious heresy, found himself in a dilemma. Given the seriousness of the situation, he decided to canvass the opinions of other territorial princes, city councils, and theological faculties.[16] The replies were carefully weighed along with the deliberations of the territorial estates, the Hessian theologians, and court advisers. The outcome was the comprehensive *Visitation Order* of 1537.[17]

The *Visitation Order* addressed itself to the larger question of religious and moral reforms in the territories. Article XIV dealt specifically with Anabaptism, identified as a "foreign sect." It attributed a number of heretical propositions to the Anabaptists; among them (1) the doctrine of Christ's heavenly flesh, (2) the idea that sins against the Spirit could not be forgiven, (3) polygamy, (4) the community of goods, (5) the refusal of the oath, (6) that a Christian could not be a part of the political order, (7) the rejection of all authority, (8) preaching without authority, and (9) rejection of pedobaptism.[18]

Not surprisingly, these charges created consternation among the rank and file of the loosely organized Melchiorites primarily because the Melchiorites lacked a normative statement of beliefs, but also because the Melchiorites shared a number of doctrines with the Münsterites, from whom they sought to distance themselves. Led by Schnabel, the imprisoned Melchiorites drafted an *Apology (Verantwortung)*.[19] It is in this context that Peter Tasch emerged as the resource person and liaison between the imprisoned Melchiorites and the larger movement. Tasch, who in all probability joined the Melchiorite movement in early 1533, was from the area of Cologne.[20] By the summer of 1534 he baptized others in his house at Geyen near Cologne,[21] and by 1538 he had emerged as a pivotal figure in the amorphous Melchiorite movement that stretched from Münster to Amsterdam, to Oldekloster, to England, to Strasbourg and Marburg.

An analysis of the *Apology* indicates that the imprisoned Melchiorites relied heavily on information provided by Tasch. The discussion of the articles on baptism, the oath, and Christology encouraged the reader to consult Tasch's "little booklets."[22] A letter by Tasch to the prisoners confirms that they had requested his help on the issue of Christology, the oath, and sins committed after baptism.[23] We can conclude that the Melchiorite *Apology* originated as a response to general accusations against Anabaptists made in the *Visitation Order* of 1537.[24]

II. The Marburg Disputation, October 30 to November 3, 1538

The discovery of the *Apology* with Tasch's letter and other written materials, as well as the disclosure that the prisoners had come and gone from the jail like "homing pigeons after a day's or even a week's evangelistic tour,"[25] jolted the landgrave and his advisers into new measures against the Anabaptists. Those at large were rounded up, the leaders transferred to stricter confinement. Still reluctant to enforce exile without a proper hearing, Philip ordered new efforts at turning the Anabaptists from their errors. However, initial discussions between the Hessian divines and the imprisoned Melchiorite leaders did not augur well. In spite of "mighty arguments" drawn from Luther, Melanchthon, Oecolampadius, Zwingli, Bullinger, Capito, and Bucer, the prisoners remained unimpressed. If Lose's reaction is any indication, the lack of persuasiveness had to do less with the logic of the arguments than with their source. The report sent to the landgrave complained that Lose, one of the prisoners, "raged...with a great poisonous and caustic tongue" against all the pastors of Hesse as "lost idolatrous fellows," identifying them as the "fornicators, coveters, idolaters, railers, drunkards and extortioners" of 1 Thessalonians 3:6 and 1 Corinthians 5:11. True followers of Christ could have no fellowship with them.[26] Challenged to be more specific, he named the church supervisor, "Magister Adam including his entire company," and suggested that Melanchthon's *Loci communes*, highly regarded by the theologians, should be burned. When the discussion turned to justification by faith alone, Lose shouted: "Whoever says that our works do not justify us before God is damned."[27]

While Lose proved the most obnoxious, discussions with the others fared little better. Leonhard Fälber[28] thought of the clergy as "enemies and destroyers" of God's kingdom, as "erring spirits and false prophets." According to one participant in the dialogue, Fälber considered the clergy "in general fornicators, adulterers, drunkards, given to greed...and declares our faith, baptism, sacrament, preachers and community as heathenish, yes, idolatrous and devilish."[29] While these reports may have been exaggerated, they underline the anticlerical feeling among the Melchiorites. And although Schnabel and especially Bastian proved more congenial, it is not surprising that the preliminary discussions failed to establish a rapport between the Hessian divines and the Melchiorites.

During the discussions, if not before, it must have become obvious that the prisoners were not Münsterites but Melchiorites, that is, followers of Melchior Hoffman, who was then a prisoner at Strasbourg. Perhaps as a last resort, it was decided to bring in Martin Bucer, the reformer of Strasbourg, who had disputed with Hoffman in person and refuted him in print.[30]

Bucer agreed to a public debate with the prisoners.[31] The disputation that followed at Marburg (October 30 to November 3, 1538) has received considerable attention and needs no detailed analysis here.[32] Suffice it to say that while Bucer came prepared to argue against schism and separation on the basis of a doctrinal agenda, Schnabel, as spokesman for the prisoners, used the first opportunity to reiterate grievances against the lack of practical piety and discipline in the territorial church. He insisted that preaching and correct beliefs must have an impact on the moral and economic life of the community.[33] He reiterated charges made earlier in the *Apology* that in the Reformed church, usury had increased to the detriment of the poor. Interest was now double what it had been in the Catholic church.[34] These complaints obviously touched popular issues which Bucer could not ignore.

In his pastoral treatise, *On the True Care of the Soul (Von der waren Seelsorge)*,[35] published only two months previously, Bucer had candidly admitted that only a "small beginning" had been made in matters of social justice, welfare of the poor, and church discipline. In the same treatise he clearly recognized discipline as the "third mark" of the true church.[36] He specifically lamented the lack of the latter in the Reformation churches. Now at Marburg Bucer conceded: "There can be no church without the ban. When there are fornicators, usurers, and other sinners among the brethren, who after brotherly admonition in accordance to the gospel, as mentioned above, refuse to desist, one should have no fellowship with them."[37]

But Bucer insisted that discipline should be dispensed within the context of the territorial church. The ban should be administered by the entire congregation and not a self-selected few. Imperfection within the church should not become a pretext for self-righteous separation. He admitted that the territorial church was still far from the ideal, and reiterated his commitment to the proper institution of discipline. However, he refused to separate the deliberations on discipline from sound doctrine. For the latter, he advocated acceptance of the Augsburg Confession. "For we do not want to treat the ban slightingly, nor approve of usury. We preach a penitent life. We dispense the sacrament in accordance to the context of the Scriptures and as given in the Augsburg Confession."[38]

Bucer's concessions on practical concerns set the stage for a frank exchange on other issues such as Christology, baptism, and obedience to authority. The net result was that the disputation opened into dialogue. Apart from Lose, whose antics provided amusement for the spectators, the prisoners indicated willingness to take a second look at Bucer's doctrinal agenda. Bastian, the most conciliatory, seemed ready to curb his condemnation of pedobaptism.[39] At the conclusion of the disputation the prisoners were provided with Bibles and a copy of the Augsburg Confession for further study.

On November 2, 1538, Bucer sent a candid report of the proceedings to the landgrave, admitting the legitimacy of Anabaptist complaints regarding the lack of discipline. "The most persuasive objection of these people is by far that, unfortunately, we do such poor housekeeping. With this argument they deceive many people." He urged that the upcoming synod at Ziegenhain, set for November 25, 1538, should "in all seriousness deal with the housekeeping in the church" in the hope that out of it would come "improvement of the church, of the Anabaptists and others."[40]

From the above it is clear that at the upcoming synod Bucer intended to deal not only with the symptoms, but also with the causes of Anabaptist alienation, namely, discipline in the church. His project received support from unsuspected quarters. Unknown to Bucer, Tasch had witnessed the entire disputation from the spectator gallery. His state of mind may be surmised when it is remembered that he was largely responsible for the notions the prisoners sought to defend. Earlier in the year he had been party to discussions between Strasbourg Melchiorites and the enigmatic David Joris.[41] The discussion ended in schism.[42] At that time, if not earlier, Tasch had come to the realization that Lienhard Jost, an acclaimed prophet of the Melchiorite movement and "Elder in Israel," lacked "discernment of spirits."[43] After debates with Joris and Jost about the nature of religious authority, Bucer's sober argumentation and conciliatory tone must have been attractive to Tasch. He requested a private meeting. During the hours of conversation that followed, Bucer learned more about the extent of the common people's alienation from the church and came to appreciate Tasch's leadership qualities. In his report to the landgrave, Bucer described Tasch as a "great and very gifted leader." Recognizing the generally low esteem in which the clergy were held by the common people, he wrote, since "we preachers are so distrusted by this rabble, I truly wished that we could use these people."[44]

The conversations between Tasch and Bucer must have turned to the question of reconciliation. As reported by Bucer, Tasch feared that the arrogance and insensitivity of the clergy, coupled with their laxity in lifestyle and lack of pastoral zeal, would remain the major stumbling block. He

expressed apprehension that a return to the territorial church might prove
spiritually debilitating for the brethren. He feared accommodation and
assimilation to the ways of the world. He feared the coercion of consciences by
the imposition of conformity in belief and the enforcement of attendance at the
sacraments. He wished the process of reconciliation to take its natural course
without coercion, and held out against humiliating public recantations. Above
all, he implored Bucer to use his influence for the introduction of stricter discipline in the territorial church.

A gentleman's agreement on these points brought almost immediate
results. Upon discussions with Tasch, Bastian asked to be restored to fellowship with the local congregation. We are told that the entire congregation wept
when Bucer announced Bastian's request for reconciliation. Lose, the most
defiant and obnoxious during the debate, now wanted to follow Bastian's example.[45]

Meanwhile, the local authorities discovered Tasch's identity. Since his letter had become a matter of high politics and since his name figured prominently in the *Apology*, he was promptly arrested.[46] A report sent to Philip
associated Tasch with Jan van Leiden,[47] and Bucer's attempts to gain his
release were met with stiff resistance. Finally Tasch was dispatched to the
court of Philip so that the landgrave should "hear him out" in person; for "he is
unable to explain his case with brevity."[48] Unfortunately, Tasch's case history
as related to Philip has not been preserved. But the meeting must have gone
well for Tasch, because he was allowed to participate at the subsequent Synod
of Ziegenhain. A brief reference that has gone almost unnoticed in previous
scholarship suggests that at Ziegenhain the clergymen in attendance reached
an agreement with Tasch.[49] The reference appears in an *Evaluation*[50] by
Bucer and the Hessian church superintendents of the December *Confession*
submitted by the Anabaptists following the synod.[51] The reference implied
oral discussions between the clergy and Tasch, and reads: "as we agreed with
Peter Tasch at Ziegenhain, which agreement we do not consider contrary to
the confession which we send herewith."[52]

The allusion to an agreement between the Hessian divines and Tasch at
Ziegenhain places both the *Order of Discipline*[53] and the December *Confession*
of the Melchiorites into a new light. As noted above, Bucer wanted the synod,
which met November 25-30, 1538, to address issues raised by the Anabaptists.[54] With Tasch present during the deliberations, we can say that the *Order
of Discipline*, which was the product of the synod, originated in dialogue with
the leader of the Melchiorites. The *Confession*, dated December 11, must in
turn be viewed as a Melchiorite response, not only to the Marburg Disputation
of October as previous scholarship was wont to do, but also to the agreement
reached at Ziegenhain.[55]

III. The Ziegenhain Agreement, November 25-30, 1538

A. *The* Order of Discipline
       As noted earlier, Stalnaker saw the significance of the *Order of Discipline*

primarily in political terms as a further extension of central authority and social control in a linear development with preceding Hessian church regulations of 1526, 1529, and 1537. For him the Anabaptists were at best pawns in a game for higher stakes of political centralization. Concessions in their direction were little more than shrewd, tactical maneuvers by Philip and his advisers. Moreover, Ziegenhain failed to bring the promised reformation in manners or morals. These came only later, imposed by a newly educated second and third generation of state pastors. From the perspective of Stalnaker's hardheaded realism, the only concrete achievement coming out of the Bucer-Anabaptist dialogue was therefore the demise of the Melchiorites, who "ceased to be a dangerous competitor for the religious allegiance of the Hessian populace." This was not because the original cause of alienation had been removed, but because the inspirational leaders, including Tasch, were lost.

However, Stalnaker's conclusions tell only part of the story. True, reality failed to conform to the expectations of Ziegenhain, but none of the participants had the benefit of hindsight. Their motivation and intention must be assessed on the basis of an analysis of the agreement and not on the basis of its failure of implementation; and, whatever the mixed motives of Bucer may have been, the *Order of Discipline* went some way toward meeting Melchiorite criticisms.

The opening statement of the *Order of Discipline* identified widespread "decadence and godforsakenness" as the reason why so many have become estranged.[56] The aim was to bring "such erring sheep" back into the fold. The true fold was defined as possessing the three marks of (1) right doctrine, (2) proper administration of the sacraments, and (3) discipline. Anticlericalism was to be overcome through model pastors: "truly learned, sensible, modest, and diligently pious" pastors. Their role was not only to preach the gospel but also to "teach, admonish and chastise."

The real novelty came in the proposal for the creation of the office of lay elders and of the introduction of the rite of confirmation.[57] Only the "most sensible, most modest and most diligent in the Lord and also the most trusted and best liked in the *Gemeinde*" were to be chosen for the office of elder. Their role underlined the importance of the *Gemeinde* and was intended to go some way in overcoming anticlerical feelings.[58] For this purpose the elders were to monitor the behavior and performance of the pastor. It was also their duty to defend him against false slander and to cooperate with him in the enforcement of church discipline. The list of sins against which the ban was to be invoked included blasphemy, swearing, negligence of family duties, immorality, drunkenness, and debauchery. Concerns about usury, raised by the Melchiorites at the Marburg Disputation, received special attention. Those involved in "quick usurious finances against all that is proper...in common lending, buying and selling or in interest and rents" were to be banned.[59]

The *Order of Discipline* called for a sensitive if vigorous application of the ban. A friend, relative, or the pastor should first admonish the offender. Public humiliation was to be avoided. In serious cases the superintendent of the district had to be called in to assure fair play. The person banned could not receive communion and was disqualified as a godparent. The most drastic resolution stipulated that children should be taken from ungodly, unfit parents and placed with God-fearing relatives, friends, or other persons of godly repute.[60] Children of those living under the ban were to be brought to baptism by "believing friends" or persons appointed by the elders. At baptism the pastors were to review with parents, godparents, and relatives the meaning of the ceremony as well as the responsibilities to nurture the child in the Christian faith. Unsuitable godparents were to be "faithfully admonished and kindly turned away."

The duty of the elders included also vigilance in regards to attendance at catechism classes, a prerequisite to confirmation. The Ziegenhain setting suggests that confirmation was conceived of as a surrogate form of believer's baptism.[61] As such, it meant the personal and public affirmation of baptism and confession of faith by the confirmant as well as his/her acceptance by the congregation as a mature member of the fellowship.[62]

The congregational thrust was also noticeable in regards to the celebration of the eucharist. Surprisingly, little was said in the *Order of Discipline* about the controversial nature of Christ's presence. The emphasis was placed on the "highest and most intimate fellowship with each other,"[63] and on the unity of the participants as one bread and body in Christ. Without question, this thrust of solidarity with Christ and one another as a disciplined community was amiable to Melchiorite concerns. It seems fair to suggest, therefore, that given the assumed inclusivist perimeters of the territorial church, Melchiorite complaints had received a fair hearing.

B. *The* Confession *of December 11, 1538*

Turning to the *Confession* signed by the Melchiorite leaders on December 11, 1538,[64] it becomes at once obvious that this document must be understood as a response to the situation created by the disputation at Marburg as well as the agreement of Ziegenhain. If the Hessian divines, prodded by Bucer, were putting their house in order, the onus shifted to the Melchiorites, who had cited the lack of discipline as the major reason for their separation. Since Bucer and the Hessian divines assumed that reconciliation could proceed only by agreement on sound doctrine, attention turned to doctrinal differences. Because Philip of Hesse had been a signator to the Augsburg Confession, the territorial church was committed to its teachings. During the earlier disputation Bucer had repeatedly sought to make it the basis for doctrinal discussions,[65] and a copy had been given to the prisoners for their study. Since their response was delayed until Tasch returned from Ziegenhain,[66] it may be assumed that the agreement reached there influenced the attitude of the signatories and the content of the *Confession*.

The introduction indicates that the *Confession* constituted a response to specific questions, "Upon the items inquired and demanded of us we answer as follows." Since the *Confession* was drafted and written in Tasch's own hand, it may be assumed that Tasch brought the questions from Ziegenhain. The composition was divided into seven unequal parts, dealing with matters of faith and good works, the sacraments, separation, some errors attributed to the Anabaptists and reconciliation with the established church.[67] A comparison with the Augsburg Confession reveals that the Melchiorites had been asked to respond to articles II, IV, XVIII, and XX of the same.

One of the key questions must have concerned original sin, because the December *Confession* opens not with the doctrine of God or Christ but with a statement on original sin. A discussion of justification, free will, and human merit followed. But concessions to the Augsburg Confession on these points were at best equivocal. The peculiar Melchiorite concern with "sin unto death" was reformulated. Since only God knew those guilty of unforgivable sin, it was no longer deemed a divisive issue. Curiously, nothing was said of Melchiorite Christology. It is possible that an oral agreement had been reached at Ziegenhain on that issue,[68] or that the signatories remained divided on the subject and chose to ignore it. The chief concern of the signatories remained practical. They feared that an overemphasis on original sin, predestination, and justification by faith alone would weaken ethical moral concerns.

The section on the sacraments opens with an acknowledgment of sacraments as "true signs of grace" to be received "with true faith," but one looks in vain for a substantive theological explanation. Somewhat surprising is the discussion on baptism. While the signatories regretted that baptism had become a cause of division and conceded that pedobaptism was not intrinsically harmful or anti-Christian, they reiterated that baptism of the immature was a chief cause of the lack of spirituality in the church. No connection was made between the earlier discussion on original sin and baptism. While the signatories no longer condemned those who permitted their children to be baptized, they could not find the ordinance of pedobaptism in the New Testament. At best, the statement on baptism indicated a softening of positions.

As far as the eucharist was concerned, the exclusion of open sinners remained of greater import than questions of the nature of Christ's presence. The latter received short treatment: "One eats the bread and drinks the wine with the mouth; the body of Christ and his blood, however, with the spirit (*gemüt*)." In this connection application of the ban continued to be a key concern. The ban had been introduced on December 1 by princely decree, but only in key urban parishes.[69] Fearing procrastination, the signatories of the December *Confession* called for its universal implementation without delay "so that this time no excuses by the prince and the officials were to be made regarding possible unrest or the lack of [true] Christians among so many evil people, etc."

Other articles of the *Confession* defended against accusations made previously in the *Visitation Order* of 1537, among them the Münsterite notion of the destruction of the godless and of polygamy (III), also the accusation that Anabaptists rejected all authority (IV) and the oath (V). Not surprisingly, on these points the *Confession* simply reiterated the denials made earlier in the *Apology*.

Without elaboration article VI committed the signatories to the Apostles' Creed (12 *artikulen des christlichen glaubens*). The last section brought a sum-

mary of positions with pledges of obedience to authority as well as a conciliatory gesture: "Finally we are also mindful and offer ourselves to behave
serviceably, fraternally, yes, justly toward the whole community and everyone,
just as we desire everyone else to behave towards us."[70]

As a whole, then, the *Confession* constituted a conciliatory document but
not a total surrender. It is possible to read the *Confession* as standing in a
revisionist line with the earlier *Apology*. None of the original concerns with
discipline were compromised, and even the derivative issue of baptism was not
entirely conceded. Although Tasch may have been its prime mover, the *Confession* claimed to be a consensus statement. As such it presumably
represented a minimal agreement, which helps to explain why some issues such
as the Melchiorite Christology were not discussed. Tasch, Schnabel, Fälber,
Lose, and several others affixed their signatures.

Like all documents conceived for purposes of compromise, the *Confession*
remained open to interpretation. From their subsequent cooperation with
Bucer we may infer that at least Tasch, Schnabel, and Bastian fully supported
its conciliatory intention. The case of two other signatories, Fälber and Lose,
remains less clear. If our sources can be trusted, Fälber returned to the Julich
area and resumed his baptismal activities.[71] More than ten years later, in 1551,
Peter Lose was back in court because he continued to boycott church services
and encouraged others to do the same. Lose justified his action with the claim
that the truth had not yet been preached in Hesse. He based his opinions
solely on the Bible, rejecting all other literature. For his opinions he received a
reprimand and was told to stay out of religious controversy, to mind instead his
business of "castrating pigs" and "fixing pots!"[72]

As noted, the *Confession* was examined by Bucer and the superintendents
of the Hessian church.[73] Not surprisingly, the theologians found its content
somewhat disappointing. No doubt they would have liked to see an unequivocal acceptance of the Augsburg Confession. The Melchiorites were, of course,
theologically uneducated artisans. This may have inclined the divines, led by
Bucer, to accept the *Confession* in good faith and laud its good intention in
spite of considered shortcomings. Accepted by the landgrave and his advisers
as a document of reconciliation, the *Confession* of the former Melchiorites
became the official yardstick of tolerable dissent in Hesse. All those able and
willing to accept the *Confession* were to be released and permitted to remain in
the land.

IV. The Demise of the Melchiorite Movement in Hesse

If scholars disagree about the Anabaptist influence on the *Order of Discipline*, a consensus exists that Tasch's collaboration with Bucer led to the
demise of the Melchiorite branch of Anabaptism in Hesse.[74] Subsequent Swiss
and Hutterite penetration remained insignificant and localized. Thanks to the
efforts of Tasch, Schnabel, and Bastian, approximately two hundred Anabaptists accepted the *Confession* and joined the territorial church. A reconciliation
or compromise on this scale remained unparalleled in Anabaptist history.
Obviously a variety of interpretations are possible. The reaction of the Hut-

terite missionary Peter Riedemann, who arrived on the scene in early 1539, documents one possible response. He wrote: "As we came to Hessia, we found great distress; because the Anabaptists had been a large company, but now almost all are lost because of false erring spirits. They are led back again to the temple of idols, pedobaptism, eating of idols [eucharist], to war and other horrible things."[75] However, Riedemann's understanding of the urban Melchiorites was at best limited. His appraisal of the events assumed a sharp dualism between the kingdom of God, as represented by the Hutterite community in Moravia, and the rest of the world. Some modern scholars have seen a genuine process of reconciliation at work in the above events. They have argued that the reconversions were not "one-sided and forced subjections" but that they constituted a "reunification."[76] Granted that the Melchiorites had been primarily an urban movement for whom strict separation from the rest of society was a difficult option, the willingness of so many to accept the compromise *Confession* becomes more easily explicable. Meanwhile, encouraged by the landgrave, the former Melchiorite leaders began a ministry that sought the release of prisoners of conscience by gaining their agreement to the December *Confession*. Among those visited was the veteran Melchior Rinck.[77] While Rinck remained intransigent, efforts on his behalf led to more comfortable conditions for him. In the months and years that followed, the former Melchiorites undertook numerous similar missions.[78] Concerns for a single prisoner could span years. The case of Endres Gutte may serve to illustrate the point.

Gutte, baptized by Schnabel, had been imprisoned since 1535.[79] His jailor, the local lord, Philip of Solms, initially refused to cooperate with the would-be visitors. On August 23, 1539, the landgrave directed that Tasch or Schnabel should be permitted to visit the "simple and pious" prisoner. When Schnabel, Bastian, and four or five others arrived, they found Gutte dressed in rags and the stench of his prison unbearable. Permission was granted to shift the meeting to the local inn, but the visitors failed to gain the prisoner's release or to have his confinement improved. The suspicious governor reported to the landgrave that Gutte refused to be instructed, and that the visitors had actually encouraged him in his error.[80] As proof, he cited the fact that the former Melchiorites commiserated with the prisoner and actually sent him new clothes!

In a letter dated Christmas Day 1539, Bucer begged the landgrave to take the prisoner into his own custody. He asked permission for Schnabel and Bastian to brief Philip on Gutte's situation,[81] but Gutte remained in the hands of the lord of Solms. Two years later, a petition supported by Gutte's entire home community failed to gain his release.[82] Still, Schnabel and Bastian did not give up. In 1543 they complained once more to the landgrave that Gutte was still held "without mercy in hard, strict confinement."[83] In February 1544, under pressure from the landgrave, discussions were renewed with Gutte. Although he had spent almost a decade under most despicable conditions, Gutte continued to maintain that the baptism he had once received from Schnabel was indeed "the correct baptism."[84] Unfortunately the documents concerning Gutte break off at this point, and his fate remains unknown.

However, even if the former leaders failed to bring about a favorable change in Gutte's circumstances, their five-year effort speaks well for their intentions. Surely, then, their collaboration with Bucer cannot be written off as mere opportunism and accommodation. The leaders obviously cared about the fate of their former charges.

Interestingly, the former Melchiorites concerned themselves not only with the fate of their own brethren, but they also monitored the implementation of the *Order of Discipline*. Their fear that discipline would not be administered seemed to be confirmed only too soon. They informed Bucer that immorality and drunkenness continued not only among parishioners but even among pastors. In Marburg, a site chosen for a pilot implementation of the ban, persons in authority flouted its application and contributed to the general delinquency by the indiscriminate sale of alcoholic beverages, from which they profited. It is to Bucer's credit that he consistently sided with his new allies, the former Melchiorites. In 1540 Bucer suggested that Schnabel should be appointed assistant to the church superintendent Kraft.[85] Two years later he urged the calling of another synod to deal specifically with the implementation of discipline agreed upon at Ziegenhain in 1538. Following the pattern of Ziegenhain, Tasch was to be brought in to represent and assure the cooperation of the former brethren, and he, Bucer, would sway the pastors.[86] Thus Bucer's alliance with the former Melchiorites was operative into the mid-1540s. According to Hessian Anabaptist records, the December *Confession* of 1538 remained an instrument of reconciliation well into 1546.[87]

By way of summary the points of this paper may be reiterated as follows:

1. Bucer's conciliatory attitude on popular grievances and his concessions at the disputation of Marburg on the need for stricter discipline encouraged Peter Tasch, the intellectual leader of the Melchiorites, to risk dialogue. It should be noted that earlier in 1538 most of the original members of Tasch's home conventicle at Cologne had made their peace with the established church under less favorable conditions. Tasch's encounter with David Joris and the "Elders of Israel" at Strasbourg had proven disappointing. Given this evidence of a general malaise in the Melchiorite movement, it becomes difficult to consider Tasch's decision to cooperate with Bucer as mere opportunism, accommodation, or betrayal.

2. Tasch's presence at the Synod of Ziegenhain and the mention of an agreement reached between him and the Hessian divines gives some credence to an Anabaptist input on certain aspects of the *Order of Discipline*, specifically the introduction of the office of lay elders, the rite of confirmation, and the ban. Without overstretching the historical imagination it is possible to argue that grass-roots support for Melchiorite grievances applied indirect pressure on the Hessian divines to deal with continuing abuses in the church.

3. The Melchiorite *Confession* of December 1538 is best understood as a response to the *Order of Discipline*. As such the *Confession* proved conciliatory and accommodating but did not constitute a simple surrender on doctrinal issues, on discipline, or even on baptism. The *Confession* was accepted by the

landgrave and his officials as a yardstick of minimal conformity within Hesse. The adoption of such a flexible formula remained unique in the history of the territorial Reformation. It is not surprising, therefore, that a number of prominent "heretics" soon sought asylum in Hesse. The fact that practically all the Hessian Melchiorite leaders and a large number of the followers accepted the agreement and joined the territorial church could suggest that they believed that their grievances had received a proper hearing and positive response at Ziegenhain.

With hindsight it is possible to see that the Hessian Melchiorite leaders had been co-opted by Bucer for a reform project that failed to live up to its promise. But the implementation of the reforms or the lack thereof did not live up to Bucer's expectations either. It would be wrong to infer, therefore, that the Melchiorites had been duped by "a devious, none-too-scrupulous manipulator of men and ideas, who threatened the weak and fawned on the powerful."[88] Certainly Bucer's continuing concern with the implementation of the agreement, his intercessory engagement on behalf of Anabaptist prisoners, and his consistent support of the former Melchiorites seem to suggest that he too could be motivated by more than mere political advantage.

4. Finally, the question of the historical significance of the Bucer-Tasch, Reformed-Anabaptist dialogue remains illusive. Anabaptist influence on Bucer and the entire "Reformed" tradition was not as straightforward as Littell and Davis thought. Key events in the dialogue, the Marburg Disputation and the subsequent agreement at Ziegenhain, led to the disintegration of the branch of Anabaptism involved. In the sixteenth century true dialogue as between equal partners was rare if not impossible. Tasch and the Melchiorites were treated at least as junior partners and expected to sacrifice their separateness in favor of a uniform confessional church. Is it possible that an influence survived without the Melchiorite survival as a distinct party? Without overstating the case, it seems possible to answer in the affirmative. The impact of the dialogue lived on in concerns with church discipline as well as the rite of confirmation.

It can only be hoped that under the more favorable circumstances of the twentieth century, the descendants of the senior partners in the sixteenth-century dialogue will listen once more and hear the other points made by the junior partner, the Anabaptists. Few have worked harder to articulate some of these points in the contemporary dialogue than the man honored by the essays in this *Festschrift*.

NOTES

1. Christian Hege, "The Early Anabaptists in Hesse," *Mennonite Quarterly Review (MQR)* 5 (1931), 157-178; reproduced in *Mennonite Encyclopedia (ME)*, II: "Hesse," 719-727.

2. George H. Williams, *The Radical Reformation* (Philadelphia: Westminster Press, 1962), 448-451.

3. Franklin H. Littell, "New Light on Butzer's Significance," in *Reformation Studies: Essays in Honour of Roland Bainton*, ed. Franklin H. Littell (Richmond, Va.: John Knox Press, 1962).

4. Kenneth Davis "No Discipline. No Church: An Anabaptist Contribution to the Reformed Tradition," in *Sixteenth Century Journal*, 13 (1982), 43-58. Davis relied on Littell for the significance of the Marburg Disputation and was strongly influenced by Jean Runzo, "Communal Discipline in the Early Anabaptist Communities of Switzerland, South and Central Germany, Austria and Moravia, 1525-1550" (Ph.D. diss., University of Michigan, 1978).

5. "Discipline as a Mark of the True Church in its Sixteenth Century Lutheran Context," in *Piety, Politics and Ethics: Reformation Studies in Honour of George Wolfgang Forell*, ed. by Carter Lindberg (Kirksville, Mo.: Sixteenth Century Journal Publishers, 1984), 119-138, esp. 129, 137.

6. John Stalnaker, "Anabaptism, Martin Bucer and the Shaping of the Hessian Protestant Church," *Journal of Modern History* 48 (1976), 601-643, esp. 606.

7 Still the best treatment is that by Ruth Weiss, "Herkunft und Sozialanschauungen der Täufergemeinden im westlichen Hessen," *Archiv für Reformationsgeschichte* 52 (1961), 162-187; also Allen W. Dirrim, "The Hessian Anabaptists: Background and Development to 1540" (Ph.D. diss., University of Indiana, 1959), esp. 211; "The Hessian Anabaptists," *MQR* 37 (1964), 61-62; and "Political Implications of Sixteenth-Century Hessian Anabaptism," *Mennonite Life* 19 (1964), 179-183. Dirrim's fine work did not receive the recognition it deserved in the 1960s.

8. This was a major shortcoming of Hege, "Early Anabaptists in Hesse." Weiss, "Herkunft und Sozialanschauungen," 162-163 and Dirrim, "The Hessian Anabaptists," *MQR*, differentiated between the various groups, as did Williams, *The Radical Reformation*, 435.

9. Stalnaker, "Anabaptism, Bucer and the Shaping of the Hessian Church," 610-611.

10. See the statements by Ludwig Spon, Adam Ergkel, Peter Spidtel, and Curt Schenck in Günther Franz, ed., *Urkundliche Quellen zur hessischen Reformationsgeschichte*, IV: *Wiedertäuferakten, 1527-1626* (Marburg: N. G. Elwert, 1951), 65, 73, 97, 147 (hereafter cited as *TA, Hesse*).

11. Cited by Günther Vogler, "Das Täuferreich zu Münster als Problem der Politik im Reich," *Mennonitische Geschichtsblätter* 42 (1985), 13.

12. They had been arrested before May 18 at a meeting in an old forsaken church. *TA, Hesse*, 90-91.

13. *Ibid.*, 37-38.

14. *Ibid.*, 74.

15. *Ibid.*, 91. On May 28, 1536, the main points of the 1531 *Regulations* were reiterated (pp. 100-101).

16. *TA, Hesse*, 98-128. Hans Hillerbrand, "Die Vorgeschichte der hessischen Wiedertaufordnung von 1537," *Zeitschrift für Religion und Geistesgeschichte* 15 (1963), 330-347.

17. *TA, Hesse*, 139-146, esp. 140. This document had been completed by August 1536, although it was not published and made official until 1537.

18. These were listed in article XIV under subpoints (a) to (g). *Ibid.*, 140-141.

19. The full title reads: *Verantwortung und widerlegung der artikel, so jetzund im land zu Hesse uber die armen Davider (die man widertaufer nennt) usgegangen sind*; in *TA, Hesse*, 165-180. English translation in Walter Klaassen, ed., *Sixteenth Century Anabaptism: Defences, Confessions and Refutations*, trans. Frank Friesen (Waterloo, Ont.: Conrad Grebel College, 1981), 74-86.

20. Leonhard Ennen, *Die Geschichte der Stadt Köln*, IV (Cologne, Düsseldorf, 1875-80), 338; Hans H. Stiasny, *Die Strafrechtliche Verfolgung der Täufer in der Freien Reichsstadt Köln, 1529 bis 1618* (Münster Westfalen: Aschendorff, 1962), 17. About Tasch, see my article "Peter Tasch: From Melchiorite to Bankrupt Wine Merchant," *MQR* 62 (1988), 276-295.

21. Hans of Cologne testified in Amsterdam on July 27, 1535, that he had been baptized a year earlier by Peter van Geyen "in his house in the village of Geyen about one mile from Cologne." Albert Mellink, ed., *Documenta Anabaptistica Neerlandica, I: Friesland en Groningen*, (Leiden: E. J. Brill, 1975), 136.

22. *TA, Hesse*, 240-41. "Weiter van der tauf ordenung und auflösung der gegenwurf les, wer da wil, im buchlein van der tauforderung Jesu Christi Peter Thess," 169; "Van disem underscheid des schwerens und eids lis, wer da wil, im buchlein vam eid Peter Thesch," 171; "Van auflösung der gegenwurf leis im buchlein van der menschwerdung Peter Thess," 173.

23. *TA, Hesse*, 158-161. Tasch had written before, since he refers to his letters in the plural. Unfortunately, several books and letters of comfort which were found and sent to the landgrave, written by both "male and female" hands, have not survived. *Ibid.*, 188.

24. The correlation between the *Apology* and the *Visitation Order* is illustrated by the fact that the Lord's Supper is not addressed in either document.

25. Williams' description in *The Radical Reformation*, 444.

26. *TA, Hesse*, 187, 189.

27. *Ibid.*, 187, 191.

28. Theodor Fabricius thought he could convert Fälber if only he could spend two weeks with him. *Ibid.*, 188, 193-194.

29. *Ibid.*, 211. See also the statement by Herman Schneider, p. 209.

30. Max Lenz, ed., *Briefwechsel Landgraf Philipps des Grossmüthigen von Hessen mit Bucer*, I (Leipzig, 1880), 45. The decision to bring Bucer into the discussion was made before August 23. Bucer replied from Basel on September 20, 1538, that he hoped to be in Kassel by mid-October.

31. He was presumably briefed by the irenic Dionysius Melander, who traveled with him from Kassel to Marburg. *TA, Hesse*, 237.

32. *Ibid.*, 213-237; trans. Franklin H. Littell, "What Butzer Debated with the Anabaptists at Marburg, 1538," *MQR* 36 (1962), 256-276.

33. Williams noted that the debate seemed to center on "such questions as usury, the ban and the common weal rather than baptism." *The Radical Reformation*, 448-449.

34. Cf. *TA, Hesse*, 174-175, 215, 223. A loan of twenty gulden (Rheinish florins) was now expected to bring a measure of corn equivalent to two and a half gulden or 12.5%.

35. Robert Stupperich, ed., *Martin Bucers Deutsche Schriften*, VII (Gütersloh: Gerd Mohn, 1964), 90ff., esp. 115-116 (hereafter cited as *MBDS*).

36. *Ibid.*, VII, 187.

37. *TA, Hesse*, 215.

38. *Ibid.*, 228.

39. *Ibid.*, 197-199. Bastian had earlier signaled his willingness to return to the church if only greater emphasis were to be placed on instructions and discipline.

40. *Ibid.*, 237-39, esp. 239.

41. About him, see James Stayer, "David Joris: A Prolegomenon to Further Research," *MQR*, 59 (1985), 350-61; and S. Zijlstra, "David Joris en de doperse stromingen (1536-39)," in *Historisch Bewogen* (Groningen: Wolters-Noordhoff, 1984), 133-34.

42. Tasch functioned as secretary and drew up the "Twistredt," our major source on the meeting with Joris. The "Twistredt" is no. 836, p. 156ff., in Marc Lienhard, Stephen F. Nelson, and Hans Georg Rott, eds., *Quellen zur Geschichte der Täufer*, XV: *Elsass, III. Teil* (Gütersloh: Gerd Mohn, 1986).

43. *Ibid.* The statement is attributed to Eisenburg, but Tasch recorded it.

44. *TA, Hesse*, 239-41.

45. *Ibid.*, 241-42.

46. Letter by the Befehlshaber at Marburg to Philip, on November 4, in *ibid.*, 242-244. The authorities remained suspicious of Tasch. It seemed to them that he was either deceiving them or the Anabaptists.

47. *TA, Hesse*, 244-45. See the Nov. 5, 1538, letter by Valentin Breul.

48. *TA, Hesse*, 241.

49. Lenz believed "auf der Synode zu Ziegenhain gab Peter Tasch eine Erklärung ab, welche die versammelten Prädikanten fast völlig zufrieden stellten." *Briefwechsel Philipps mit Bucer*, I, 324, n. 2.

50. *TA, Hesse*, 257-61.

51. *Ibid.*, 247-57; translation in *Sixteenth Century Anabaptism*, 103-112.

52. *TA, Hesse*, 260.

53. Known as the *Ziegenhainer Zuchtordnung*, the full title of the published version reads: *Ordenung der Christlichen Kirchenzucht. Für die Kirchen im Fürstenthumb Hessen*; in *MBDS* VII, 247-278.

54. After Marburg, Bucer traveled on to Wittenberg on a delicate mission concerning Philip's bigamy. Thus Philip was much obliged for a number of reasons, not only his tolerant attitude. Bucer had written on November 17 from Wittenberg, urging again that the synod address the problem of "Christliche haushaltung und zucht."

55. Williams was apparently unaware of the close connection between Ziegenhain and the Confession. *The Radical Reformation*, 450.

56. The comments by the editor, Hannelore Jahr, that the reference to the *Epicurär* refers to Anabaptists misses the point. The Anabaptists are here more likely referred to as "viel armer leut," alienated from the church. *MBDS* VII, 261, n. 5.

57. From Hesse this practice spread to other territorial churches: in 1542 to Calenberg–Göttingen, in 1553 to Württemberg, in 1556 to Waldeck, in 1569 to Braunschweig-Wolfenbüttel, in 1581 to Hoya. *Ibid.*, 264, n. 25.

58. Stalnaker believed that, given the strong anti-clerical feeling among the laity, it would have been futile at this stage to put more power into the hands of the clergy. "Anabaptism, Bucer and the Shaping of the Hessian Church," 622.

59. *MBDS* VII, 269. This article depended obviously on a separate note appended to the landgrave's response to the resolutions of Ziegenhain. These had been discussed by the landgrave and his advisers. The note reads: "Auch das man nit allein die, so in offenlichem ehebruch, hurerei and volsaufen legen and nit ablassen wollen, banne, sonder auch die, die da so diff im giez stecken, die da in offnem wucher sizen, die da mit fruchten and ander war ufhalten und nit verkofen wollen, den armen man zu erstegern, die da uber unser ordenung wucherliche zinse nemen, auch in kaufhendeln so gar hohe finanzische erstegerung machen." *TA, Hesse*, 245-

247.

60. *Ibid.*, 245. The landgrave feared that these measures would meet with resistance and prove socially disruptive.

61. See Hege, "Early Anabaptists in Hesse," 169; see also Emil Händiges, "Konfirmation," *Mennonitisches Lexikon*, III, 533-36.

62. *MBDS* VII, 264. This provision earned Bucer the title of "Father of evangelical confirmation." Charles B. Mitchell, "Martin Bucer and Sectarian Dissent: A Confrontation of the Magisterial Reformation with Anabaptists and Spiritualists" (Ph.D. diss., Yale University, 1960), 374-376. Mitchell saw the *Order of Discipline* as "incarnating Bucer's own ideas" while "trying to meet" the sectarian's most serious criticism.

63. *TA, Hesse*, 273.

64. *Ibid.*, 247-257. Written in Tasch's hand, it was signed by Jorg Schnabel, Ludwig Schnabel, Lenart Fälber, Thönis Möller, Christian van Odenhausen, Junghen von Geissen, Contz Schymt and Peter Löss.

65. *Ibid.*, 221-222; 233; 238.

66. Williams was wrong when he thought that the *Confession* came a year later. *The Radical Reformation*, 450-51. It was completed by December 11, 1538. *TA Hesse*, 247.

67. This was the summary given by Bucer and his colleagues in their *Evaluation (Erklärung)*, in *TA, Hesse*, 257.

68. An inference made from the statement by Bucer and the superintendents that the *Confession* was in keeping with an oral agreement reached with Tasch at Ziegenhain. *TA, Hesse*, 259-260.

69. In responding to the resolution of Ziegenhain, Philip had expressed fear that the ban would be misused to settle local scores. He therefore wanted it first introduced in churches where the best-educated ministers presided. *Ibid.*, 245.

70. *Ibid.*, 256.

71. Weiss, "Herkunft und Sozialanschauungen," 168.

72. Weiss questioned whether this was the same Lose. *Ibid.*, 172. But the ideas expressed fit our Lose. On justification he allegedly held closer to the papists, but he expressed a low view of the sacraments. He was adept in using the Bible to contradict the efforts of the pastor. *TA, Hesse*, 329-330.

73. The *Evaluation* was signed by Bucer, Johannes Kymüs, Dionysius Melander, Johannes Pistorius Niddanus, and Justus Winther. All had been present at the synod as superintendents, although Winther's and Bucer's names do not appear among the ten signatories of the *Order of Discipline*. Cf. n. 9 above.

74. Stalnaker, "Anabaptism, Bucer and the Shaping of the Hessian Church," 601.

75. *TA, Hesse*, 266.

76. Weiss, "Herkunft und Sozialanschauungen," 170.

77. Rinck, the leading Anabaptist in Eastern Hesse had been imprisoned for seven years. *TA, Hesse*, 261-63. Erich Geldbach, "Toward a More Ample Biography of the Hessian Anabaptist Leader Melchior Rinck," *MQR*, 68 (1974), 371-384.

78. In March 1541 he had been responsible for the release of Caspar von Giessen. Giessen reported "wie das Peter Desche mit irem lerer ein disputacion gehalten, und Peter habe iren lerer in allen artikeln und stücken uberwunden." It is not clear whether this was a reference to Matheias Hasenhan. *TA, Hesse*, 280.

79. *Ibid.*, 90. He was also identified as "Endres, ein streuschneider von Girms."

80. Dated Jan. 8, 1540; in *Ibid.*, 267-68.

81. *Briefwechsel Philipps mit Bucer*, I, 120-122; *TA, Hesse*, 288, n. 1.

82. *Ibid.*, 291, n. 1.

83. Before Oct. 8, 1543, because on that day Philip forwarded the letter to the councilors of Solm. *Ibid.*, 287-288.

84. *Ibid.*, 288-91.

85. Weiss, "Herkunft und Sozialanschauungen," 171.

86. Letter, Apr. 14, 1542. *Briefwechsel Philipps mit Bucer*, II, 77.

87. *TA, Hesse*, 316-17. Schnabel remained active on behalf of imprisoned Anabaptists as late as March, 1544 (pp. 296-301).

88. R. Emmet McLaughlin, *Caspar Schwenckfeld, Reluctant Radical: His Life to 1540* (New Haven: Yale University Press, 1986), 129.

CHAPTER 2

The Confession of the Swiss Brethren in Hesse, 1578

C. Arnold Snyder

The story of Hessian Anabaptism is a rich and interesting one, encompassing most of the historical manifestations of the early movement. In its earliest phase Hessian Anabaptism owed much to the social tensions which erupted in the Peasants' Revolt. Early Hessian Anabaptism shared peasant anticlericalism, and its most significant early leader, Melchior Rinck, had once been a follower of Thomas Müntzer.[1] In a second phase Melchior Hoffman gained considerable following, Melchiorites becoming the dominant Anabaptist group in Hesse. Leaders among the Hessian Melchiorites of the 1530s included such able men as Peter Tasch and Georg Schnabel. After the fall of Münster, Hesse became a noted place of refuge for fleeing Münsterites, but when the Melchiorite leadership was reincorporated into the state church in 1539,[2] the field was left to small numbers of clandestine Swiss Brethren and Hutterites, who competed for adherents in the Hessian territories. In the end, this small remnant was eradicated by the Thirty Years' War.

The rich variety of Anabaptist activity in Hesse was due in no small measure to the tolerant policies of Landgrave Philip of Hesse, policies which were continued by his four sons and heirs. Throughout Philip's long life (d. 1567), he resisted applying the death penalty to religious dissenters, preferring rather to persuade the dissidents to rejoin the state church. He had notable success in his efforts, and he urged his four sons to continue walking the same path--advice which they took to heart and followed. As a result, the space for tolerable dissent remained much wider in Hesse than in any other part of Europe, save perhaps for Strasbourg and Moravia.[3]

The 1578 "Confession of the Swiss Brethren in Hesse" which is treated in this essay is a document representing the later, minority phase of the Anabaptist movement in Hesse, long after the demise of the Melchiorite movement.[4] The activity of the Swiss Brethren which is documented in the confession involved the rural jurisdictions of Landgrave Wilhelm of Lower Hesse (capital, Kassel) and his brother Landgrave Ludwig of Upper Hesse (capital, Marburg).[5]

Several features make this material worthy of further examination. In the first place, a study of this explicitly Swiss Anabaptist "confession of faith" continues the earlier work of C. J. Dyck and the more recent work of Howard J. Loewen on Anabaptist-Mennonite confessions of faith.[6] More specifically, this 1578 confession represents an important Swiss Brethren doctrinal statement, all the more significant given the relative scarcity of such statements among the Swiss. The Swiss Brethren Confession of 1578, standing as it does roughly at the midway point between the Schleitheim Articles of 1527 and the Dordrecht Confession of 1632 (later adopted by the Swiss), allows us to examine at close view one of the steps in the "confessional" line of development: how does "Swiss" teaching in 1578 compare with the original Swiss Brethren outline of Schleitheim? What has changed in substance or tone? One notes immediately the strongly credal nature of the Swiss Brethren Confession of 1578, so unusual in the Swiss tradition.[7] How should this manifestly credal Swiss confession be understood and interpreted?

In the second place, and in a more general way, we learn more about the lives and the teachings of the "Swiss Brethren" in Central Germany at this late date, for this material also offers us an unusually intimate glimpse into the lives of this small and beleaguered group of Swiss Anabaptists in the last quarter of the sixteenth century. Finally, the Confession of 1578 represents an extended conversation between Swiss Brethren representatives and Lutheran divines in Hesse. Such conversations and disputations with Lutherans are relatively rare in the source literature.[8] It cannot be our purpose here to detail the Lutheran arguments or to compare them with the Lutheran polemical tradition.[9] Nevertheless, the material we have at hand relating to this Lutheran-Anabaptist dialogue is informative, detailing the concerns on either side of the discussion.

From among the many issues prompted by this material, we must be content here to introduce the confession, placing it in the perspective of Swiss Anabaptist doctrine, with minimal comment relating the confession to the later Mennonite confessional tradition or the Lutheran context. In what follows, then, we will describe and discuss the confession itself in light of the Anabaptist tradition which preceded it, after which we will be able to pose some questions calling for further study.

The Hessian Anabaptist Confession of 1578 is properly called a confession of faith; it was so understood by its authors and was entitled by them "Confession of the Christian Faith and Brotherly Union in the Faith of Some Reborn Christians and Elect Children of God, who are scattered here and there."[10] Supporting documents identify the primary Anabaptist author and spokesman as one Hans Pauli Kuchenbecker, called a leader of "the Swiss Brethren."

That Kuchenbecker identified himself, and was identified by others, with the "Swiss Brethren" is a fact not open to question. The interrogation protocol of June 1578 says that Pauli Kuchenbecker of Hatzbach distinguished himself and his brothers from the Hutterites, because the latter "take the property of their brethren, separate marriages, love their leaders better than their brother, have all things in common. Also that they have no ban, and that they do not restore anything to those who leave."[11] To the contrary, the protocol states, "he and his group are Swiss Brethren."

It is hard to argue with this latter statement: surely Kuchenbecker knew to which group of Anabaptists he belonged! Furthermore, Christof Eckhardt, the revenue officer of Alsfeld who provided much written information on local Anabaptists, also knew of two Anabaptist groups who operated in the area, namely, Hutterites and "Swiss Brethren." Sometimes these competing groups held nocturnal meetings in the same woods--on different nights, of course. Although Eckhardt knew only of a meeting of eight "Huttite Brethren" and fifteen "Swiss" around Eastertime in 1578, he reports that around two hundred and fifty people came from neighboring villages because "they wanted to watch" the midnight proceedings.[12]

The term "Swiss Brethren" has always been problematic, and this self-proclaimed "Swiss" confession does little to clear up the confusion. The *Mennonite Encyclopedia* informs us that the designation apparently began with the Hutterites in Moravia, as a way of identifying non-Hutterite Anabaptists.[13] This may well explain the confusion of nomenclature in the earlier years, during which some historians claim to find "Swiss Brethren" among the *Schwertler*, or sword-bearing followers of Balthasar Hubmaier in Moravia. In this case the name "Swiss Brethren" would refer more to "non-communal Anabaptists" than to followers of Schleitheim. The "Swiss Brethren" are also said to have appeared in Württemberg, Hesse, Alsace, and, of course, Switzerland. In these latter cases the designation would appear to refer more to direct followers of the Schleitheim tradition.[14]

This picture becomes even more clouded by the apparent "conversion" of some Philippite brethren following the persecutions of 1535 in Moravia. In 1537 some sixty Philippites were imprisoned at the castle of Passau; the songs they wrote formed the basis of the *Ausbund*, a later songbook of the Swiss Brethren and still in use among the Amish. The conclusion that offers itself is that some of these Philippites managed to get out of prison, and subsequently became "Swiss Brethren."[15] Furthermore, it may be that some of the Philippites who fled Moravia for Germany following the persecutions of 1535 also joined the Swiss Brethren.[16]

In short, membership in the "Swiss Brethren" for the decade of the 1530s is difficult to pinpoint--it was certainly more of a loose doctrinal fellowship than a strictly "Swiss" one, contrary to what the name might imply. It appears, however, that by 1540 the doctrinal content of this fellowship had solidified. There is explicit evidence that by 1539 significant numbers of the non-Hutterite Anabaptist fellowship in Moravia coould no longer be considered theological adherents of Hubmaier, but had thoroughly embraced the Schleitheim Articles.[17]

There are fundamental points of doctrine which help to identify the "Swiss Brethren," particularly from 1540 onward. Some of the more obvious distinctions follow. Stated negatively, from the start the "Swiss" do not agree with the Hutterite ordinances which legislated community of goods, nor do they agree with Melchiorites on christological or eschatological matters. We could add that the earlier "Swiss" also had points of difference with Hans Denck, Hans

Hut, and Pilgram Marpeck. Hans Denck criticized the divisive nature of reliance on "outer ceremonies," a clear rejection of Schleitheim and later Swiss emphases;[18] Hans Hut did not agree with the introduction of external "ordinances" of the Swiss concerning sword, oath, and clothing;[19] Pilgram Marpeck found the Swiss too legalistic and harsh in their application of the ban,[20] but for the later Dutch, on the other hand, the Swiss were too lenient in their view of shunning.[21]

By way of positive teachings, the Swiss Brethren have generally been understood to follow the outlines of the Schleitheim Articles, particularly the strong emphasis on separation from the world. The Swiss stress on separation colored their understanding of baptism as the outward commitment to the separated community, the Supper as the celebration of unity for that community, use of the ban to maintain purity (which was also maintained by absence from state church services), and rejection of both sword and oath. It is also apparent that the Swiss Brethren located in Switzerland and South Germany early on began to elaborate further ordinances concerning behavior and clothing which also served as marks of separation.

If we take the Hessian Confession at face value then, as a statement of Hessian "Swiss Brethren" beliefs in 1578, we are faced with several surprises, and not a few questions. In the first place, it is noteworthy that the Confession of 1578 is very credal in nature. In fact, the initial articles of this confession are built around a core that turns out to be, on inspection, the Apostles' Creed. While the Swiss Brethren of any era would also have had no trouble subscribing to what is affirmed in the traditional Trinitarian creeds,[22] it is rare to find Swiss documents affirming the standard formula in full detail.[23] Before celebrating (or bemoaning) the emergence of "high church" Swiss Brethren in Hesse, however, we must note the apparent fact that the Hessian Anabaptists were here following a Protestant formula, and not their own.

Landgrave Ludwig wrote to his brother Wilhelm on June 13, 1578, that Pauli Kuchenbecker "allowed himself to be instructed and informed by our preachers in several points, but concerning one part he asked for time to think, and fourteen days were granted to him."[24] The landgrave received a reply from his brother expressing doubt about the outcome, repeating the common saying, "It's not easy to tame an old wolf" (ein alter wolf nicht wol bendig zu machen sei).[25] In a document dated July 16, we are informed in convoluted fashion that Pauli Kuchenbecker and his Anabaptist brothers "met last Sunday [July 13] in his house at Hatzbach, read what was sent them by the learned men, compared it with the writing they handed in yesterday [July 15]; on the Monday following [July 14] he, Pauli, had formulated this writing."[26] In other words, in their confession Kuchenbecker and his brothers were responding to a document sent by Lutheran theologians who, to all appearances, were intent on carrying out a rather formal and standard test of orthodoxy.

This is not surprising in itself, for the Lutheran church was in the midst of confessional struggles of its own. At the time of these Lutheran-Anabaptist conversations in Hesse, Lutheran theologians elsewhere were putting the finishing touches on the Formula of Concord, the confession designed to end decades of bitter controversy in the Lutheran church. The Book of Concord was finally published in 1580.[27] Thus on the basis of contemporary documentary evidence it is immediately doubtful that the "credo" nature of this extended confession stems from "high church" Anabaptists in Hesse. Rather, it would appear that the Anabaptists in Hesse had no trouble affirming the orthodox creed as such, when they were questioned in that manner.[28]

In light of later developments in the Anabaptist-Mennonite confessional tradition, it is worthy of note that, in contrast to the omission of traditional credal affirmations in the Schleitheim Articles, and the virtual absence of such points in earlier disputations,[29] by the 1570s the Anabaptists were being pressed into credal statements of orthodoxy. A possible reason for this is that as the Protestant denominations moved into their own period of confessional orthodoxy, this had a corresponding effect on Anabaptist apologetics, resulting in the reactive adoption of standard confessional forms. The study of later Mennonite confessional activity would seem to support the conclusion.[30] However, where the Hessian Anabaptists did encounter trouble was not in the affirmation of the orthodox creed, but in what they wished to affirm beyond that creed. It is here that we can learn more about these Anabaptists: what elements did they feel were necessary to add to the traditional creed to which they also ostensibly subscribed? How did they interpret that creed in its particulars?

The first element to strike the reader, already in the first line of the introduction, is the phrase "reborn Christians and elect children of God" (*neugebornen christen und auserwelten kinder gottes*).[31] This phrase will be repeated throughout, and its centrality also will be drawn out explicitly, as will be noted shortly. In the second place, the foreword strikes a prolonged and strongly apocalyptic note: these are the last days, when false prophets abound, when many fall away to their damnation, when the Antichrist takes seat in the temple, and when vices dominate the earth. The answer is, quite simply, that the true reborn believers have no choice but to separate from such (*von solchen mir uns abwenden sollen*).[32] It is in the fear of God and in view of the abomination and evil of these last days that this confession is being written. "We hope for the salvation of the souls of all our enemies and friends, which we desire from our hearts through Jesus Christ, our Lord and Savior."[33]

The foreword serves notice that the entire discussion must be understood in the context of the last days, when apostasy will be the rule, and when the reborn and elect children of God will be called upon to separate from the evil that has come. It is within this apocalyptic context, then, that the credal affirmations follow. This emphasis on separation as a necessary step in the end times is completely in harmony with the approach of Schleitheim and the Swiss tradition generally. There is no attempt to identify key prophets or to establish a calendar of end times events, but rather the emphasis falls on a pure, separated Bride, patiently awaiting the Bridegroom, who is about to return.[34]

The appearance of such a strong, explicitly apocalyptic expectation in 1578 is somewhat surprising, and calls for further reflection. By this late date Hans Hut's predictions had long since proven false and the Münster debacle

was more than one generation past. And yet it is clear that the expectation of
the end had remained alive and well among the Swiss Brethren of Hesse. How
did this expectation play itself out in the later tradition?

There are some interesting additions to the creed itself that are worth
noting. Concerning God the Father, the Hessian Anabaptists affirm that God
is the Father of Jesus Christ, but go on to add that God is also the Father of
"all believing, reborn Christians, who have been reborn through his Word and
the power of the Holy Spirit, who believe the word of God in their lives and
have turned to God in repentant living." Just in case their Protestant inter-
locutors missed the point, the next article states unequivocally that "God is *not*
the Father of the unbelieving and unrepentant world and heathen, who persist
in their sin in unbelief, and remain in their evil and unrepentant lives until the
end, who refuse to accept Christ and refuse to turn to God."[35] Those who wish
to inherit eternal life "must recognize and confess their sins and die to them."[36]
This emphasis on conversion, rebirth, and a new ethical walk is extremely significant; it runs through the entire document and indicates that for these
brethren, creation is divided into two fundamental camps, the one belonging to
God, the other belonging to Satan. These are familiar Swiss Anabaptist
affirmations, although not exclusive to the Swiss; nevertheless they indicate the
continuation of these central doctrines in the later Swiss tradition, demonstrat-
ing that the disciplinary concerns of Tasch and Schnabel remained very much
on the later Hessian Anabaptist agenda as points of criticism.[37] Some forty
years after the Ziegenhain Agreement, the Swiss Anabaptists could still argue
that the state church had failed to become a church of serious, disciplined
believers.

The first major section of this Swiss Brethren Confession of 1578 is, as we
have indicated, a summary and elaboration of the Apostles' Creed. But the
very next article following that credal affirmation is an article on repentance,
followed immediately by articles on baptism and the Lord's Supper. It is clear
that it is at this point that the real Hessian *Anabaptist* confession begins. This is
reinforced textually by the fact that the credal section is set apart from the
more traditionally Anabaptist topics by the interposition of "Amen. Amen.
Amen."[38] Thus if the first part of the document is the elaboration of an
orthodox "confession of faith," the second part is the elaboration of an Anabaptist "Brotherly Union," a twofold emphasis already suggested by the document
title.

Central to the second half of the confession is the stress on two realms, a
theme already introduced in the credal introduction. There is no ambiguity or
invisibility about these realms: the realm of God is visibly present in those who
"confess with their lives" their status as reborn children of God. Those who do
not so live cannot claim to have God as their Father. The stress on separation
from the world has strong roots in the Swiss tradition, dating back to the
Schleitheim Articles of 1527--although it is curious that Schleitheim's
unequivocal language of separation is pitched in a lower key in this later confession.[39]

When we compare the second and "Anabaptist" half of this confession with the earlier Swiss tradition, there are both clear continuations and evident and significant shifts in content and emphasis. The article on baptism contains few surprises, emphasizing an inner baptism of the Holy Spirit and an outer baptism of water for those who have repented, believe in the gospel, confess their faith, and so request baptism.[40] By contrast, the article on the Lord's Supper takes us into unfamiliar territory for "Swiss Brethren."

The Supper, affirms the confession, "is a powerful sealing of the saved community of all believers with the Lord Jesus Christ, for just as the bread and wine is received with the mouth, so also *the heavenly flesh and blood of Jesus Christ is received spiritually, by faith, in the believing soul.*"[41] Here the interpretation of the Lord's Supper, although still "communal," has taken on very spiritualistic tones. This is no straightforward Zwinglian "memorial," but a spiritual communing in the souls of believers. Such an emphasis definitely is not present in the earlier Swiss documents concerning the Supper--certainly not in the Schleitheim Articles or the earliest Swiss interpretations.

The early Anabaptist understanding, following Zwingli, emphasized first of all the nonsacramental nature of the elements and the Supper as a memorial. Conrad Grebel noted in his letter to Thomas Müntzer, for instance, that "the bread is nothing more than bread."[42] Along with this emphasis came a corresponding stress on the Supper as an act of unity for the Anabaptist fellowship of believers.[43] Said another way, the Supper also was to be, along with baptism, an outward witness to repentance and a sign of willingness to love one's neighbor.[44] Thus the emphasis in the early Swiss testimonies, as at Schleitheim, falls not on a "spiritual presence of Christ" or an inner spiritual communion, but rather on the memorial, nonsacramental nature of the Supper, the repentance of believers, their physical and spiritual unity of love in the church (the visible body of Christ), and their separation from the world. As Schleitheim states, all who wish to partake of the Supper "must beforehand be united in the one body of Christ, that is the congregation of God, whose head is Christ, and by baptism. For as Paul indicates, we cannot be partakers at the same time of the table of the Lord and the table of devils."[45] In short, the appearance of a strongly spiritualist interpretation of the Lord's Supper in a "Swiss Brethren" confession poses some interesting questions of origin and influence.

A spiritualist understanding of the Lord's Supper was not unknown in Anabaptist circles, of course, even though it was not present among the early Swiss. Hans Denck affirmed just such a position in his "Recantation," and Melchior Hoffman's nuptial imagery could also lead to such an interpretation.[46] Given the strong Melchiorite presence in Hesse in earlier years, there is a possibility of such a tradition surviving also among the Swiss of that region. This possibility, however, is remote, particularly since the trademark Melchiorite christological teaching is emphatically rejected by Kuchenbecker and his compatriots and apocalyptic speculation is missing.[47] Had a spiritualist Gabrielite strand emerged among the Hessian Swiss Brethren, or was there some influence from another spiritualist or Schwenkfeldian tradition, or even from the Calvinist branch of the Reformed tradition? Or do we have here evidence of Dutch influence, given that some of the Dutch shared a remarkably similar conception and language of spiritual presence in the Supper?[48] While this is not the place in which to attempt detailing the development of this doctrine in the complete corpus of Swiss sources, there are significant pointers along the way that suggest a growing internal sophistication in the Swiss understanding of the Supper, and the emergence of further layers of understanding beyond the Schleitheim formulation.

One interesting Swiss Brethren confession dating from 1539 in Moravia offers us a unique glimpse at the way in which the Swiss Brethren elaborated their understanding of the Supper beyond the Schleitheim formulation, for the confession of these Moravian Anabaptists begins its discussion of the Supper by a verbatim citing of Schleitheim's article III. This brief statement is, however, further elaborated upon in a manner which will also appear in later Swiss documents; namely, the brethren say that "here one must understand the Word of Christ in a spiritual manner, as it stands written, 'my [sic] flesh is of no avail, rather the word(s) which I speak, they are spirit and life.'"[49] The Swiss Brethren in Moravia go on to clarify that when we have faith in Jesus Christ we then "truly eat of Christ and are made alive, saved, made holy and participants in Christ through the Holy Spirit."[50] Not only is eating the true bread a matter of participation in Christ by faith, but the "cup of the New Testament is suffering." The true followers of Christ drink from the same cup of suffering as their Lord.[51] Christ, conclude the brethren,

> celebrated the remembrance of his suffering and death with his disciples and also established that they were members of his body and of his flesh and limbs. They are one body and one bread in Christ.... Therefore they may truly celebrate the remembrance of his suffering and death and may properly break the bread in truth, in remembrance of the broken body of Christ, in which they have been made one bread through faith.[52]

The "spiritual" understanding of the Supper of these Swiss Brethren in Moravia in 1539 retains the communal and separatist emphases of Schleitheim, but elaborates further the interior, "spiritual" role of faith. Such a view is visible already in Hubmaier's writings, and may have entered the Swiss tradition in that way.[53]

The development of Swiss views beyond these simple affirmations concerning the Supper is difficult to trace, since the majority of the later Swiss were neither inclined to elaborate their views in writing nor had they the leisure to do so. Furthermore, the majority of theological disputations involving the Swiss put them in conversation with the Reformed, who were in basic agreement with the Anabaptist view of the Supper.[54] Nevertheless, it must be noted that at the disputation with Lutheran theologians at Pfeddersheim in 1557, where the issue of the Sacrament of the Altar was on the agenda, a fascinating "difference of opinion" surfaced between two Anabaptists concerning the question of a "real presence" in the Supper.

The Anabaptist defense concerning the Supper, presumably by the Swiss leader Diebold Winter, begins with the traditional Zwinglian and Anabaptist position, recognizing bread as only bread, and the Supper as a memorial, and goes on to appeal to John 6:63, as had the Swiss Brethren in Moravia in 1539. At some point in the discussion, however, an unnamed Anabaptist interposes that "in the Lord's Supper I understand the word 'this is my body' spiritually." This same Anabaptist goes on to clarify, "Just as the bread is eaten physically, so also one participates spiritually, albeit internally, in the body of Christ." This spiritual participation allows one to "participate in the suffering of Christ."[55]

Unfortunately, the Pfeddersheim protocol copy suffers from the apparent disinterest or laziness of the scribe in charge of documenting the exchange, so we do not know much more about this "difference of opinion" between the two Anabaptist participants. For instance, we cannot know whether the Pfeddersheim "spiritualist" considered himself Swiss, Melchiorite, or something else, although the slim evidence would argue for membership in the Swiss tradition.[56] Nevertheless it is significant that by 1557 a more "spiritualist" Anabaptist position concerning the Supper has emerged in the Rhineland. The spiritual "presence" of Christ and communion that makes an appearance at Pfeddersheim is also defended some twenty years later by Kuchenbecker and the Hessian Swiss Brethren, as we have seen.[57] Kuchenbecker's use of the phrase "himmlischen leib, fleisch und blut Jesu Christi" may well provide some further clues concerning the origins of his doctrine, but significant questions also remain concerning the influence of his view. Did this spiritualist understanding of the Lord's Supper find expression in the later Swiss tradition? Did it disappear completely, or did it survive in later doctrine or liturgical practice?

Returning to the Hessian Confession of 1578, the article on civil authority and the subsequent article on the duties of a subject suggest, at first glance, a growing distance from Schleitheim's famous article VI on the sword. The emphasis in the Hessian Confession falls entirely on obedience to the authorities, with appropriate and extensive citations from the Old Testament and the ubiquitous Romans 13. A subject is to pray for the authorities, pay all taxes, tolls, etc., and to serve the authorities "in all that is not against God."[58] This brief caveat is the only hint that the Hessian Anabaptists might refuse to take up the sword at the magistrates' behest. In fact, the matter of sword bearing and the question of whether a magistrate may be a Christian are not mentioned in this confession. They apparently did not even come up for discussion, even though such would have been very natural questions stemming from the Hessian Anabaptists' insistence on a separated church. These "errors" also are earmarked in the Augsburg Confession and the Formula of Concord as prototypical Anabaptist errors. They received full play at Pfeddersheim and were a consistent point of contention in the Reformed disputations.[59] Thus the omission of any mention of the sword in this confessional document and discussion is all the more puzzling.

It is clear that Kuchenbecker was very sensitive to the issue of Anabaptist violence, as might be expected in Hesse some forty years following the Münster episode. In earlier testimony Kuchenbecker goes to great lengths to distance himself from any "uproar" or any Anabaptists accused of such. He says he did not learn his faith from other Anabaptists, but rather came to his faith through grace; he did not eat or drink with other Anabaptists, and he adds that "those at Münster made a terrible mistake" (*haben gross unrecht gehabt*). He again denies that his separation from worldly things has any connection with uproar, and mentions having read about the Peasants' War, adding "may God protect us all from that." In this earlier testimony, as in his later confession, Kuchenbecker underlines that civil authority is established by God.[60] At any rate, Kuchenbecker did make it his practice to pray publicly for all authorities at his nocturnal Anabaptist meetings, as reported by a Lutheran pastor who attended one such meeting.[61]

The evidence is a little clearer concerning the oath, again a commonly disputed point in all the Anabaptist disputations and again condemned explicitly in the Lutheran confessions both preceding and following 1578. Although there is no mention of the oath in the Hessian Confession nor in the reply by the Marburg theologians, in the interrogation protocol of June 1578 Kuchenbecker concludes by saying that he wishes not to swear an oath to the prince; "he hoped that, as a Christian, he would be allowed to stay with no and yes."[62] It is not clear from this if Kuchenbecker had had a previous arrangement with his lord, or whether he had somehow escaped having to take an oath of allegiance. But in any case his opposition to the swearing of oaths is clear in his testimony, even if it did not form an explicit part of his confession.

This anomaly sheds some important light on the document as a whole, and helps explain the absence of an article on the sword in the confession. Articles of faith forbidding "legitimate" sword bearing, holding government office, and oath taking would have been extremely inflammatory in a Lutheran setting. Kuchenbecker and his compatriots were doing their best to remain in their home territories, and were thus being as accommodating as they could be in stating their position. Such an aim, however, colors the resulting "confession." Such a confession reveals how far these Swiss Brethren were willing to go in their accommodation, and what specifics they were willing to leave unstated, but the resulting apologetic "confession" is not a reliable guide for telling us exactly what Kuchenbecker and his group believed in detail. The conciliatory atmosphere in Hesse probably also explains the omission of explicit discussion on the sword and oath by the Marburg theologians.[63]

There is an interesting series of articles on economic matters, dealing with community of goods, the poor, labor, and usury.[64] The upshot of the first two of these articles is that reborn Christians may in fact own private property, as long as they also help out the poor and needy. Immediately following comes the confession that reborn Christians should be engaged in honest hand labor, avoiding merchandising and the like. Likewise concerning usury, the reborn children of God should not invest their money to get interest, but should use their surplus to help the poor, "to lend and give to them, and expect the reward from God."[65] This approach is consistent with the earlier Swiss position, which although it avoided ordinances enforcing the strict community of goods of the Hutterites, nevertheless was far from a blanket acceptance of capitalist principles and enjoined a very active mutual aid program.

The two final articles give a definite "Swiss" stamp to this confession. The penultimate article deals with pride in a peculiarly Swiss way: "We believe, recognize and confess that all pride, conceit and splendor of this world is an abomination and is hated by God. Therefore the believing, reborn Christians and elect children of God should flee them, be it in word, works, clothing, or behavior."[66] This point of doctrine is a close reflection of articles XX and XXI of the Strasbourg Discipline of the Swiss adopted in 1568.[67] Finally, closing out the confession is an article reaffirming the correctness of the ban in the Christian community. Such a conclusion is appropriate, in light of the essence of the "Anabaptist" half of the confession, for the thrust has been unequivocally in the direction of the necessary establishment of a visible, pure, and separated community.

Two rather unusual inclusions in the Confession of 1578 should be mentioned. There is an article concerning food, which affirms that all food may be eaten, as long as God is thanked for it.[68] Inclusion of this article is curious, since such an issue was not under debate, as far as we know, in either Anabaptist or Lutheran circles. There is a more interesting inclusion in a series of articles concerning family life. Two articles concerning marriage and divorce treat those subjects in standard ways, praising marriage and not allowing divorce except for adultery.[69] On this latter point, the Hessians make a point of saying that nothing, not even the ban, is cause for separation (nichts scheiden mag) of those who have become one flesh. More interesting still are the articles which follow, dealing with teaching of children, the obedience of children, disobedient children, and the salvation of young children. Discussion of these topics gives us an unusual window into the life of these Hessian brethren.

Again, it is not clear to what specific situation or question Kuchenbecker has addressed these articles with their corresponding citations from the Bible, but he makes it clear that Christians are ordered by God to teach their children to fear God and to keep God's commandments. Children, for their part, are to obey their parents and be submissive to them. In fact, children who disobey their parents and do not follow God's Word are hated and damned by God and are an abomination, for which reason their parents should restrain them all the more with punishment. As might be expected, Proverbs is cited several times.

While this sounds rather severe, Kuchenbecker apparently was successful in raising his own children to follow him in his Anabaptist beliefs. Hans, "Kuchenbecker's own son," is listed as one of the Swiss Brethren and under questioning acquitted himself well.[70] His father admitted that he had had Hans baptized as an infant, but since his own baptism had occurred only ten years previous, he maintained that he had acted in ignorance; otherwise he never would have had the infant baptism done.[71]

We also know something of Kuchenbecker's daughter, thanks to an account by the preacher at Speckswinkel. According to this divine, in 1575 Kuchenbecker's daughter was engaged to be married to a neighbor's son, surnamed Neidenstein. This was proclaimed in the Lutheran church, the bride-to-be renounced her father's faith, became a zealous church attender, and even partook of the Lutheran Supper prior to her wedding. But after being married a year and a half, she left her husband and turned away from the state church. When asked why, the preacher reports, "she answered that she was warned by an angel to leave her former ways or she would not be saved, so she returned again to the faith of her father."[72] This background may explain the article on disobedient children and Kuchenbecker's two citations of advice from Jesus ben Sirach concerning ill-mannered and stubborn daughters.[73] It is apparent that Kuchenbecker took his duties as a parental teacher very seriously, and that he had some success in inducing obedience to his wishes. One cannot help but wonder, furthermore, whether Kuchenbecker himself had something to do with the sending of the Anabaptist "angel" which prompted the return of his errant daughter to the fold.

In conclusion, when we compare the doctrinal statements of this Swiss Brethren Confession of 1578 with earlier Swiss teachings, we find primarily differences of emphasis and tone, and a natural further elaboration of earlier themes. The strongly credal nature of the first part is explained by the historical circumstances which dictated the writing of the confession; there is no reason to conclude that Kuchenbecker and his Anabaptist brethren would have freely chosen to begin their own confession with a traditional creed. In the Anabaptist part of the confession we find present the central Swiss tenets of repentance, baptism into the body of Christ, separation from evil, continued obedience to Christ's commands, and acceptance of the discipline of the body. The growing Swiss emphasis on ordinances defining the proper visible forms of expression of humility and mutual aid also are plainly visible in the confession. The strong concern with the education of children in the faith is interesting and indicative of the developments necessary to the survival of second- and third-generation Anabaptism. While the Hessian Anabaptists clearly continued their missionary activity of public preaching, they also were taking steps in the direction of developing a *Familienkirche*.[74]

It is worthy of note that although the number of baptized Anabaptists was, according to all evidence, rather small,[75] the number of interested onlookers was huge. In the estimation of one observer, three hundred people attended a nocturnal Anabaptist meeting and two-hour-long preaching, at which a Lutheran pastor was also present "out of interest."[76] This wide interest among the common people indicates that even at this late date in Hesse, the faith, message, and missionary activity of the Anabaptists probably was a real, and not an imagined, threat to the state Lutheranism promoted by Philip of Hesse's sons.[77] The magistrates certainly treated the Anabaptists with a seriousness that far exceeded the actual numbers of rebaptized Hessians, most likely because of the popular appeal of the Anabaptist message and the viability of their critique.

Two apparent doctrinal anomalies, namely, the exclusion of any article dealing with the prohibitions relating to sword and oath, such as are found in Schleitheim articles VI and VII, would appear to be, on examination, studied omissions rather than indications of doctrinal movement on these issues. This is an irenic confession, a plea for acceptance, and an attempt to reach accommodation with the vacillating and irenic state Lutheranism of Hesse. As such there is every attempt to smooth, rather than ruffle, theological feathers.[78] The one dramatic theological anomaly that remains is the interesting doctrine of a spiritual presence and communion with Christ at the Lord's Supper.

The Confession of the Hessian Swiss Brethren of 1578 frames at least three questions which deserve further study:

1. How did Swiss Brethren doctrine develop and change over time, and in what ways was this doctrine passed on in the tradition?[79] More specifically, how did Swiss Brethren teaching on the Lord's Supper develop in non-Hessian locales? What specific elements of the doctrine of the Supper enter the later Swiss tradition?[80]

2. What happens to the lively expectation of the end times, and how is this late apocalyptic conviction expressed (if at all) in the later confessional tradition?

3. How much or how little do the later Mennonite confessions owe to the confessional *Zeitgeist* present in Protestantism generally? Or to state the same in another way, is Mennonite confessionalism the result of an inner dynamic, or is it a response to a social need for organized apologetics? Although this issue remains to be taken up another time, a study of the Swiss Brethren Confession of 1578 suggests that the "confessional" mode of expression in Hesse owes more to external apologetic requirements than to internal theological dynamics.

NOTES

1. On the Anabaptism of this region, see John S. Oyer, "Anabaptism in Central Germany," part I: "The Rise and Spread of the Movement," *MQR* 34 (1960), 219-248; part II: "Faith and Life," *MQR* 35 (1961), 5-37.

2. See Werner O. Packull, "The Melchiorites and the Ziegenhain Order of Discipline, 1538-39," in this volume; and "Peter Tasch: From Melchiorite to Bankrupt Wine Merchant," *MQR* 62 (1988), 276-295.

3. Christian Hege, "Hesse," *ME* II, 719-727. Philip wrote the following in his last will and testament: "It is also our view and wish that no one be killed as punishment for reasons concerning faith, unless [such a one] foments uproar or bloodshed." Philip goes on to urge persuasion and conversion, citing the cases of Tasch and Schnabel as positive examples. Günther Franz, ed., *Urkundliche Quellen zur hessischen Reformationsgeschichte, IV: Wiedertäuferakten, 1527-1626* (Marburg: N. G. Elwert, 1951), 262 (hereafter cited as *TA, Hesse*). See also Philip's "Landesordnung" of 1537, in *ibid.*, 138-146.

4. The confession has been available in print since 1949, when an edition in the German language was published in the *Mennonite Quarterly Review*; a critical edition was published in 1951 in the *Täuferakten* volume for Hesse. See Theodor Sippell, ed., "Confession of the Swiss Brethren in Hesse, 1578," *MQR* 23 (1949), 22-34 (hereafter cited as "Confession," *MQR*); full text in *TA, Hesse*, 404-440.

5. As Hege notes, "after Philip's death his country was divided into four districts. Wilhelm received the principality of lower Hesse with its capital Kassel, Ludwig received upper Hesse with its capital Marburg, Philip received the lower county of Katzenellenbogen with St. Goar, while George received the upper county of Katzenellenbogen with Darmstadt," *ME* II, 726. Landgrave Wilhelm's policy in particular continued to feature banishment and persuasion rather than execution. See Wilhelm's "Ordnung" of Aug. 1, 1572, in *TA, Hesse*, 373-77.

6. C. J. Dyck, "The First Waterlandian Confession of Faith," *MQR* 36 (1962), 5-13; "The Middleburg Confession of Hans de Ries, 1578," *MQR* 36 (1962), 147-161; and "A Short Confession of Faith by Hans de Ries," *MQR* 38 (1964), 5-19. Also Howard J. Loewen, *One Lord, One Church, One Hope, and One God: Mennonite Confessions of Faith* (Elkhart, Ind.: Institute of Mennonite Studies, 1985). One must agree with Loewen's statement, "If Mennonites want to engage in historical and theological studies, they must take seriously their confessional tradition, for it provides one significant angle of vision on the historical unfolding of Mennonite life and thought" (p. 47). Much more work needs to be done, however, in unravelling the sixteenth-century prehistory of later Mennonite confessions.

7. The South German and Swiss movements are noted for producing statements relating to "Christian conduct and church regulations" rather than doctrinal or credal statements. C. Neff, J. C. Wenger, and H. S. Bender, "Confessions of Faith," *ME* I, 680.

8. See John Oyer, "The Pfeddersheim Disputation, 1557," in *Bibliotheca Dissidentium*, no. 3, ed. J.-G. Rott and S. L. Verheus (Baden-Baden: Valentin Koerner, 1987), 449-465. Virtually all Anabaptist disputations of the formal variety occurred with the Reformed branch of Protestantism. Oyer identifies only one Anabaptist disputation held with Lutherans, namely, the Pfeddersheim Disputation. While Kuchenbecker did have a private verbal exchange with the Lutheran divines, the material here documents a written exchange, not a public and verbally disputed one. Kuchenbecker's discussion and confession would not qualify as a "disputation" in the

formal sense; nevertheless the written exchange of ideas between Anabaptists and Lutherans adds to our knowledge in this area. See also John Oyer, ed. and trans., "The Pfeddersheim Disputation, 1557," *MQR* 60 (1986), 304-351, for a transcription and translation of the Pfeddersheim protocol.

9. See esp. John Oyer, *Lutheran Reformers against Anabaptists* (The Hague: Martinus Nijhoff, 1964).

10. "Bekantnus christliches glaubens und bruderliche vereinigung im glauben, etlicher neugebornen christen, und auserwelten kinder gottes, die itzt hin und her zerstreuet seind." *TA, Hesse,* 404.

11. "Confession," *MQR,* 22; *TA, Hesse,* 393. Swiss Brethren-Hutterite polemics had already assumed fixed forms by this time. See Leonard Gross, *The Golden Years of the Hutterites* (Scottdale, Pa.: Herald Press, 1980), 164-193. The Swiss rejected community of goods, arguing that people were defrauded by Hutterite practices; they objected to the Hutterite practice of "double honour" for leaders in which the *Vorsteher* were given better food, clothing, and shelter than the rest of the brotherhood; and they objected to the separation of husband and wife. The objection concerning the ban may refer to a perception of laxity in its application among the Hutterites.

12. *TA, Hesse,* 390. "Uf den ostermontag in Jorg Dieden geholz, die 'Spangenbergische dicke' genant, uf einer platten, welche von E. F. G. grenz 60 ruden weit ist, acht wiederteufer, so sich Huttische bruder nennen, und uf den pfingstdinstag 15 Schweitzerbruder im selben geholz bei einem bronnen...in mitternacht zuesamen kommen. Denselben sind aus den nechst umbliegenden dorfern als gericht Ottra und andern orten ungefehrlichen anderthalbhundert personen zuegelaufen, dero meinung, wie sie sagen, das sie ihnen zuesehen wollen."

13. According to Harold Bender, the first mention of the term appears in the Hutterite Chronicle for 1543, "where a certain Hans Klöpffer is stated to have 'formerly been a minister of the Swiss Brethren.'" *ME,* IV, 670. Klaus Deppermann states, without citing evidence, that the name came into use first at the end of the 1530s. *Melchior Hoffman* (Göttingen: Vandenhoeck und Ruprecht, 1979), 160, n. 69.

14. William Klassen notes, "Just how widely to apply the term and how precisely it was used in the sixteenth century are debatable. Johann Loserth finds evidence that even the Schwertler were called Swiss Brethren at Nicolsburg (*ME,* III, 338, 884)." *Covenant and Community: The Life, Writings and Hermeneutics of Pilgram Marpeck* (Grand Rapids, Mich.: Eerdmans, 1968), 89, n. 65. Loserth's articles ("Liechtenstein, Leonhard von" and "Nikolsburg") in *ME* III, 338, 883-886, cite little explicit evidence connecting the remnants of Hubmaier's followers with the later "Swiss Brethren" of Moravia. It may well be that the name "Swiss Brethren" takes on clearer doctrinal significance in later years.

15. The *Ausbund* says "Some Christian Songs as they were written and sung in the Castle Prison at Passau by the Swiss Brethren." Apparently, by the time of the first printing of the *Ausbund* (1564) the Philippites were identified as Swiss Brethren.

16. See the articles "Philippites" and "Plener, Philipp," by Robert Friedmann in *ME,* IV, 166-167, 192-193.

17. See "Rechenschaft und bekanntnus des glaubens....," in *Glaubenszeugnisse oberdeutscher Taufgesinnter, I. Teil,* ed. Lydia Müller (Leipzig: M. Heinsius Nachfolger, 1938), 190-205 (hereafter cited as *TA, Glaubenszeugnisse, I*). This confession of faith, although preserved only in the Hutterite manuscript tradition, is manifestly a "Swiss" confession. It contains extensive verbatim citations and further paraphrases from Schleitheim, and has no mention of community of

goods. Note especially p. 198ff. in the sections dealing with separation, the sword, and the Supper.

18. See Denck's comments regarding separation and ceremonies in his "Widerruf," in *Hans Denck: Schriften, II. Teil*, ed. Walter Fellmann (Gütersloh: C. Bertelsmann Verlag, 1956), articles VI and VII, pp. 108-109; also his comments in the exegesis of the Prophet Micah, in *Hans Denck: Schriften, III. Teil*, ed. Walter Fellmann (Gütersloh: Gerd Mohn, 1960), 82ff. Denck emphasizes faith and love as taking priority over "ceremonies," including baptism and the Supper. Cf. the comments of Depperman, *Hoffman*, 166-167.

19. "Ettlich hettenauch vermaint, die christen solten kain woer tragen, wie sy dann derhalben in Schweitz ain ordnung gemacht. Solhs hette er auch abgestelt und angezaigt, das solhs nit wider got, auch nit verpoten were. Dergleichen mit den klaidern, hetten ettlich anzaigt, wie man ainfeltig in den klaidern solte geen, solhs er inen auch durch got nit verpoten zu sein anzaigt hette, sonder man solte jeden lassen gen, wie er wolt." Christian Meyer, "Zur Geschichte der Wiedertäufer in Oberschwaben," part I: "Die Anfänge des Wiedertäufertums in Augsburg," *Zeitschrift des historischen Vereins für Schwaben und Neuburg* I (1874), 228.

20. Klassen, *Covenant*, 89 ff. See Walter Klaassen, ed., *Anabaptism in Outline* (Scottdale, Pa.: Herald Press, 1981), 222-225, for Marpeck's objections directed to the Swiss Brethren in 1542.

21. Christian Neff, "Ban," *ME* I, 219-223, esp. 221. Note the Swiss Brethren objections to the Wismar Articles of 1554, which enjoined a strict ban and avoidance (shunning) of the banned member, even by the marriage partner. "The Wismar Articles of 1554," in *The Complete Writings of Menno Simons*, ed. J. C. Wenger (Scottdale, Pa.: Herald Press, 1956), 1041-42. Compare the letter of the Swiss representatives Zylis and Lemke to Menno Simons in 1557, requesting leniency in the application of the ban. *Anabaptism in Outline*, 231.

22. Perhaps the most notable "heterodox" Anabaptist teaching was docetic Melchiorite Christology, which did not enter the Swiss tradition. The use of credal patterns certainly was not unknown in Anabaptist writings, but since most Anabaptist "confessions" were extracted in prison, as replies to questioning, the usual pattern was not an extended, reasoned argument. The most notable "Swiss" example of a confession built upon the credal pattern is Balthasar Hubmaier's "Die zwelf Artickel Christenlichs glaubens," written in 1527; in *Balthasar Hubmaier: Schriften*, ed. Gunnar Westin and Torsten Bergsten (Gütersloh: Gerd Mohn, 1962), 215-220 (hereafter cited as *TA, Hubmaier*). For a Hutterite example, see Peter Riedemann, *Account of Our Religion, Doctrine and Faith*, written in 1542 (London: Hodder and Stoughton, 1950). In the Hessian context, Tasch's "Confession of Faith" of 1538 included the simple acceptance of the "twelve articles of the Christian faith." *TA, Hesse*, 255.

23. When we paraphrase the first series of articles (leaving out the repetitious phrases and scriptural quotations) we find the following pattern. Following an opening article affirming faith in Holy Scripture as the revealed Word of God, the Hessian Anabaptists confess their faith in one, eternal, almighty God, creator of heaven and earth, and of all creatures therein, Father of our Lord Jesus Christ. Further, they affirm their faith in Jesus Christ, only Son of God, born of the Father, God of Glory, of the essence of God, having God's power, strength, and glory, the eternal Word of the Father, through whom all things were made. Jesus Christ is affirmed again as the Messiah and Word of the Father, who came in the flesh, begotten by the Holy Spirit, born of the Virgin Mary. Jesus Christ is both true God and true man. He suffered under Pontius Pilate, was crucified, dead, and buried; he descended into hell, but rose again from the dead on the third day, and sits at the right hand of God the Father. He will come again to judge both the

living and the dead. They confess further their faith in the Holy Spirit, who proceeds from the Father and the Son, also true God; thus God the Father, Son, and Holy Spirit are one godhead, three in one. The Hessian Anabaptists confess their faith in "one holy Christian church" of the reborn Christians; they confess the forgiveness of sins through the death and blood of our Lord Jesus Christ; they await the resurrection of the body and the life everlasting which God will grant to all the faithful and elect. Paraphrased from "Confession," *MQR*, 27-31; full text in *TA, Hesse*, 404-440.

24. *TA, Hesse*, 396.

25. *Ibid.*

26. *Ibid.*, 403; translation from "Confession," *MQR*, 22, with some editorial notes.

27. See F. Bente, ed., *Concordia Triglotta* (St. Louis: Concordia Publishing House, 1921), esp. the historical introduction, pp. 10-56. Although Philip of Hesse's sons were involved in the doctrinal controversies, and sponsored Jacob Andreae's preliminary efforts to produce a definitive confession in 1567 and 1570, they did not sign the final Formula. See *ibid.*, 243-250.

28. The Marburg theologians, in their response to the Swiss Brethren Confession of 1578, make mention first of the articles concerning God, Christ, etc. They go on to cite most of the Apostles' Creed, and several points besides, which they say "require no answer, since we recognize these points to be correct and Christian (as long as no other interpretation of them was intended)." *TA, Hesse*, 441-442. The Book of Concord also begins by reproducing and affirming the "ecumenical" creeds.

29. The Frankenthal Disputation of 1571, rather close in time to our present confession, could be considered an exception. The Anabaptists at this disputation also had no trouble affirming the "Twelve Articles of the Faith." See Jesse Yoder, "The Frankenthal Disputation: Part II," *MQR* 36 (1962), 116. Also Heinold Fast, "Die Täuferbewegung im Lichte des Frankenthaler Gespräches, 1571," *Mennonitische Geschichtsblätter*, n.s. 23 (1971), 7-23, esp. 15.

30. See *ME* I, 679-686.

31. *TA, Hesse*, 404.

32. *Ibid.*, 405-407.

33. *Ibid.*, 407.

34. Walter Klaassen writes concerning earlier Swiss apocalyptic expectations, "This tremendous pressure of events as it was experienced by the Sattler circle clearly illuminates the radical duality and separationism of the Schleitheim Articles. In that sense the *Brüderliche Vereinigung* is an apocalyptic document." He adds further, "Swiss Anabaptist apocalyptic was intense in its expression and expectation, but none of the principals identified themselves as specific actors in the events by which a timetable could be identified. They knew the end was near; they knew that they constituted the faithful, persecuted church; they waited for Christ to return and bring justice." "Visions of the End in Reformation Europe," in *Visions and Realities*, ed. Harry Loewen and Al Reimer (Winnipeg: Hyperion Press, 1985), 47ff.

35. *TA, Hesse*, 411.

36. *Ibid.*, 424.

37. Cf. Packull, "Ziegenhain," passim.

38. *TA, Hesse*, 424.

39. In this connection, the use of the ban is also affirmed, rather quietly, at the end of the document. *Ibid.*, 439-440.

40. *Ibid.*, 424. Cf. Schleitheim article I: "Baptism shall be given to all those who have been taught repentance and the amendment of life and [who] believe truly that their sins are taken

away through Christ, and to all those who desire to walk in the resurrection of Jesus Christ and be buried with Him in death, so that they might rise with Him." J. H. Yoder, trans. and ed., *The Legacy of Michael Sattler* (Scottdale, Pa.: Herald Press, 1973), 36.

41. *TA, Hesse*, 426. Emphasis added.

42. "dass brott nüt anderss ist dann brot." L. von Muralt and W. Schmid, eds., *Quellen zur Geschichte der Täufer in der Schweiz*, I: *Zürich* (Zurich: S. Hirzel Verlag, 1952), 15 (hereafter cited as *TA, Zurich*). Also in Hubmaier: "*das brott brot ist unnd wein wein, wie ander brott und wein.*" *TA, Hubmaier*, 162. This point of view was still being affirmed at the Pfeddersheim Disputation of 1557. See "Pfeddersheim Disputation," *MQR*, 335 ff., esp. 337 for this point.

43. George Blaurock clearly understood the Supper as an act of "union": "*sprach er, wölcher mit inen wölte in dise vereinigung gan, der sölte von disem brot essen.*" *TA, Zurich*, 38. Blaurock said further regarding the Supper: "*es söll sin ein brott der liebi und christenlichen gmuts.*" *Ibid.*, 40.

44. Jorg Schad reports how he had been a sinner; how God called him and said that if he stopped sinning, he would be forgiven. "Das habe inn bewegt und heig das zeichen bruederliche lieby begert, das er sin nechsten als guts thun wetti als im selbs und habe sich lassen güssen mit wasser." *Ibid.*, 41. The Supper was understood in much the same fashion: "das sy gott allweg im hertzen habenn und an inn dencken wettind, darzu gegen jederman bruederliche lieby erzeigen." *Ibid.* Felix Mantz emphasized that the Supper signified the unity of brothers and sisters in Christ: "*das wir ouch also eins werind ie einer des anderen brueder und schwester in Christo unsserem herren.*" *Ibid.*, 50. The twofold emphasis, on the Supper as a remembrance and as a commitment to brotherly love, is strongly present in Hubmaier. See Hubmaier's small tract of 1525, "Etliche Schlussreden vom Unterricht der Messe," in *TA, Hubmaier*, 101-104; also pp. 317-318 in *TA, Hubmaier*. Cf. *ibid.*, 113-114; 161-162; 284-304; 317-318; 355-365.

45. *Legacy of Michael Sattler*, 37. This explicitly separatist understanding of the Supper is commonly elaborated further in Switzerland. See, for example, the document written around 1546, most likely by a native Swiss author, in *Quellen zur Geschichte der Täufer in der Schweiz*, II: *Ostschweiz*, ed. Heinold Fast (Zurich: Theologischer Verlag, 1973), 141-165; esp. 153-156.

46. See Denck, "Widerruf," 109-110; translation in *Anabaptism in Outline*, 195-196. On Hoffman, see *ibid.*, 197-199; and Deppermann, *Hoffman*, 204: "In Hoffmans Konzeption von Taufe und Abendmahl wird kaum etwas ausgesagt über die Bedeutung dieser Sakramente für die Stiftung und Selbstdarstellung der Gemeinde. Ihn interessieren eigentlich nur die Folgen, die sich aus diesen beiden 'Sakramenten' für das Verhältnis Zwischen Gott und der einzelnen Seele ergeben." On Hoffman's development on the question of the Supper, see also *ibid.*, 45, 63-65, 105ff., 114-115, 152ff., 189ff., 200.

47. Articles IX and X of the Swiss Brethren Confession of 1578 seem to be explicit rejections of Melchiorite Christology, affirming that Jesus Christ "ist ins fleisch komen und ist entpfangen vom heiligen geist, hat den samen Abrahe nach der verheissung an sich genomen, ist in der junkfrawen Maria mensch worden." Also that Jesus "das wort des vaters, so mensch worden ist, ist geboren aus Maria der reinen junkfrawen, warer gott und mensch." *TA, Hesse*, 414-415.

48. See, for instance, Dirk Philips on the Supper: "Whoever believes in the Lord Jesus Christ...eats the flesh and drinks the blood of Jesus, but spiritually with the mouth of the soul, and not physically, with the mouth of the body. For spiritual food--that is what the body and blood of Christ are—must be spiritually received." *Anabaptism in Outline*, 206. Hans de Ries (1553-1638), coauthor of the most important early Dutch confessions, wrote in 1610 of the Sup-

per that it was, first, an act of remembrance; but further, the external Supper signifies "that in his glorified state [Christ] is the living bread, food and drink of the soul. The external Supper brings to our mind the office and function of Christ in glory, his institution of the spiritual Supper with believing souls, feeding them with truly spiritual food. Likewise the external Supper teaches us to rise above the external in holy prayer, longing for the reality of the gift of Christ." "A Short Confession by Hans de Ries," *MQR*, 17-18. In this formulation de Ries goes beyond the earliest Mennonite confessional statements. Compare the statements on the Supper in the 1577 Waterlandian Confession of Faith and the Middelburg Confession of 1578, both of which were also coauthored by de Ries. "The First Waterlandian Confession," *MQR* 12; "The Middelburg Confession," *MQR*, 153.

49. *TA, Glaubenzeugnisse*, I, 200. The marginal reference is to John 8, but the paraphrase indicates rather John 6:63.

50. *Ibid.*

51. *Ibid.*, 201.

52. *Ibid.*, 202.

53. In one of his later writings, "Ein Form des Nachtmals Christi," published in 1527, Hubmaier uses very similar language and also refers to John 4, 6 and 7: "Probiere sich der mensch, ob er einen rechten inwendigen und inbrünstigen hunger und durst hab nach dem brot...und nach dem tranck...sy bayde zeessen und trincken im geyst, glauben und warhait, wie unns Christus leert, Joan. 4, 6, 7. Wo das geystlich essen und trinckhen nit vorgeet, da ist das eüsserlich brot brechen, essen und trincken ein todtender buchstab." *TA, Hubmaier*, 357.

54. In the three earlier Swiss disputations, namely the disputation with Pfistermeyer (1531), the Zofingen Disputation (1532), and the Bern Disputation (1538), the issue of the Supper enters the discussion only tangentially. Thus these earlier documents afford us no opportunity to note developments in doctrine concerning the Supper. See Martin Haas, ed., *Quellen zur Geschichte der Täufer in der Schweiz, IV: Drei Täufergespräche* (Zurich: Theologischer Verlag, 1974) (hereafter cited as *TA, Drei Täufergespräche*). Likewise at the Frankenthal Disputation of 1571 there was total agreement between the Reformed and Anabaptist parties on the Supper, a fact which made the Reformed suspicious. See Yoder, "Frankenthal, II," 119.

55. "Pfeddersheim Disputation," *MQR*, 341 and 340, n. 44.

56. Although forty Anabaptists participated, we know the name of only one participant, Diebold Winter. *Ibid.*, 306. On the basis of the teachings defended by Winter it is clear that he stands within the Swiss Brethren tradition. The fact that he was chosen by the group to be their spokesman suggests that the majority of the participants were of the same persuasion.

57. A general development toward an inward piety in later Anabaptism was noted some time ago by Robert Friedmann, and it may be that we have here concrete and early instances of movement in such a direction. See his *Mennonite Piety through the Centuries* (Goshen, Ind.: Mennonite Historical Society, 1949).

58. *TA, Hesse*, 428.

59. Cf. the Augsburg Confession, article XVI: "Of Civil Affairs they teach that lawful civil ordinances are good works of God, and that it is right for Christians to bear civil office, to sit as judges, to judge matters by the Imperial and other existing laws, to award just punishments, to engage in just wars, to serve as soldiers, to make legal contracts, to hold property, to make oath when required by the magistrates.... They condemn the Anabaptists who forbid these civil offices to Christians." *Concordia*, 51; see also the Formula of Concord, article XII, in *ibid.*, 841. Also "Pfeddersheim Disputation," *MQR*, 325-329; John Oyer, "Die Täufer und die Confessio

Augustana," *Mennonitische Geschichtsblätter*, n.s. 32 (1980), 7-23, esp. 15ff; Yoder, "Frankenthal, II," 118, 127ff.; *TA, Drei Täufergespräche*, passim.

60. See *TA, Hesse*, 394.

61. See *ibid.*, 401.

62. *Ibid.*, 395.

63. The tactic of omitting mention of points on which no agreement was possible was also apparently practiced in 1538-39, when Tasch et al. and Bucer fail to mention anything in writing concerning docetic Melchiorite Christology. See Packull, "Ziegenhain," 7.

64. *TA, Hesse*, 434-438.

65. *Ibid.*, 437.

66. "Wir gleuben, erkennen und bekennen, das aller hoffart, stolz und pracht der welt, von gott verhast und ein greuel ist. Derhalben die gleubigen neugebornen christen und auserwelten kinder gottes denselben meiden sollen, es sei mit worten, werken, kleidung und geberden." *Ibid.*, 439.

67. "20. Tailors and seamstresses shall hold to the plain and simple style and shall make nothing at all for pride's sake. 21. Brethren and sisters shall stay by the present form of our regulation concerning apparel and make nothing for pride's sake." H. S. Bender, "The Discipline Adopted by the Strasburg Conference of 1568," *MQR* 1 (1927), 65. Note also the economic provisions of the Strasburg discipline in articles II, IV, V, VI, XVI, XXI, XXII.

68. *TA, Hesse*, 438.

69. *Ibid.*, 429-430.

70. He replied to his questioners that he had been rebaptized one year earlier by one Hans Grecker who "lived on the Rhine in the Alsfelt district." The brethren gathered together, he said, to admonish one another to love according to God's Word. He denied that they taught sinlessness, but maintained that he saw "no improvement following Lutheran preaching." Concerning civil authority he said it was of God, as Paul says. *Ibid.*, 403.

71. *Ibid.*, 394-395.

72. *Ibid.*, 385-386.

73. He cites Ecclesiasticus 26:10: "Keep close watch over a headstrong daughter; if she finds you off your guard, she will take her chance." Also 42:11: "Keep close watch over a headstrong daughter, or she may give your enemies cause to gloat, making you the talk of the town" (NEB).

74. See the comments of H. Fast, "Die Täuferbewegung im Lichte des Frankenthaler Gespräches, 1571," 17.

75. Kuchenbecker states that there were no more than 10 Anabaptists in the entire region. *TA, Hesse*, 393. This estimate is almost exactly half of the actual number of Anabaptists the authorities managed to round up by July 20, 1578. See *ibid.*, 403-404.

76. See *ibid.*, 399-401.

77. Perhaps part of the reason for the popularity of Anabaptism with the common people was the continued ineptitude of local Lutheran preachers. Certainly Tileman Nolte, Lutheran pastor at Schwarz who went to hear Kuchenbecker preach, was no credit to the pastoral profession. The editors of the Hessian *Täuferakten* note that, according to one source, the pastor was an incompetent and eccentric exmonk, a windowmaker by trade, whose ignorance of the Bible remained deep and thorough some thirty-six years after his departure from the monastery of Fulda. In 1604 he was finally removed from the pastorate. "Tileman Nolte kam, nachdem er 14 Jahre Priester im Stift Fulda gewesen war, 1568 nach Schwarz und wurde 1604 als 'ein

ungeschickter ebenteurer,' ein 'choresel und seines handwerks ein fenstermächer,' der nicht wisse, wo das Vaterunser in der Bibel stünde und wer es gemacht hat, abgesetzt." *Ibid.*, 400, n. 1.

78. In his reply to the response of the theologians, Kuchenbecker argues again for a visible and separated church of repentant believers, but concludes with a plea for mercy and toleration. Even though there was no agreement on all things, he says, there is no difference between us on the "main things and the high articles of faith." Surely, he says, we will not be driven from the land because of disagreement on a few minor points, treated like unbelieving Jews or people who reject Christ and the faith. *Ibid.*, 472. Mention of the "unbelieving Jews" was not without economic significance, for, traditionally, Jews in Hesse were not to own land, and convicted Anabaptists were to be subject to the same regulation as the Jews. See *ME* II, 719-720.

79. The relevance of this question is underlined by the recent book of Beulah Stauffer Hostetler, *American Mennonites and Protestant Movements* (Scottdale, Pa.: Herald Press, 1987), in which the author claims that the Schleitheim Articles functioned as the "charter" for North American Mennonites: "The first common statement of values and beliefs for the Swiss-South German Anabaptists who came to America was the Schleitheim statement of 'Brotherly Union' in 1527" (p. 77). See especially chap. 2, pp. 75-124, where the argument is developed. While Hostetler's thesis may yet prove true, more study is needed of post-Schleitheim doctrinal development among the Swiss Brethren in Europe prior to migration.

80. It is interesting to note that the article on the Lord's Supper in the Dordrecht Confession underlines the memorial aspect and the love of neighbor, but contains no hint of a "spiritual communion." See Loewen, *One Lord*, 67.

CHAPTER 3

Community as Sacrament in the Theology of Hans Schlaffer

Stephen B. Boyd

It might be said that the Reformation began, in part, as a response to a disillusionment with the church's sacramental system and spawned various efforts to reform that system. This essay is concerned with one such effort by Hans Schlaffer, a secular priest in Upper Austria who resigned his office, became an Anabaptist, and was executed in the Tirol in 1528.[1] My thesis is that Schlaffer developed an implicit sacramental theology which identified the believing community as sacramental and all of its concrete acts as potential sacraments. In the conclusion I want to suggest some possible implications of his view for ecumenical and liberationist discussions of ecclesiology, Christology, and hermeneutics.

Before turning to Schlaffer's position, I want to sketch one of the contexts of his effort by treating, very briefly, the dynamics of Martin Luther's sacramental theology--a theology to which Schlaffer specifically responded. In an effort to understand Luther's objections to the church's sacramental system, particularly his repeated criticism of the sacrament of penance, scholars have explored, among other aspects of late-medieval theology and practice, the fourteenth- and fifteenth-century preaching traditions and the confessors' manuals, as they reflected scholastic theologies of justification.

Ian Siggins has argued that scholarship has virtually ignored one of the most important influences on the young Luther's spiritual development--the parochial preaching he heard in early adolescence while living with his relatives in Eisenach.[2] Having surveyed a number of the fourteenth- and fifteenth-century preaching manuals which served as models for that preaching, Siggins suggests that the homiletic theology reflected in them sheds light on Luther's objections to the church's penitential practice.

With respect to salvation, or the forgiveness of the sinner, the sermon books focus on the need for true contrition of the heart. Siggins notes that this stress on contrition draws on a medieval tradition, flowing from Peter Lombard and Thomas Aquinas, "which located the efficacy of penance in the prior sincerity of the contrite heart."[3] This inner contrition brings forgiveness "before and apart from sacramental penance," if one intends to submit to the sacrament in obedience to the church. One might even say that these manuals teach a doctrine of "justification by contrition alone."[4] To evoke this sincerity, the preachers repeatedly encouraged their listeners to think on their deaths (*memoria mortis*). Because "there is no justification without fear," the preachers described the physical and spiritual horrors of death in order to move consciences to the grief of contrition, which attends continually to specific sins, as well as the pervasive state of sin.[5]

According to Siggins, the doctrine and spirituality of this preaching "drove young Martin Luther to abandon his legal studies at Erfurt...to seek the mercy of God in a life of devotion and penitence."[6] Because of his dissatisfaction with his spiritual state and consequent fear in the face of death, Luther became a monk:

> I was never able to be consoled about my baptism. "How (I thought) can a person become pious even once?" And so I became a monk.[7]

Uncertain of his forgiveness through the sacrament of baptism, Luther entered what was, according to the authors of the preaching manuals, the safest way to forgiveness and holiness--the religious life.

However, even in the monastery Luther could not be assured of his justification. The sacrament of penance, developed to deal with postbaptismal sins, seems to have been inadequate to his needs for assurance. Indeed, a study of the day's confessors' manuals reveals a Scotist pastoral theology which grounds the efficacy of the sacrament of penance in the power of the priest to forgive.[8] Even if the penitent came to the sacrament with attrition, motivated by fear, the priest, by virtue of his office, could, through words of absolution, complete and transform it into contrition. But Luther could never reach the perfection of contrition required by the preachers; therefore, the promise that his inadequate sorrow would be made up by the authority of the priest seemed hollow.

As Siggins observes, Luther's superior and confessor, Johann von Staupitz, helped him out of this dilemma by finally convincing him that he was expecting too much of himself and that forgiveness was to be found neither in the quality of his own contrition nor in the power of the priest to forgive, but in the "sweet wounds of Christ."[9] One realizes that Christ, prior to and apart from one's sorrow and contrition, died for one's sins. This is the *extra nos* aspect of Christ's salvific work; the act did not, and the offer of forgiveness does not, depend on the quality of one's contrition. But one also realizes that Christ died for one personally. This is the *pro me* aspect of Christ's work; it evokes both gratitude and honest self-examination resulting in true sorrow for and hatred of sin (contrition), rather than fear of its penalties (attrition). In faith the "happy exchange" takes place; what belonged to the sinner becomes Christ's, and what belonged to Christ becomes the sinner's.[10] For Luther, faith in Christ encompasses both the *extra nos* and *pro me* aspects of Christ's work and presence. Faith, then, is essentially relational; it mediates the "exchange" whereby the grace and person of Christ, which is outside the believer, comes into the believer.

It might be said that the Reformation began because of a crisis in the church's sacramental system; the church's preaching evoked an urgent spiritual striving for personal change, which, for some, the church's sacramental system did not satisfy. Put another way, the *pro me* and *extra nos* aspects of Christ's benefits and presence had been so sundered in the sacraments that parishioners were caught in a false dilemma.

For example, when Luther became a pastor to lay people and monks he saw clearly the ambiguous message reaching their ears. They were told that their contrition must spring from love and be true, but were offered indulgences which short-circuited the process of self-examination and change. This was the foundation for Luther's objection to the penitential practice of the day. On one hand, in the name of contrition, or the *pro me* aspect of faith, Luther assaulted "the citadel of priestly authority in sacramental penance, with all its attendant cheapening of grace, empty or trivial satisfactions, and indulgences."[11] In the *Ninety-five Theses* he asserted:

1. When our Lord and Master Jesus Christ said, "Do penance," he wanted the whole life of believers to be penance.

2. That word cannot be understood of sacramental penance (that is, confession and satisfaction, celebrated by the ministry of priests).

In opposition to the cheapening of grace, he insisted on a vigilant, rigorous contrition. On the other hand, perceiving the danger of overemphasizing the *pro me* aspect, Luther declared:

3. No one is certain of the truth of his own contrition.[12]

Therefore, when one's conscience is uncertain, one should simply trust in Christ, who says, "Whatever you shall loose on earth shall be loosed in heaven."[13] One should go to confession and gain absolution in faith--opening oneself to the *extra nos* aspect of Christ's presence available in the sacraments of the church. Faith in Christ's work and his presence grounds both true contrition and trust in Christ's promise of forgiveness through those who hold the keys. Both poles of the sacraments must be held in tension lest the believer's conscience and life be torn asunder.

Luther's sacramental theology can be seen as an attempt to hold together the *extra nos* and *pro me* aspects of Christ's work and presence, thereby maintaining the relational character of faith in the same. Jaroslav Pelikan claims that Luther argued for infant baptism against the Anabaptists and the real presence against the Sacramentarians based on the principle that "faith builds and is founded on the Word of God, rather than God's Word on faith."[14] In other words, Christ is there not because one believes it, but because Christ has said that he would be. Here, Luther emphasizes the *extra nos* character of Christ's presence. Christ is "out there," in the elements, and is offered by the church and its officer, who says the words of institution and consecration.

In fact, by 1520 Luther reduced the number of sacraments from seven to two, baptism and the Lord's Supper, because of the particularly strong *extra nos* character of Christ's presence in them. For him, sacraments were only those acts specifically instituted by Christ, which involved material elements, and to which Christ promised his presence. These conditions were met only by baptism and the Supper, whose efficacy rested not on the quality of human faith, but on God's promise. Because penance involved nonmaterial elements and received no explicit promise of Christ's presence in Scripture, Luther considered it to be a means of grace rather than a sacrament.[15]

However, Luther's sacraments were not without a *pro me* aspect. Even with infant baptism, Luther admits the necessity of a personal element in the sacrament when he argues against the Anabaptists that the burden lay with them to prove that faith is not present in infants. With respect to the Supper, as with penance, Luther opposed a strictly mechanical understanding of the sacrament. In his 1531 tract, "Concerning the Private Mass and Papal Ordination," Luther insists that the body and blood of Christ are present in the Supper only when it is carried out in the fashion prescribed by Christ. That is, the elements must be consecrated, distributed, and received by at least one congregant.[16] He therefore not only rejects the mass as sacrifice, but also doubts that "solitary masses" for the dead are sacraments, because there is no distribution and reception. There must be an exchange in order for the Supper to be sacramental; there must be a flow of grace from the consecrated, distributed, and received elements to the believer through faith.[17] Sacramentality necessarily involves relationality. Again, Luther's sacramental theology can be viewed as an effort to restore relationality to the sacraments.

It is clear that, in Luther's mind, the flow of grace, at least in the sacraments, was uni-directional; it flowed from the elements consecrated by the duly called, educated, and ordained officer to the recipient. During the controversy about *Hauskommunion*, Luther adamantly linked the Supper to the pastoral office. Emphasizing the public character of that office, Luther wanted to secure the tender conscience in something outside the self--the publicly called and ordained ministry of the church.[18]

Hans Schlaffer, ordained in 1511, left the secular priesthood in 1526, because of a similar disillusionment with the sacramental system of the late-medieval church and the officers who administered it.[19] He confessed that his ordination vows of poverty, chastity, and obedience meant nothing to him and his ecclesiastical colleagues. He observed that he received, in addition to board and clerical exemptions from taxes, tolls, and interest, a salary of forty to fifty guilders, and still wanted more. In this context of excess food and drink, he found celibacy an unreasonable expectation.[20] As for the preaching office, he later could not remember what he preached, for as much as a year would pass without his reading so much as a page of the Old or New Testament.[21] His understanding was that, through his good works and reading of the mass, he could make not only himself blessed, but also his parishioners.[22] However, he often experienced "anxiety and restlessness." He, therefore, considered joining the Carthusian Order and "ran again and again to the Roman grace, confession, and did things, I know not what." Nevertheless, he could not still his conscience before God.[23]

Through the agency of Luther, Schlaffer claims that God's eternal Word was opened to him in the "testimony of the Holy Scripture." Encouraged by Luther's tracts and sermons, the anxious priest began to read "the Bible, the Gospels, and the letters of the apostles."[24] In them Schlaffer discovered that one is not justified nor made blessed by works of the law, but by "faith in Jesus

Christ." Consequently, he stopped celebrating the mass, resigned his office, and retired to the castle Weinberg of the Protestant Lord von Zelk near Freistadt in Austria.

Schlaffer's involvement in the religious ferment of the 1520s was brief but eventful. Although he had earlier spoken out against the Anabaptists, he was attracted to Hans Hut in Nicolsburg and later took his side in a controversy Hut had with Balthasar Hubmaier. In 1527 Schlaffer had contact with Jacob Wiedemann and Jacob Kautz in Augsburg, Ludwig Hätzer and Hans Denck in Nuremberg, and Oswald Glait and Wolfgang Brandhuber from Linz in Regensburg. From Regensburg, Schlaffer traveled to Rattenberg on the Inn and stayed with a family friend in nearby Brixlegg.[25] The length of Schlaffer's stay in the Rattenberg area is uncertain, but he probably had contact with the Anabaptist group there and may have been responsible for founding the congregation which enthusiastically received Leonhart Schiemer.[26] Probably because of Archduke Ferdinand I's mandate against the Anabaptists, published in November, and Schiemer's subsequent arrest, Schlaffer decided to travel to Hall. On December 6, 1527, he was arrested in Schwaz.

During the nearly eight weeks of his confinement leading up to his execution on February 4, 1528, Schlaffer wrote all but one of his extant works. In those writings he develops a theology in which he articulates the means by which his conscience found peace. Because, in his case, it did not effect a personal, inward justness or transformed life, Schlaffer rejected the *ex opere operato* character of the old church's sacramental system, as well as Luther's real presence. As an alternative, he developed an implicit, or functional, sacramental theology which identified the community of gathered, baptized believers as the sacramental medium of God's transforming grace. We shall view his idea of the sacramental community in the context of his understanding of sin, the work of Christ, and its appropriation by the believer.

Although his brief writings do not yield an extensive anthropology and doctrine of sin, Schlaffer assumes that all human beings are in a state of sin, that is, they are "always turned toward [their] own desires."[27] He asserts,

> We are all by nature [as soon as we are able through reason to know the difference between good and evil] an evil tree and are incapable of doing good.[28]

This state does not prevail at birth, but is activated later, when one is able to know the difference between good and evil. Sin, then, is natural, not in the sense that human beings are born in it, but that it seems inevitable that human beings choose evil. This rejection of original sin allowed Schlaffer to deny the necessity of infant baptism for forgiveness and its effects, and to ascribe, as we shall see, a different role to baptism.

Responding to human sin, Christ accomplishes a threefold work, in Schlaffer's view--a view that sees Christ both as an *extra nos* and *pro me* reality. Christ suffered and died "on account of our sins and rose for our justness (*gerechtigkait*)."[29] As for Christ's death and blood, Schlaffer calls it a "sufficient sacrifice" which "achieved an indulgence for your sins...and freed and purified your evil conscience."[30] It was through Christ's death that God "erected also an eternal covenant with those believers."[31] There is then a certain vicarious, *pro nobis* character to Christ's death through which human beings have gained pardon and a purified conscience. But Christ also rose "for our justness," or, as Schlaffer elsewhere says, "so that one could and should not live in himself, but that Christ might."[32] For Schlaffer, justification brings a transformation of one's mode of living--rather than being turned toward one's own desires, one lives as Christ did, indeed Christ lives in one. Justification, therefore, involves not only a forensic imputation, but also an intrinsic impartation of righteousness, or justness. Christ's suffering and death purifies the conscience, preparing one to receive the living presence of the resurrected Christ.

Christ is also an exemplar for Christians in that he "testified to us of a model with his life that we also should live and act as he...."[33] But for Schlaffer, Christ is an exemplar, because he is first a sacrament:

> For he [Christ] has from you [the Father] all power in heaven and on earth and he shows us through him and from your goodness the way, the truth and the life *to* him and *in* him.[34]

One can follow him, because one has received him.

For Schlaffer, suffering is required to change the sinful nature of the human being which is turned in on the self, in order that one might receive the transforming reality of Christ. "Whoever does not suffer with him [Christ] will not share the inheritance."[35] Both Scripture and nature testify to this necessity. Schlaffer attests, "The whole Scripture speaks only of suffering." Abraham, Isaac, Jacob, and others came to faith only through affliction.[36]

However, one does not have to be one of the "scriptural experts" (*schrift geleerten*), or even literate, to learn this important truth. For example,

> with a hen or fish or other animal, that you want to eat, it is clear that it (according to its own will and pleasure) cannot prepare (*rechtfertigen*) itself, that is, it may not lay itself out, open itself, clean itself and boil or fry itself. But you must do it according to your will, which it must suffer. You must prepare (*rechtfertigen*) it according to your will.[37]

Ordinary creatures are a living book teaching the same lesson. The pain experienced with everyday obstructions to the intentions of one's will awakens the human being to the fact that one is "always turned toward his own desires."[38] One recognizes that one's highest end is not achieved by the exercise of one's own will. One sees that "he cannot come farther through himself, for as he knows, a wild tree cannot become better without a gardener." Only God can and "must make [one] pious, just, and virtuous"; therefore, one "must subject himself to God and suffer his will."[39] Much suffering and affliction is required for one to come "to that for which he was originally created."[40]

The state originally intended for human beings was a communal participation, characterized by receiving what one needs from others and giving to others in the context of God's grace. That original state is now a renewed possibility through Christ. Schlaffer articulates the two dynamics of this participation by stressing the inward coming of Christ and the outward body of Christ.

As we have noted previously, Christ not only died *for* us, but also rose to live *in* us. "The same Word became flesh and dwelt *in* us"; "the devil, death and hell are only overcome through Christ *in* us."[41] Simultaneously the believer is incorporated into a larger body of Christ through faith, "which is a work and gift of God within us."[42]

For Schlaffer, the "great mystery (*grosse geheimnuß*)" of the Christian faith is Christ's relationship not to the bread and the cup, but to the believing community.[43] The body of Christ is "the believing community of Christ,"[44] in which "we are members of his body, of his flesh, and of his bones and become two in one flesh."[45] Christ "is conceived and born, suffers, dies and is raised in their own bodies," and they become one body with him, "members of his body, from his flesh and from his body."[46] The gathered, believing community is where the present reality of Christ is experienced and where mutual giving and receiving takes place. Schlaffer had a quite concrete notion of the presence of Christ in the community. Having received what is needed from others in the name of Christ, the believer is free "to maintain the community, to give for his brother as Christ gave for him." This mutual sharing involves love and suffering, wealth and poverty, honor and humiliation, sorrow and joy, death and life, or "all that has body and life."[47] In each aspect of the community's everyday life, the Christian serves the sister and brother as Christ served her or him. The communal life of Christians carries, then, sacramental significance.

In fact, Matthew 28:18-20 seems to have served Schlaffer a similar purpose as John 6:48ff. did Luther. It contains the words of institution for the only implicit sacrament (though never so called by Schlaffer) he affirmed--the gathered community of baptized believers. For Luther, if the pastor said the words of institution in the presence of at least one believer, Christ promised his presence. So with Schlaffer, if one went, taught all people, and baptized them (i.e., those who had been taught), Christ promised his presence in the community.[48] Consequently, for Schlaffer baptizing infants (i.e., those who were incapable of receiving instruction) would be like Luther's intentionally changing the words of institution, to which Christ had promised his presence. For this reason Schlaffer sided with Hut against Hubmaier in Nicolsburg, criticizing the latter for baptizing anyone who came after his preaching without asking about personal confession. The result, according to Schlaffer, was that one sees little *besserung*.[49]

As we have observed, Schlaffer never explicitly referred to the community as a sacrament, but he seems to have had an implicit or functional sacramental theology which imbued the everyday life of the believing community with sacramental significance. As for Luther's two sacraments, baptism and the Supper, Schlaffer was critical of his defense of infant baptism and assertion of the real presence of Christ in the Supper.

As noted above, Schlaffer views infant baptism as disobedience to Christ's instructions, which, therefore, assures his absence, rather than his promised presence. Rather than an *ex opere operato* medium of grace, Schlaffer sees baptism as the means by which one is incorporated into the body of Christ.[50] It is the outward, public sign of an inner, "correct penance (*rechte bueß*)."[51] By "correct penance" Schlaffer means that water baptism is a sign that one has turned away from the world. In contrast to the Roman confessional, to which

Schlaffer had repeatedly returned without satisfaction, believers' baptism was the public confession that one was "a follower of Christ and his teaching," which marked a "separation from the world" and a "betterment of life."[52] Baptism is, then, a vow similar to that taken by Luther upon entering the monastic life. With it one enters the sacramental community, or body of Christ, wherein one receives that which is Christ's and shares it with others.

As Schlaffer could attest from his jail cell, following Christ's teaching leads to opposition by the world and usually to persecution and death, or the baptism of blood.[53] Schlaffer believed the renewal of believers' baptism in his own time had eschatological significance:

Therefore God, in this last dangerous time, through his Son, constituted again a public, Christian, holy community. So he also desires that it be made public and before the world through the outer sign of the baptism.[54]

God was reconstituting a holy community, like those of early Christianity.

Schlaffer testified that his early reading of Luther convinced him that the mass was not a sacrifice. On the basis of Scripture (Hebrews 8:10-13), he affirmed the Supper as a memorial of Christ's "covenant and new testament," to which one commits oneself in baptism.[55] Just as baptism does not effectuate a change in the individual, but is a testimony of that change, so too the Supper is not a sacrifice, but a testimony to one's desire "to have community and be a participant in all things with the body of Christ."[56] He also rejected Luther's insistence on the real presence in the bread and wine:

They make so many glosses about the word of the Lord in John and want to have the body of Christ or his flesh in the bread and his blood in the cup and say it is not hard or difficult to eat and drink daily. The reason is, it creates good and peaceful days and they live in sumptuous eating and drinking...remaining in their fleshly lives.

But,

Christ says, "Whoever eats my flesh and drinks my blood, remains in me and I in him."...

Here one sees well that the eating and drinking is something new, different from worldly lives.[57]

For Schlaffer, Christ is not outside in the elements, but inside believers whose lives are being transformed and in the community where the sharing of love and suffering, wealth and poverty, honor and humiliation, sorrow and joy, death and life takes place.

It might be said that Schlaffer's disillusionment with the power of the church's sacramental system to effect personal, moral transformation, as evinced by his own life as a cleric, led him to assert the necessarily mutual character of sacramental acts. Further, this led him to a democratization of the sacraments which was more extensive than Luther's.

Luther wanted to correct certain abuses of the *ex opere operato* character of the sacraments, such as masses for the dead, by insisting that, for the sacrament to be effective, the pastor not only had to say the words of institution and consecration, but also that the elements must be distributed and received by at least one believer. For him, a sacrament is a sacrament only when it is both given and received. But, according to Luther, it must be given by an ecclesiastical officer who has received his vocation and investment of authority to preach, teach, and administer the sacraments from a superior. This pastoral office required a relatively high level of education and brought to its holder a corresponding economic and social status.

Schlaffer's criticism of Luther's defense of infant baptism and insistence on the real presence in the Supper might be seen as an implicit critique of Luther's criteria for determining who is able to perform, or offer God's grace in, the sacraments. In Schlaffer's view, education, money, and social status, rather than enhancing one's ability to experience the transforming presence of Christ, obstruct the process. In fact, wealth and social standing tend to encourage people to see Christ as a reality outside themselves, for that view "creates good and peaceful days" and allows them to "live in sumptuous eating and drinking...remaining in their fleshly lives." Rather than opening themselves to the transforming presence of Christ, they keep Christ at a distance, remaining unchanged.

Schlaffer agrees with Luther that relationality is necessary for grace to be conveyed in sacrament, that is, that it must be offered and received. However, he insists that the sharing is not uni-directional; grace does not flow only through the duly called, educated, and ordained ecclesiastical officer. In a sacramental act anyone is a potential giver and anyone a potential receiver. The prerequisites for giving or receiving have nothing to do with one's educational level, financial status, or social power. One is prepared for radical receptivity and liberal giving by a process of suffering. This suffering is caused by the deprivation of the object of one's desires, which brings the recognition of one's limitations, that is, that one "cannot come farther through himself." Convinced that one cannot supply all of one's own needs, one opens oneself to receive what one needs from others within the body of Christ. By doing so, one receives Christ himself.

Because the wealthy are more likely to convince themselves that they can supply their own needs, the poor and oppressed, who "have a natural affinity to the suffering of Christ," are more likely to enter into the mutual sharing of the "holy," or as I have suggested, sacramental community.[58] This fact may have been behind Schlaffer's polemical use of the gospel of all creatures:

> For Christ taught the gospel to the poor, lay people in terms from their own occupations and work and not with a lot of bookish circumlocutions. He cited Scripture only for the purpose of convincing the stiff-necked scriptural experts (*schrift geleerten*). For the common man (*gmeineman*) is more easily convinced through creatures than through Scripture.[59]

Using Christ as the example, Schlaffer denies the exclusive right to preach the gospel to those who are less likely to respond to it and enter into the transforming mutual sharing of the body of Christ, that is, the "stiff-necked" clerical interpreters of Scripture. In fact, the gospel is most convincingly preached, not by proof-texting or even an erudite exegesis of the scriptural text, but by the use of images, metaphors, or similes which refer to the natural world.

Conclusions and Implications

I have argued that Hans Schlaffer, responding to a crisis within the sacramental system of the late-medieval church, developed an implicit, pervasive sacramental theology. He agreed with Luther that the sacramental mediation of grace is necessarily relational, but insisted further that there must be mutuality within that relationality. One receives the benefits of Christ and Christ himself in the context of the mutual sharing of a transformed and transforming community. This notion of Schlaffer's insistence on the mutual character of the sharing also entailed a certain democratization of the communal life; anyone is a potential giver and anyone a potential receiver.

With reference to the traditional Reformation principles of *solus Christus, sola gratia*, and *sola scriptura*, I would like to suggest some possible contributions Schlaffer's view might make to discussions of ecclesiology, Christology, and hermeneutics in ecumenical and liberationist circles.

As the traditions identified as the believers' churches have not generally given a great deal of attention to sacramental theology, the recognition and analysis of an implicit or functional sacramental theology may be of some ecumenical significance. For example, the Roman Catholic bishop of Würzburg, Hans-Werner Scheele, has recently described a similar view of sacramentality in the early Luther. Quoting one of four 1519 sermons in which Luther says, "The picture of Christ is nothing else but that of Christ on the cross and of all of his dear saints," Scheele argues that Luther believed that "the 'once for all' work of Christ is co-completed by his saints."[60] Rather than abrogating Luther's insistence on *solus Christus* and *sola gratia*, this notion of the role of the saints is interpreted by Luther as fully consistent with the same. Again, according to Luther, "when the saints act like Christ and act with Christ so that their engagement in the work of salvation becomes fruitful, then that happens through Christ." Further, with respect to the mediation of grace, "...through the same sacraments, you are included and made one with all the saints..." and are "also drawn and changed into a spiritual body...of Christ and all the saints and by this sacrament [Supper] put into possession of all the virtues and mercies of Christ and his saints."[61] Scheele concludes that for Luther, "to go to the sacrament" means "to take part in this fellowship."[62]

Schlaffer, I think, would agree. As for salvation in Christ alone, Schlaffer affirms the "once-for-all allness" of Christ's work--not in the sense that Christ and his work remain external, limited in space and time to Palestine fifteen hundred years previously, but in the sense that the incarnation first initiated the ongoing existence and work of the salvific community, or body of Christ. For Schlaffer, one is saved by Christ alone, who has been embodied in the lives of Christians through the successive generations since the resurrection of Christ. Those Christians and those concrete communities which birthed them could be viewed as "a prolongation of the incarnation."[63] This view might have interesting implications for those who insist that Christ's maleness delimits the Christian apostolate, or for those women who wonder whether a male Christ can be a savior for them.[64] From Schlaffer's christological perspective, Christ is both male and female, in that Christ has been, is, and will be embodied in the lives of men and women.

As for salvation by grace alone, Schlaffer, too, insists that grace is not experienced in isolation, but only in relation to others. Grace is necessarily relational and is experienced in a community characterized by mutuality. The ground for this mutuality is prepared by the recognition and acknowledgment of one's own vulnerability and that of others which issues from the experience of suffering. From Schlaffer's perspective, the church can do nothing with more potential to revitalize itself than to exercise a "preferential option for the poor."[65]

As for another principle of Reformation theology--*sola scriptura*--in Schlaffer's view, personal transformation comes not from the force of logic derived from an argument based on an authoritative text, nor from the authoritative weight of the superior educational, social, or ecclesiastical status of the interpreter. Rather, transformation is effectuated when a person opens himself or herself to the grace offered by God, initiated by Christ, and mediated through the contemporary body of Christ--the concrete, believing community. This receptivity is most often facilitated when the witness connects the viator's own experience of suffering to that of Christ, as revealed in Scripture, by means of images from the natural world--also a part of the viator's immediate experience. For Schlaffer, Scripture, like Christ, means nothing if it remains external, that is, if it is not connected to one's personal experience of suffering. The scriptural testimony to God's grace in Christ is authenticated by the believing community, which, empowered by Christ's presence, responds to the openness and needs of the viator.

In this sense Schlaffer's position concerning a reliable authority for doctrine and practice might be more closely associated with certain late-medieval Catholic than with Protestant notions.[66] That is, he seems to imply that Scripture alone, without the authenticating testimony of tradition, is insufficient. However, the kind of tradition which authenticates the scriptural witness to Christ is not the cumulative theological reflection passed on in learned texts interpreted by the Roman magisterium. Rather, it is the transformed and transforming life of the community which has been received by those in the believing community and passed on to the viator. This transforming life is experienced in every aspect of the community's life--physical, emotional, psychological, and spiritual.

NOTES

1. On Schlaffer's life and writings, see Robert Friedmann, "Schlaffer, Hans," *ME* IV, 457-459. For a brief summary of his theology, see W. Wiswedel, *Bilder und Fürhergestalten dem Täufertum*, II (Kassel: J. B. Oncken, 1952) 191-201.

2. See his *Luther and His Mother* (Philadelphia: Fortress Press, 1981) for details.

3. Ian Siggins, "Luther and the Catholic Preachers of his Youth," in *Luther: Theologian for Catholics and Protestants*, ed. George Yule (Edinburgh: T. & T. Clark, 1985), 65.

4. Siggins, *Mother*, 61-62.

5. Siggins, "Preachers," 67.

6. *Ibid.*, 68.

7. Quoted in *ibid.*, 69.

8. See Thomas Tentler, *Sin and Confession on the Eve of the Reformation* (Princeton: Princeton University Press, 1977).

9. Siggins, "Preachers," 69.

10. See Ian Siggins, *Martin Luther's Doctrine of Christ* (New Haven: Yale University Press, 1970), 152-153.

11. Siggins, "Preachers," 71.

12. Quoted in *ibid.*

13. Quoted in *ibid.*

14. "Luther's Defense of Infant Baptism," in *Luther for an Ecumenical Age: Essays in Commemoration of the 450th Anniversary of the Reformation*, ed. Carl S. Meyer (Saint Louis: Concordia Publishing House, 1967), 200-218.

15. Jaroslav Pelikan, "The Theology of the Means of Grace," in *Luther for an Ecumenical Age*, 124-147. Luther later divided the traditional sacrament of private penance into public forgiveness (the liturgical general confession and absolution), private pastoral confession, and mutual, lay correction.

16. E. F. Peters, "Luther and the Principle: Outside the Use There is No Sacrament," *Concordia Monthly* 42 (1971), 643-652. Against his perception of the Zwinglians, Luther also asserts that the body and blood are present throughout the ceremony rather than just with the reception.

17. Roland Bainton observes that Luther continually maintained that whatever mode of physical presence there was, there was no benefit without faith. "Luther and the Via Media at the Marburg Colloquy," *Lutheran Quarterly* 1 (1949), 394ff.

18. See Peter Manns, "Amt und Eucharistie in der Theologie Martin Luthers," in *Amt und Eucharistie*, ed. Peter Bläser (Paderborn: Bonifacius-Druckerei, 1973), 68-173.

19. Lydia Müller, ed., *Glaubenszeugnisse oberdeutscher Taufgesinnter, I. Teil* (Leipzig: M. Heinsius Nachfolger, 1938), 119 (hereafter cited as *TA, Glaubenszeugnisse*, I).

20. *Das Kunstbuch (KB)*, 1561, Bürgerbibliothek, Bern, Mss. Codex 464, 117v: "...wolt ich mich nit alein mit meine vermeinten guten werckhen als meslesen und beten (mit fassten ließ ich mir nit wee gschechen) selig machen, sonder ouch andern als ein mitselsorger, darzu hilflich sein." Having discovered a manuscript of this devotional book of the Marpeck circle, Heinold Fast is preparing a critical edition. All citations from the *Kunstbuch* are from the notes to this edition, which Dr. Fast made available to me.

21. "Ein einfaltig gebet durch ein gefanngnen armen b[rude]r imherren zu Schwatz gebetet

unnd betreubt bis inn denn Tod." *KB*, 117v-118r: "Wie und was ich aber glernt und gebredigt, o herr, so bekenn ich, das ich inn etlich jaren nit ein blat weder im alten noch neuen testament nach der ordnunng glensenn hab, ja nit wissen kapt, was testament sey."

22. *Ibid.*, 117v.

23. *Ibid.*, 118r: ...oft inn angst und unfrid meiner gwissen gstossen...darinnen ich mir zu ermalen furnam, ain kartheiserr zu werden, lief hin und wider inn römischen gnaden, beichtet und thet waiß nit was. Aber inn dem allem konth ich mein gwissen nit zufriden stellen gegen dir, mein ewiger got."

24. *Ibid.*, 118r-118v: "...do befannde ich, das nit die werckh, ja herr, ouch die werckh des gsatz, so du uns durch Mosen geben, ich gschweige von menschen erdachte und gutdunckende werckh nit rechtfertigen noch seligmachen mochten, sonnder alein der gloub inn Jesum Christum, deinen einigen sun, o himlischer vater."

25. *TA, Glaubenszeugnisse*, I, 120.

26. Schlaffer's traveling companion, Ulrich Moser, was an employee of the Fuggers, the Augsburg banking family which had interest in the Rattenberg smelting works, so Schlaffer probably had contact with the mining community.

27. *Ibid.*, I, 94.

28. *Ibid.*, 86.

29. *Ibid.*, 115. Although *gerechtigkeit* is often translated "righteousness" in a theological context, I translate it here as "justice" or "justness" to convey the sociomoral component which is important to Schlaffer. See a similar translation by Bengt Hoffman, *The Theologia Germanica of Martin Luther* (New York: Paulist Press, 1980), 184, n. 177, in the *Theologia Deutsch*, which may have served as a source for Schlaffer.

30. *KB*, 125v-126r: "Das ist, wie euch Christus mit seinem tod und plutvergiessen ablaß eurer sunden erlanngt hat und mit dem vaterr, weil ir feind warn, versuent, eure bose gwissen dadurch besprengt und gereinigt."

31. *TA, Glaubenszeugnisse*, I, 111.

32. *Ibid.*, 114.

33. *Ibid.*, 89; 114-115.

34. *KB*, 112r. Emphasis added.

35. *TA, Glaubenszeugnisse*, I, 88.

36. *Ibid.*

37. *Ibid.*, 86.

38. *Ibid.*, 94.

39. *Ibid.*, 94.

40. *Ibid.*, 94.

41. *Ibid.*, 107, 96. Emphasis added.

42. *KB*, 124v-125r.

43. *Ibid.*, 122r: "O, das ist ein grosse geheimnuß inn Christo und seiner gmein. Dieweil nun Christus als das houbt im sterblichen fleisch lept, aber on sundt, must es nur gelitn und getödtet sein. Seyen wir nun seine glider und mitsampt im ein gantzer leib, so muessen jee di glider dem houpt allennthalben nachvolgen, welches aber nit allenthalben mit got, das ist kein glid am leib nit."

44. *TA, Glaubenszeugnisse*, I, 109.

45. *KB*, 122r: "Dann wir seyen glider seines leibs von seinem fleisch und von seinem gebein und werden zwey inn einem fleisch sein."

46. *TA, Glaubenszeugnisse*, I, 95.

47. *Ibid.*, 109.

48. *Ibid.*, 111: "Erstlichen spricht Christus, mir ist geben aller gwalt im himmel und auf erden; darumb geet hin, leeret alle völker und tauft sie (zu versteen, welche ir geleernet habt) im namen des vaters, suns und des heiligen geists und leeret sie halten alles, was ich euch bevolhen hab. Nembt war, ich bin bei euch bis zu ennd der welt usw." Also, in his *Von der Art und Gestalt Christi, was er geistlich und leiblich sey geformieret*, Schlaffer cites Jesus' promise to be present "where two or three are gathered" (Matt. 18:20) in his name. Archiv mesta Bratislavy, Bratislava, CSSR, Signature: Codex Hab 6 (1581), 133r.

49. *TA, Glaubenszeugnisse*, I, 123. See also Werner O. Packull, *Mysticism and the Early South German-Austrian Anabaptist Movement, 1525-1531* (Scottdale, Pa.: Herald Press, 1977), 113.

50. *TA, Glaubenszeugnisse*, I, 117.

51. *Ibid.*, 122.

52. *Ibid.*, 114, 122.

53. *Ibid.*, 114: "Der sie [wassertauf] aber annimbt, ja sonderlich jetzt zur zeit des großen anstoßs, ist nemlich im geist und feuer von Christo zuvor getauft, das er nachmals zu dem tauf des bluets auch komen mag."

54. *Ibid.*, 93.

55. *KB*, 118v.

56. *TA, Glaubenszeugnisse*, I, 109.

57. *KB*, 123r-123v: "Die machen der glosn sovil uber deß herrn wort im Johanne und wellen den leib Christi oder sein fleisch im brot und sein plut im kelch haben und ist nit hart unnd schwer, teglich zu essen und trinckhen, ursach, es schaffet gut, ruehig tag und leben inn wolessen und trincken, inn allem wollusst und hocher wirdigkeit...doch Christus spricht: Wer mein fleisch isset und mein plut trincket, der pleibt in mir und ich in im.... Hie sicht man wol, das essen und trinckhen ein anders neues, dann wie di welt lebt, ist."

58. See Packull, *Mysticism*, 116.

59. *TA, Glaubenszeugnisse*, I, 95.

60. "'A People of Grace': Ecclesiological Implications of Luther's Sacrament-Related Sermons of 1519," in *Luther's Ecumenical Significance: An Interconfessional Consultation*, ed. Peter Manns and Harding Meyer (Philadelphia: Fortress Press, 1984), 130-133.

61. Quoted in *ibid.*, 127.

62. *Ibid.*, 130.

63. Neal Blough uses this formulation to characterize a similar position in the thought of Pilgram Marpeck. *Christologie Anabaptiste* (Geneva: Labor et Fides, 1984), 105.

64. According to sections 5 and 6 and Commentary 30 of the *Inter Insigniores*, issued in 1976 by The Congregation for the Doctrine of the Faith, since sacramental signification requires a natural resemblance between the sign and thing signified; and since the priest, in the specific and unique act of presiding at the eucharist, is a sign; and since Christ was and remains a man, therefore it is fitting that priestly ordination be reserved to men. Cited in the first draft of "Partners in the Mystery of Redemption: A Pastoral Response to Women's Concerns for Church and Society," issued by the National Conference of Catholic Bishops. See chap. 5, "Christology: Can a Male Savior Save Women?" in Rosemary Ruether's *Sexism and God-Talk: Toward a Feminist Theology* (Boston: Beacon Press, 1983), 116-138, esp. 138, where she articulates a christological affirmation similar to that of Schlaffer: "Christ, as redemptive person and Word of God, is not to

be encapsulated 'once-for-all' in the historical Jesus. The Christian Community continues Christ's identity."

65. See Deane William Ferm, *Third World Liberation Theologies* (Maryknoll, NY: Orbis Books, 1986), 11f., for a brief historical introduction to this formulation as first articulated by the General Conference of Latin American Bishops held in Medellin, Colombia, in 1968.

66. That is Tradition II as outlined by Heiko Oberman. *The Harvest of Medieval Theology: Gabriel Biel and Late Medieval Nominalism* (Durham, N.C.: Labyrinth Press, 1983), 372-373.

CHAPTER 4

Oath Refusal in Zurich from 1525 to 1527: The Erratic Emergence of Anabaptist Practice

Edmund Pries[1]

This study arises out of a larger examination of Anabaptist oath refusal which concentrates on the sociopolitical context of Zurich.[2] The larger context makes it clear that for early modern Europeans, oaths defined and legitimated the relationships between governing authorities and their constituents or subjects, regulated the relationships between fellow citizens and fellow peasants, and served as the glue that held both urban and rural sociopolitical structures in place. The existence of a community without an oath was unthinkable. Thus the refusal of the oath seemed like a repudiation of society. It invited social enmity and charges of anarchy and insurrection, and virtually guaranteed persecution.

The authorities certainly felt threatened by the "insurrectionist practice" of oath refusal. George Williams claims that "disastrous civic consequences [would take place as a result] of the Anabaptist refusal to take the annual oath to uphold the constitutions of the city republics...."[3] Hence it becomes clear why historians like Martin Haas would point to the rejection of the oath by the early Swiss Anabaptists as a decisive factor that transformed the Anabaptists into a separatist sect.[4] To reject the oath indicated a "giant step toward 'separation from the world,'"[5] because it signified a severance from the very bonds which held society together and legitimated all legal and sociopolitical relationships and transactions. Haas is correct. But why did the Anabaptists reject the oath? Was it purely a statement of separation, or were there other implications and reasons? At what point did a statement of protest and perhaps even rebellion, made by other radicals as well, become a statement of separation? At what point did oath refusal become a principled Anabaptist position and standard practice?

The Anabaptists have usually been characterized as a group that refused the oath on principle; furthermore the oath was said to be one of the most consistent points of agreement among the various branches of sixteenth-century Anabaptism.[6] This is largely an inference from the mistaken conclusion that the points articulated by Michael Sattler and agreed to by several others at Schleitheim in 1527 were normative for Anabaptism prior to their formulation into the Schleitheim Articles. The Articles, it has been assumed, represented a consensus statement of Swiss Anabaptists.[7] But that was hardly the case. Rather, as recent scholarship has pointed out, the Articles defined the "correct" views as understood by Sattler and some of the others present. The Articles therefore implied a censure of those whose views did not correspond.

As noted above, a number of important early Anabaptists were not in agreement with the Schleitheim view of the oath. Most of these, e.g., Hubmaier, Denck, Hut, Marpeck,[8] were only tangentially related to Zurich Anabaptism. However, diverse attitudes towards the oath persisted also in the Canton of Zurich. It seems that some Anabaptists continued to swear, while some refused. Even where refusal took place, the reasons for doing so varied.

The swearing of the *Urfehde* represents a special case, but may be used here to illustrate the original diversity of Anabaptist attitudes. The fact that some swore the *Urfehde* has drawn some attention and begged for an explanation. John Howard Yoder, in his usual thoroughness, provided at least three:

(a) the rejection of the oath was the least clear of the Anabaptist distinctives in 1525; (b) it was not a clear common conviction of the Anabaptists...that the *Urfehde* was identical with the swearing which Jesus and James forbid; and (c) Anabaptists, being human, sometimes weakened under persecution.[9]

If oath rejection was not a clearly held principle in 1525, when did it become so? Is there any evidence to suggest that the Anabaptists did not consider the *Urfehde* an oath? Or to put it more succinctly, why should the *Urfehde* be considered differently than other oaths?

It will be the purpose of this study to answer some of the above questions and to trace the erratic emergence of oath refusal among Anabaptists in Zurich and its subject territories. Since this study is based primarily on the court records *(Täuferakten)*, the type of oath in question concerns above all the *Urfehde*, that is, the sentence given to Anabaptists for their faith. Where possible and plausible, inferences will be made to oath swearing in general, and to the crystallization of Anabaptist practice in this regard.

The *Urfehde* varied according to place and circumstances. The *common Urfehde* was a simple oath usually rendered after an imprisonment or legal custody in which prisoners acknowledged their guilt, accepted their sentence and punishment, and promised by oath not to seek vengeance, thereby renouncing all claims to wrongful or unjust treatment and absolving their captors of all responsibility. It was an oath of truce to keep the peace and respect the due process of law. Those who had committed a lighter offense were usually released on a common *Urfehde*. The common promise not to complain about treatment nor seek legal damages remained a part of all other *Urfehden*.

Depending on the nature of the crime, other promises were tagged onto the common *Urfehde*. A frequent case in point concerned the sentence of exile. A specific clause concerning the nature of an exile was added to the common *Urfehde*. Generally it meant the additional promise not to return. In some areas of Europe *Urfehden* became almost synonymous with a sentence of exile.

For Anabaptists the *Urfehde* frequently included the renunciation of their "rebaptism" and a promise to refrain from teaching, preaching, or baptizing. In areas with a high concentration of Anabaptists, *Urfehden* with specific anti-Anabaptist content became synonymous with a recantation.

Many other conditions could be attached to the *Urfehde*, depending on the circumstances of the person sentenced. Anabaptists from outside the territory of Zurich were frequently exiles, whether they recanted or not, and thus had to swear not to return. Residents or offenders with citizen status were not exempt from exile and certainly not from recantation if they hoped to remain. Breaking the terms of exile meant perjury and could be punished by death.

The consequences of breaking the oath, or *Urfehde*, were usually spelled out in the *Urfehde* for purposes of legal recourse in case the oath was broken. Like all other oaths, the *Urfehde* was sworn according to the proper religious formulas, with upraised fingers to God and the saints.[10]

An examination of a few instances of oath swearing and oath refusal in Zurich by Anabaptists from 1525 to 1527 may illustrate the above points and allow for a somewhat fuller understanding of the diverse attitudes exhibited.

I

On January 18, 1525, in response to the previous day's public disputation on baptism, the Zurich Council issued a mandate which required all unbaptized children to be baptized within the following eight days.[11] On January 21, as a precaution against further unrest, several radical leaders who had come from outside the city were exiled.[12] Meanwhile, a number of the radicals at Zurich decided not only to defy the mandate requiring infant baptism but initiated adult baptism by rebaptizing each other. As a consequence, on January 30 Felix Mantz, Georg Blaurock, and twenty-five others were arrested in the Zollikon area just south of Zurich.[13] Mantz and Blaurock were kept in prison, while the others were transferred to the old Augustinian monastery in Zurich for discussions with a team of three city preachers--Huldrych Zwingli, Leo Jud, and Kaspar Grossman (or Megander)--and three council members. All except Mantz and Blaurock were released on February 8, 1525, after swearing the common *Urfehde*, promising to refrain from rebaptism and posting a joint bond of one thousand guilders.[14]

Blaurock's sentence, handed down on February 18, indicated that he was to be released upon swearing an *Urfehde*, but first he was required to appear before the council, and in the presence of Zwingli prove his claims that Zwingli had done greater harm to Scripture than the old pope. The outcome of the discussion would determine the final nature of the sentence against Blaurock.[15] The council sentencing of Mantz, also on February 18, indicated that in order to attain release he would have to pay the costs relating to his custody and post a one-hundred-gulden bond, as well as promise before Zurich's large and small councils to refrain from baptizing, breaking bread, and holding private meetings.[16]

On February 25 the council reaffirmed the earlier sentence against Mantz. Insofar as Mantz refused to accept the conditions of his release as outlined on February 18, he would remain in prison and survive on gruel,[17] bread, and water until he had enough of it and swore the *Urfehde* for release.[18]

Blaurock, meanwhile, resumed baptizing in the Zollikon area. On March 11 the council announced that all rebaptized persons would be fined, while rebaptizers were to be arrested.[19] On March 16 a specific order to arrest the rebaptizers went out.[20] As a result Blaurock was rearrested along with nineteen others from the Zollikon area on or shortly after March 16, and rejoined Mantz, who was still in prison.[21] On March 20 Mantz and Blaurock participated in a disputation with the *Burgermeister*, five other council magistrates, three heads of monastic houses, the three city preachers (Zwingli, Jud, and Engelhart), and two schoolmasters.[22] Of the seventeen Anabaptist prisoners listed with their responses in the imprisonment summary of March 25 (four of the twenty-one must have been released earlier), only six, including Mantz and Blaurock, remained steadfast in their convictions regarding rebaptism, while one person equivocated. The rest recanted.[23] All seventeen were required to admit wrongdoing, desist from baptizing in the cities and territories of Zurich, and refrain from speaking against infant baptism. They would be released upon swearing an *Urfehde* in which they promised to pay a fine and the legal costs. If any continued to baptize, they would be required to leave Zurich's territories with their wives and children.[24]

Mantz and some others refused to swear the required *Urfehde* for release. Mantz, therefore, remained in prison until he managed to escape.[25] He subsequently made his way to Schaffhausen and then Chur, resuming the forbidden practice.

Of special interest in this context is the treatment of "foreign" Anabaptists. Six of seventeen prisoners, including Blaurock, had come from outside Zurich territory.[26] According to their sentence, all six were exiled and thus required to swear to remain out of the jurisdiction and territories of Zurich.[27] Three of the six were listed on March 25, 1525, as actually having sworn the oath; two had not yet done so.[28] Blaurock, the sixth, was to be placed on a boat together with his wife and forcibly deported to his home territory of Chur. Should he decide to return, "he would be dealt with severely, in order to silence him."[29] From Blaurock's absence in the list of those who swore the exile oath and from later evidence that referred to his March 1525 release and exile, we can deduce that Blaurock did not swear an oath to stay out of the Zurich territories at that time. He was apparently exiled without the oath.

Blaurock's testimony during his third imprisonment, during which he testifies that he had not sworn an oath to stay out of Zurich's territory, supports the view that he had refused to swear in March 1525.[30] Again, in the sentencing during Blaurock's fourth imprisonment, the statement of the authorities indicated that Blaurock had been released on the earlier occasion upon his "plain words" (promise).[31] He had been exiled, it seems, without the usual oath, or *Urfehde*. Thus Blaurock was the first documented oath dodger among the Zurich Anabaptists.[32] Interestingly, he was both an outsider and a former cleric. Presumably this influenced the council's dealings with him.

Mantz reappeared in Zurich when Chur forcibly returned him on July 18,

1525. He was promptly imprisoned,[33] and not released until October 7, 1525.[34] According to a later council report, Mantz had sworn an *Urfehde* in October 1525.[35] The fact that Mantz had sworn the *Urfehde* would prove crucial in his later trial and eventual death sentence.

One day after Mantz's release, Conrad Grebel and Georg Blaurock were arrested in the district of Grüningen on October 8, 1525. They were brought to Zurich for the disputation of November 6-8, 1525.[36] By November 8, 1525, Felix Mantz and several others had joined Grebel and Blaurock in the Zurich prison.[37] Both Blaurock and Mantz were prisoners for a third time. The records of the investigation and interrogations concerning Mantz, Grebel, and Blaurock[38] contain only one brief but significant mention of the oath. Blaurock's views are presented as follows:

> He also says that he has not *sworn* to stay out of milords' territory. He would rather die than forswear God's earth, for the earth is the Lord's [emphasis mine].[39]

The above passage is the first documented explanation of oath refusal by an Anabaptist at Zurich. Blaurock claimed he had earlier (on March 25, 1525) refused the oath. The rationale for his previous action, however, is not at all a well-developed argument against oaths in principle, but rather a general statement, implying that he considered all territorial law subordinate to the lordship of God. He also claimed that he had not promised--and never would promise--to stay out of Zurich's territory. Unfortunately Blaurock did not elaborate his views on swearing and refusing oaths. His statement reads more like a rejection of content than of oath swearing itself. He appealed to his sense of divine mission as superseding the mandate of the Zurich Council. In some ways his argument is reminiscent of peasant appeal to divine law as juxtaposed to human custom. The stubborn response reads more like a defiant reflex than a carefully thought-out and reflected-upon position.[40] It remains nevertheless unique. In no other cases of oath refusal in the city of Zurich between 1525 and 1527 was any form of ideological explanation provided.

On November 18, 1525, after a week-long trial, Grebel, Mantz, and Blaurock were sentenced to be placed together into the New Tower for an indefinite term. According to a council mandate, they were to remain there "for as long as it pleases God or seems good to the magistrates."

By March 1526 the number of prisoners had risen to twenty-five, including Mantz, Grebel, and Blaurock.[41] New interrogations took place from March 5 to 7.[42] On March 7, as a result of the intransigence of many of the prisoners, especially the ringleaders Mantz, Grebel, and Blaurock, the council handed down a sentence of life imprisonment for eighteen of the prisoners, with only a little bread and water for nourishment and beds of straw for rest. Should they decide to recant and desist from Anabaptism, however, they might gain their release.[43]

On that same day the Zurich Council passed its fateful mandate against the Anabaptists which stated that unrepentant Anabaptists--especially those who continued to baptize others--would be drowned without mercy.[44] The reasoning was as follows:

Since, however, some [Anabaptists] stubbornly persist against their oath, vows, and promises; and to the hindrance of the common order and governmental authority as well as to the destruction of the common good and true Christian order appear disobedient,[45] some of them--men, women, and daughters--have been placed under severe punishment and imprisonment by our lords. And *therefore* it is the earnest commandment, declaration, and warning of our lords named [above] that henceforth no one in their city, country, and territory, [neither] men, women, or daughters, should baptize one another. For whoever henceforth baptizes another [person], will be arrested by our lords and according to their present judgment drowned without any mercy [emphasis mine].[46]

Anabaptist breaking of the oath thus became the key legal argument for prosecution. A formulaic "Anabaptist sentence," based on the March 7 mandate, was passed on the prisoners and would henceforth be used as a formula for cases involving Anabaptists:

Whoever confesses that rebaptism is wrong and that infant baptism is correct, and admits having fallen into error, shall be released upon an *Urfehde* during which he will again be told to refrain from Anabaptism in both word and deed, nor to speak or teach about it; [also to stay away from unauthorized preaching and go to church in the correct parish; similarly to stay away from the home or property of any Anabaptist and not to give them (Anabaptists) any hospitality or provisions: no food, drink, or place to stay at any time;][47] for where they transgress and appear disobedient, they will again be arrested and from that very hour be drowned without mercy.[48]

The "life imprisonment" did not last as long as expected. Several prisoners recanted and were released. Among them was Hans Hottinger, a former prison guard, who was released upon swearing the *Urfehde* on March 21.[49] The remaining male prisoners escaped on the night of March 21, 1526, through an open shutter.[50] It was Mantz's second escape and no doubt, like the first one, led to rumors of divine intervention on behalf of the prisoners of faith.

Meanwhile, the council's position vis-à-vis the Anabaptists hardened. On November 19, 1526, the Zurich Council acted to strengthen the mandate of March 7, 1526. House meetings or secret conventicles, the nonattendance of the official church, as well as the harboring of Anabaptists, were now serious crimes.[51]

On December 13, 1526,[52] Mantz and Blaurock were apprehended once more in the Grüningen area,[53] and transferred almost immediately to custody in Zurich.[54] It was the fourth imprisonment at Zurich for both Mantz and Blaurock.

The preparatory notes for the interrogations, held between December 13, 1526, and January 5, 1527--Mantz's execution and Blaurock's banishment-- made the explicit charge that Mantz had broken the *Urfehde* which he swore on October 7, 1525. According to that *Urfehde*, he had promised to refrain from baptizing, to give no one cause for rebaptism, and to obey the will of the magistrates in general.[55] The preamble to the sentences of Mantz and

Blaurock on January 5, 1527, repeated the accusation that within fourteen days of the prison escape of March 21, 1526, Mantz had broken "the oath sworn to God" in October 1525.[56] Of Blaurock, on the other hand, it was said that he had been previously released upon an alternative promise to the oath, his "plain words," to refrain from rebaptizing others and from proselytizing. Despite those assurances, Blaurock had returned to territory in Zurich's jurisdiction and continued with his Anabaptist practices.[57]

The final sentence (January 5, 1527) reiterated the same points. Mantz, a ringleader, had been released once before on an *Urfehde*. He had broken the oath and escaped from a subsequent imprisonment.[58] According to the mandate of March 7, 1526, he thus deserved the death penalty. The final sentencing of Blaurock gave similar cause: he had given a promise in "plain words" but broken his pledge.[59]

Mantz was sentenced to drowning,[60] while Blaurock was whipped out of the city with rods and exiled. At the city gate he was required to swear an *Urfehde* with the stipulation that if he broke this oath, he too would be drowned without mercy.[61] At first Blaurock refused to swear the *Urfehde*, but when threatened with continued imprisonment he complied.[62]

The difference in treatment of Blaurock and Mantz has puzzled previous scholars. It has been suggested that "Blaurock fared better [than Mantz] because he was not a citizen of Zurich and [because] no evidence was presented that he had violated the mandate of March 7...within their city, country, and domain,"[63] or that "foreigners were [only] threatened with the death penalty *should they return to the territory contrary to the order of exile.*"[64] This focus on the oath permits us to sharpen the issues. It should be noted that being a foreigner could lead to exile sooner but did not necessarily guarantee freedom from execution.

Second, although Blaurock had not baptized anyone since the time of his promise, he had indeed violated the mandate of Zurich by continuing to teach and preach against infant baptism, and encouraging rebaptism. Furthermore, many of the charges against Blaurock were identical to those against Mantz, accusing him also of inciting rebellion, insurrection against Christian authority, and destruction of the common Christian peace, brotherly love, and harmony among citizens.[65] According to the expanded mandate of November 19, 1526, Blaurock was a more than suitable candidate for the death penalty. Third, Blaurock had broken an order of exile after having been deported to Chur. Why then the apparent leniency and a second exile rather than death as for Mantz?

Although Blaurock's "foreign" status may have played a role, it is suggested here that the key element in the lighter sentence was due to legalities. It seems that Mantz had sworn and broken a legally binding *Urfehde*, while Blaurock had not. Thus Mantz became subject to the council mandate that prescribed the death penalty for those who broke the legally binding oath of the *Urfehde*. Since Blaurock, on the other hand, had not sworn a legally binding oath but only broken a *promise*, the council lacked the proper legal recourse to execute him. Blaurock had used this legal distinction in his own defense during his third imprisonment, when he argued that he had never *sworn* to stay out of the Zurich territory.

In his *Elenchus* of 1527[66] Zwingli recounted the story of Blaurock's beating and banishment and accused the Anabaptists of attempting to use the argument against swearing of oaths to circumvent being legally bound. They would return to Zurich territory claiming that their Father in heaven called them back, and that they were therefore not legally accountable.[67] In other words, they invoked a kind of divine law to place themselves above the law of Zurich. Blaurock's behavior does indeed lend credibility to Zwingli's argument. Thus it becomes clear why the authorities forced Blaurock to swear the oath on January 5, 1527, with the stipulation that if he broke it, he too would be drowned without mercy. One can only speculate that Blaurock took seriously and understood the consequences had he broken the legally binding *Urfehde*. As far as is known, he did not return to Zurich to test the council's resolve.

Zwingli's assertion that the Anabaptists used Christ's admonition of "letting one's yea be yea and nay be nay" in their arguments against rendering oaths is of interest here. Given the context of Zwingli's statement, this form of argumentation could have been part of the defense of Blaurock and his fellow prisoners by January 1527. It is possible that this more principled form of argumentation against the oath, based on Matthew 5, if not used in Zurich prior to 1527, came to Zurich via the Grüningen district. According to surviving records, the arguments based on Matthew 5 were first made in the Grüningen area--the location of Blaurock's third and fourth arrests.

The Grüningen connection seems plausible because it was there that Ulrich Teck and Jacob Gross were active in the fall of 1525. Both had been forced to leave Anabaptist Waldshut when they had objected to the use of the sword, though they had been willing to participate in the defense of the city in other ways, including guard duty and the payment of taxes.[68] On September 20, 1525, they found themselves in the custody of Jörg Berger, the governor of Grüningen.[69] From later correspondence by Berger we learn that the two objected to swearing the *Urfehde* but offered to give their plain promise--to let their yea be yea and their nay be nay--and keep it. Berger granted their request, taking their promise in place of the oath.[70]

Teck appears to have found himself in prison for a second time, this time in connection with the November 6-8, 1525, disputation at Zurich. A council decision of November 18, 1525, exiled him upon his swearing the *Urfehde* and paying the costs of his custody. He must have again objected to the oath but received no sympathy in Zurich. The council added that if he did not want to swear, he would have to remain in prison.[71]

The argument by Gross and Teck that their plain promise (yea or nay) should be accepted in place of the oath, clearly based on Matthew 5:37, is the *first* as well as the *only* documented case in the Canton of Zurich before 1527 of any argumentation similar to the Schleitheim article on the oath. In contrast to Blaurock's early statement, which we suggested was based on objections to content, the statement of Teck and Gross contained no refusal of that which was to be sworn or promised--in fact they were willing to *promise* the content without swearing an oath.[72] It was, therefore, a straightforward rejection of the oath. Curiously, Blaurock was arrested in the Grüningen district by the same governor, Berger, only two and a half weeks after Gross and Teck were released from custody. He was also in the prison at Zurich with Teck. Thus, if Zwingli's report of Blaurock's banishment is accurate, it can be assumed that by 1527 Blaurock was not only familiar with the argument of Gross and Teck, but possibly learned it from them.

One other incident of oath refusal in Zurich's southern subject territories has been recorded. As the only documented case of pre-1527 Anabaptist oath refusal in the Canton of Zurich which did not concern the *Urfehde* but rather an oath of testimony, it is worthy of mention. Early in December 1525 a messenger arrived from the Canton of Schwyz to search for Hans am Berg, an Anabaptist from Schwyz, who had been at the November disputation and was now in the Grüningen area. When Jörg Berger, the governor of Grüningen, gave permission for the messenger from Schwyz to hold a legal court of inquiry and question local Anabaptists under oath regarding the whereabouts of Hans am Berg, four of the six Anabaptists refused to testify under oath. They refused to swear an oath to tell the truth, but offered to speak the truth without the oath.[73] The fact that the legal inquiry broke down despite the fact that the Anabaptists were willing to testify *without a sworn oath* demonstrates the legal weight and importance given to the oath in the judicial process of that time. To what extent the incidence of oath refusal was based on clearly thought-out principles remains unclear. One possible, though questionable, explanation may be that the Anabaptists were attempting to frustrate the attempts by Schwyz to extract information from them. They may also have been unwilling to submit to the legal implications and responsibilities of swearing under oath. The authorities, not surprisingly, perceived the refusal as a manifestation of rebellious and uncooperative attitudes.

In contrast to Blaurock, Teck, and Gross and the four Anabaptists near Grüningen who raised objections to the oath and attempted to refuse it, many examples could be cited of Anabaptists in the Canton of Zurich swearing the *Urfehde* without raising questions before 1527.[74] In fact, according to the records, all but the few mentioned above swore the *Urfehde*.

A noteworthy Zurich example is that of Rudolf Rutschmann and Rutsch Hottinger. Their *Urfehde*, sworn on June 29, 1525, has been preserved in full detail.[75] According to the document, Rutschmann and Hottinger, upon their "own free will, upon proper reflection, and without coercion," swore with "raised fingers bodily to God" to refrain from baptizing and proselytizing.[76] They agreed that should they be caught baptizing and preaching again, the gracious lords of Zurich would be correct in treating them as perjurers without honor.[77]

It was obviously not quite true that the Anabaptists agreed to these terms on their own "free will" and without coercion, as the prepared *Urfehde* of Rutschmann and Hottinger had stated. Anabaptists who were mistreated in prison and could only gain release by swearing an *Urfehde* were not really doing so uncoerced. The inclusion of the "voluntarily swearing" clause was widely insisted upon by governing authorities in order to protect themselves against accusations of coercion and from resultant claims by persons falling back into Anabaptism that the *Urfehde* they had sworn was therefore null and void.[78]

The conclusion above that the overwhelming majority continued to swear the oath is challenged by the account of Johannes Keßler, who related that the Anabaptists of St. Gall during May or June 1525 "did not swear, not even the obligatory civic oaths to the government. And if one transgressed herein, he was banned by them, for there was daily excommunication among them."[79] Keßler's claims suggest that oath refusal was well advanced in St. Gall by the summer of 1525--indeed that it was part of Anabaptist practice and identity. It is possible that Keßler, writing several years after the fact, imposed a later, more developed position onto the earlier time period he was describing in his chronicle. Another possibility is that Anabaptism in St. Gall had a more developed and mature position on the oath than Anabaptism in the Zurich area at this time. A third, and perhaps more likely, possibility may be that other oaths were refused much more successfully than the *Urfehde*. However, if that indeed was the case, there is a surprising absence of prosecutions for failure to swear the civic oath in the court records![80]

II

We can summarize the main conclusions of our narrowly focused study on early Zurich Anabaptism as follows:

1. The evidence surveyed certainly supports Yoder's assertion that oath refusal was not a clear-cut Anabaptist practice in 1525. But ambivalence on the oath was not limited to 1525. It extended at least up to 1527. Thus we can conclude that the Schleitheim position on the oath did not represent the consensus of the Anabaptists in Zurich's territories prior to its formulation in 1527 and likely did not become normative for some time thereafter. Evidence suggests that oath refusal developed erratically and became a distinguishing factor only gradually.

2. If oath refusal was a milestone in the Anabaptists' becoming separatist, as Haas suggests, then we must also conclude with Haas that the Anabaptists were not a consistently separatist movement in Zurich and the surrounding area before 1527.

3. Contrary to Yoder, there can be no question whether or not the Anabaptists regarded the *Urfehde* as an oath of the kind addressed by Jesus and James. There is no evidence to suggest otherwise. The terms *Urfehde* and "oath" were used interchangeably in reference to the same oath rendered. Arguments used against other oaths, biblical (particularly Matthew 5) and otherwise, were directed against the *Urfehde* as well, at least by Teck, Gross, and likely also by Blaurock. The authorities too understood the *Urfehde* as an oath. Mantz, as well as other Anabaptists after him, was accused of having broken an oath sworn to God. Breaking the *Urfehde* was considered perjury-- like the breaking of other oaths.[81]

4. Our analysis suggests that oath refusal was originally not a deliberate

means of separation from society. Oath refusal arrived in the Zurich area more as a protest or as a defensive reflex against perceived religious and social coercion. Oath refusal grew out of concrete circumstances rather than systematic theological reflection.

5. Several reasons for oath refusal can be delineated:

a. Since the legal justification for prosecution and punishment of Anabaptists in sixteenth-century Europe frequently existed in the oath, there seemed to be a strong desire on the part of the Anabaptists not to make themselves legally liable in case they could not or did not want to fulfill the obligations of the *Urfehde* or of other oaths. This appeared to have been at least one of the motivations behind Blaurock's original rejection of the *Urfehde* in March of 1525. This could also have been the reason that the four Anabaptists near Grüningen refused the oath of testimony.

b. The content of the citizenship oaths contributed to Anabaptist oath refusal. The obedience clause of the oath meant a promise to obey the laws and statutes of the council to which Anabaptists could not subscribe. This was particularly true with laws prohibiting the preaching and practice of believers' baptism, those requiring the baptism of infants and compulsory church attendance, the obligation to tell the authorities of coreligionists who were already refusing the oath, and eventually the requirement to bear the sword. Later, the obedience clause also created difficulties for the Anabaptists because it represented a rendering of authority to government which most Anabaptists could yield only to God.

c. The content of the *Urfehden* was likewise difficult for Anabaptists to submit to. The requirement not to return to an area, to refrain from preaching and baptizing, to renounce any adherence to Anabaptism, and to agree to whatever else the recantation or renunciation might contain, touched the heart of the matter, namely, Anabaptist dissent and social protest.

d. The religious element in the swearing of the oath may also have been a factor. To swear an oath was a specific form of self-cursing. If the oath, sworn in God's name, was broken, late-medieval belief held that one became guilty of blasphemy and could even endanger one's salvation.[82] Anabaptists were no doubt familiar with these assumptions since they were commonly shared notions into early modern times. Even if Anabaptists no longer believed that breaking the oath endangered their salvation--those who felt that an oath contrary to the will of God should be broken may have felt the opposite--many began to believe that swearing any oath at all represented an affront to God. It is this position which was articulated in the Schleitheim Articles. Swearing an oath was, first, contrary to the explicit command of Christ and, second, represented a promise to keep something which human beings did not have the power to fulfill. Thus the oath was an act contrary to the will of God and should not be sworn.

6. Since the oath served as the legal basis for prosecution, oath refusal effectively placed the refuser beyond the arm of the law. This undermined the legal authority of the government as well as its very ability to exist. It is for this reason that Blaurock and Teck were finally forced to swear.

7. Why did so many Anabaptists swear the *Urfehde*?

a. We have already pointed out that refusal of the *Urfehde* as well as oath refusal in general had not yet become a uniform practice before 1527. It is possible that some may not have known that the teaching regarding oath refusal was part of the Anabaptist teaching, together with rebaptism, or may have held an independent opinion on the oath. We have also mentioned that it is possible, though we cannot know for sure, that refusal of other oaths may have been more successful.

b. We must agree with Yoder that "Anabaptists, being human, sometimes weakened under persecution." It is clear that imprisonment, torture, and other forms of coercion played a significant role in Anabaptists' consenting to swear the *Urfehde*. Anabaptists who at first attempted to refuse the oath would frequently break down after lengthy imprisonment and mistreatment and swear the required *Urfehde*. They even had to agree to the "voluntarily swearing" clause which was part of the official format.

c. It is possible that some Anabaptists agreed to swear the *Urfehde* because they felt that they were not bound by the oath. The responses outlined below would indicate such an attitude for some.

8. Why did so many Anabaptists who swore the *Urfehde* or other oaths turn around and break them?

a. In response to accusations from the authorities regarding their continued transgression of the laws and mandates of the government, particularly as they applied to baptism, the Anabaptists of Grüningen responded:

Once again we witness and confess that your laws and mandates are contrary to the word of God and the teaching of Christ. For that reason we are more obedient to God than to people.[83]

Once again we encounter the contrasting of human laws and divine law--human authority versus the word of God. This argument was not that dissimilar from the arguments made by Carlstadt and Müntzer: where oaths were found to be in conflict with the will of God, the will of God should take priority.[84]

Even though the oath was not an issue raised or discussed in this submission to the Grüningen *Landtag*,[85] it is likely that similar arguments were forwarded for the breaking of an oath made to human authority. In fact, on several occasions when Anabaptists were required to swear the *Urfehde*, they replied that they would abide by the requirement to refrain from baptizing unless God directed them otherwise.[86] Similar qualifications were made about exile stipulations. Zwingli complained that the Anabaptists returned from exile because they claimed their heavenly Father had called them back.

b. It has frequently been argued that coercion made an oath legally invalid. The argument of coercion was used to seek a legal exemption from an oath or simply to claim that it was thus invalid. While the "voluntarily swearing" clause was designed to get around claims of coercion, most courts did not grant releases from oaths legally sworn to government on the basis of coercion anyway, since it was the same magistrates who had administered the oath in the first place who served as judges. According to canon law, the church considered even coerced oaths valid--though church authorities would also grant releases under the argument of coercion if it suited them.[87]

These factors do not remove the fact that most Anabaptists swore the *Urfehde* because they had been coerced and weakened under the pressure of persecution. For many, however, abandoning a movement because of being forced to swear an oath would have been a greater wrong than breaking their oath and reinvolving themselves with the movement. Many were not deterred from pursuing this course by the well-known consequences of breaking the oath.[88]

Though the peasants also broke their oaths of fealty when they joined the Peasants' War in 1525, they never rejected the oath. With Müntzer they objected to demands of obedience when the laws imposed upon them seemed to conflict with their understanding of divine law. However, like some early Anabaptists at that time, they never opposed the concept of oath swearing itself. In fact they were more concerned with getting an oath that coincided with their understanding of justice and divine law. Thus it is not surprising that when many Anabaptists eventually rejected oaths in principle, they also lost much of their popular support among the peasantry. The average commoner preferred the traditional system of working within a social structure of oath contracts, even if it meant that the occasional insurrectionist oath had to be taken in support of their rights.

The Anabaptists seemed to go more than one way on the oath. "Magisterial Anabaptists" such as Hubmaier, for example, never questioned the oath. For them the oath was not a relevant issue. On the other hand, the Anabaptists who rejected the oath also rejected society in general, and as already indicated, lost much of their popular support as a result.

The Anabaptist rejection of the oath raises additional questions. Did the Anabaptists replace the oath ceremony they rejected with another? If so, how? Preliminary investigation shows that Anabaptists who refused the oath viewed the baptismal ceremony as a replacement for the oath ceremony in which they had previously participated within the context of secular society. The sectarian church covenant community was seen to replace the secular covenant community they had left--such as a city or village. Similarly, those Anabaptists who continued to swear oaths saw the baptismal ceremony as a parallel ceremony to the citizenship oath ceremonies in secular society. The similarities are not difficult to see. It is likely that aspects of the service of initiation into the church were borrowed from the secular community and taken into the new community. The Anabaptists did not see themselves so much as joining a church within society; rather they were becoming a part of a new and alternative community which replaced the one which they had left. Thus parallels in the initiation services of a Swiss community and a Swiss Anabaptist conventicle are readily visible. In both cases the person being initiated into the community made a commitment to that community above all others, and the communal oath or the baptismal covenant to the church superseded all others.[89] Both groups exercised the ban (or exile) for breaches of certain communal guidelines. The full nature of this relationship between the baptismal ceremony and the oath ceremony still awaits further investigation.

The question regarding the larger impact of Anabaptist oath refusal on society also remains. Did the persistent refusal of oaths contribute to the eventual waning in the importance of oaths for society? This question is not easily answered, and more study is necessary to arrive at satisfactory conclusions.

NOTES

1. I acknowledge with thanks the generous assistance of Werner Packull. I also appreciate the kindness of Arnold Snyder for making available to me his own index of Leonhard von Muralt and Walter Schmidt, eds. *Quellen zur Geschichte der Täufer in der Schweiz, I: Zürich* (Zurich: S. Hirzel Verlag, 1952) (hereafter cited as *TA, Zurich*).

2. See Edmund Pries, "The Historical Context of Anabaptist Oath Refusal in Zurich: 1515-1532" (M.A. thesis, University of Waterloo, 1988).

3. George H. Williams, *The Radical Reformation* (Philadelphia: Westminster Press, 1962), 185.

4. Martin Haas, "Der Weg der Täufer in die Absonderung" in *Umstrittenes Täufertum 1525-1975: Neue Forschungen*, ed. by Hans-Jürgen Goertz (Göttingen: Vandenhoeck und Ruprecht, 1975), 70.

5. Arnold Snyder, *The Life and Thought of Michael Sattler* (Scottdale, Pa.: Herald Press, 1984), 75; Haas, "Der Weg," 70.

6. Christian Neff and H. S. Bender, "Oath" in *ME* IV, 4-5.

7. Article VII of Schleitheim opposed any and all oaths on the basis of Matthew 5:33-37. Sattler and those who agreed with him argued that it was not within human capability to guarantee that they could keep what was promised in the oath. They refuted specific arguments directed against them. The examples of God swearing to Abraham were of a different order because God was his own guarantor of and could fulfill his promise. To the qualification that Jesus had not forbidden swearing itself, but had only forbidden oaths by heaven, earth, Jerusalem, and one's head, the writer(s) of Article VII responded with the comment that since heaven was God's throne and one was not to swear by heaven, should one not also refrain from swearing by God--after all "what is greater, the throne or he who sits upon it?" Arguments that both Peter and Paul also swore were answered with the clarification that Peter and Paul were testifying to that which God had promised Abraham--something already past. The argument concluded with a repetition of Christ's statement that one's speech should be yea, yea, or nay, nay: anything beyond that comes from evil. Thus Sattler and his friends returned to the much-debated words of Jesus Christ in Matthew 5:33-37. Article VII of Schleitheim argued against the oath on the basis of Matthew 5:33-37. Heinold Fast, ed., *Quellen zur Geschichte der Täufer in der Schweiz, II: Ostschweiz* (Zurich: Theologischer Verlag, 1973), 33-34 (hereafter cited as *TA, Ostschweiz*); John H. Yoder, trans. and ed., *The Legacy of Michael Sattler* (Scottdale, Pa.: Herald Press, 1973), 41-42.

8. For an excellent summary of Marpeck's position on the oath see Stephen Blake Boyd, *Pilgram Marpeck and the Justice of Christ* (Ann Arbor: Unviersity Microfilms International, 1985), 135-138, 367-374; and "Anabaptism and Social Radicalism in Strasbourg, 1528-1532: Pilgram Marpeck on Christian Social Responsibility," *MQR* 63 (1989), 58-76.

9. *Legacy of Michael Sattler*, 16, n. 2.

10. Whether the oath was also sworn to the saints depended on whether the territory was under Catholic or Reformed control.

11. *TA, Zurich*, 34-35.

12. Those required to swear an oath to abide by the exile regulations and leave the city within eight days of January 21, 1525, were Wilhelm Reublin, Johannes Brötli, Ludwig Hätzer, and Andreas Castelberger. *Ibid.*, 35-36. Von Muralt and Schmid wrongly date this item from

January 21, 1521 (likely a typographical error).

 13. *Ibid.,* 37-51.

 14. *Ibid.,* 47.

 15. *Ibid.,* 51.

 16. *Ibid.,* 50.

 17. German: Muß or mus. Also translatable as "mush" or "pap."

 18. "...bis es im riff wirt und er selbs ußhin ficht." *Ibid.,* 51. On the basis of this statement Haas suggests that Mantz became the first Anabaptist to refuse the oath. "Der Weg," 70. Though that remains a possibility, there is no evidence to prove that was indeed the case. The emphasis was on Mantz's fulfilling the requirements for release mentioned in the earlier sentence (refrain from baptizing, etc.), in which the *Urfehde* had not been mentioned. The reference to the *Urfehde* in the February 25 reaffirmation of the earlier sentence may simply be a shorthand way of saying "until he agrees to the terms of release" or a reference to normal procedure for release from prison, not a case of oath refusal. See also n. 33 below.

 19. *TA, Zurich,* 60-61.

 20. Ibid., 61.

 21. *Ibid.,* 70.

 22. This disputation was actually more like a judicial hearing, because it was never meant to be open-ended in terms of its outcome.

 23. *Ibid.,* 73-74. Hanß Bichter agreed not to baptize in Zurich's territories any longer and swore the exile *Urfehde.* He did not, however, explicitly deny his Anabaptist convictions. It was sometimes possible for foreigners to swear the exile *Urfehde* without having to recant their views.

 24. *Ibid.,* 74-75.

 25. Ekkehard Krajewski suggests that Mantz escaped between March 25 and May 25, 1525. A more precise dating is not possible. *Leben und Sterben des Zürcher Täuferführers Felix Mantz,* (Kassel: J. G. Oncken Verlag, 1957), 99-100. See also *TA, Zurich,* 93-94.

 26. Another one of the six foreigners among the seventeen prisoners was a certain "Michael in the white coat." Scholarship has frequently identified this Michael as Michael Sattler, though this has been vigorously refuted by Sattler's foremost biographer, Arnold Snyder. For examples of the former see: *ibid.,* 73, n. 2; 74, n. 4; also Heinold Fast, "Michael Sattler's Baptism: Some Comments," *MQR* 60 (1986), 364-373. For Snyder's explanations, see his *Michael Sattler,* 76-79; and "Michael Sattler's Baptism: Some Comments in Reply to Heinold Fast," *MQR* 62 (1988), 496-506.

 27. *TA, Zurich,* 74.

 28. A further comment threatened the two who had not yet sworn with being ordered out of the territory should they refuse to swear the oath. *Ibid.,* 75.

 29. *Ibid.,* 74.

 30. Blaurock's third imprisonment lasted from October 8, 1525, to March 21, 1526. *Ibid.,* 127.

 31. Blaurock's fourth imprisonment lasted from December 13, 1526, to January 5, 1527. His sentence dates from January 5, 1527. The preamble to his 1527 sentence stated that although the authorities had believed his "plain words," without an oath, that he would abstain from baptizing and returning to Zurich territory, Blaurock had apparently broken his promise. *Ibid.,* 223.

 32. The credit of being the first oath dodger among the Zurich Anabaptists has sometimes been given to Mantz (see n. 19 above) or to Castelberger (see Snyder, *Michael Sattler,* 145). Castelberger proponents argue their case on the basis of a letter by Castelberger to the Zurich

Council found in *TA, Zurich*, 55-56. However, Castelberger was merely requesting a release from the oath of exile he had sworn earlier, on January 25, 1525 (*ibid.*, 36)–a request made due to illness and to the fact that he had suffered severe financial losses already. If he recovered from illness and the council considered him a threat, Castelberger suggested that at that time he be exiled *without an oath*. Castelberger was granted an extension to his stay in Zurich but not a full release from his oath. *Ibid.*, 56. There was no mention of any *Urfehde* when he was deported to Graubünden on June 12, 1525. It is therefore not clear whether he swore an oath on this occasion or whether he was deported and released upon his word only. *Ibid.*, 388.

33. *Ibid.*, 92-93.

34. *Ibid.*, 109.

35. Following Mantz's fourth and last arrest on December 13 (or 3), 1526. See *ibid.*, 216.

36. *Ibid.*, 111-113.

37. Mantz and the others arrested with him were all likely all taken into custody immediately after the Zurich Disputation of November 6-8, 1525. See *ibid.*, 93, n. 1; see also von Muralt and Schmid's dating of documents nos. 120-124, pp. 120-127.

38. Between November 9, 1525, and March 7, 1526. *Ibid.*, 120-127, 174-178.

39. *Ibid.*, 127.

40. Von Muralt and Schmid point out that Blaurock's comment that "the earth is the Lord's" is a quote from Psalm 24:1. *Ibid.*, 127, n. 6. That, however, does not change the tone or nature of the way in which Blaurock made his point. The question can also be asked whether Blaurock's statement relates in any way to Article VII of Schleitheim. Both Matthew 5:35 and Article VII do mention that one should not swear by the earth, because it is God's footstool. Is Blaurock making a principled argument against the swearing of all oaths based on Matthew 5, one which would later be incorporated into Schleitheim? It is unlikely. Blaurock is making an argument based on content--arguing against agreeing to exile, because God's authority supersedes human authority, and thus he could never agree to stay out of an area in which God might call him to minister.

41. *Ibid.*, 174-183.

42. *Ibid.*, 148-149.

43. *Ibid.*, 178.

44. *Ibid.*, 181.

45. "To be obedient in all things" was a key ingredient of the Zurich communal citizen's oath: Zurich 15th Century (ca. 1432). Hans Nabholz, ed., *Die Zürcher Stadtbücher des XIV. und XV. Jahrhunderts*, III (Leipzig: Verlag von S. Hirzel, 1906), No. 37, p. 150 (hereafter cited as *ZS* III). The New Citizen's Oath also included the requirement to further the good (or interest) of the city and the domain: Zurich 15th Century (ca. 1432). *ZS* III, No. 43, pp. 152-153. The rural communities of the Canton of Zurich also had to promise "to be obedient in all things" to the Zurich Council in their oaths of fealty. This became one of the key grievances of the peasants in the revolt of the rural peasant communities against Zurich in 1489. They requested to be allowed to swear "in all reasonable things" (*in allen ziemlichen sachen*). Eventually the peasants were granted a new oath which included all the ingredients of the previous oath (e.g., keep peace, defend against harm, do not seek other courts of justice, etc.), but the incriminating "obedient in all things" was now rendered "to be obedient and supportive." See Christian Dietrich, *Die Stadt Zürich und ihre Landgemeinden während der Bauernunruhen von 1489 bis 1525* (Frankfurt am Main: Peter Lang, 1985), 46-90. "To be obedient to the council" included obedience to all council statutes, and thus included the prohibition of rebaptizing, as well as compulsory church

attendance and the requirement to have one's children baptized. Legally it was the breaking of the oath which was often prosecuted. The above information suggests that the reference to the disobedience of the Anabaptists of Zurich in the mandate of March 7, 1526, might indeed have been a reference to their contravention of their citizenship oaths.

46. *TA, Zurich,* 180-181.

47. The bracketed section was added on November 19, 1526. *Ibid.,* 211.

48. *Ibid.,* 182-183. After this general sentence, rather than detail that the released Anabaptist had sworn the *Urfehde,* the documents simply state that the person agreed to the sentence as had been determined for Anabaptism-related offenses. After this point any reference to a common *Urfehde* in connection with Anabaptism disappears. In most cases the *Urfehde* then becomes synonymous with a recantation, unless perhaps an exile *Urfehde* is used for a foreigner.

49. *Ibid.,* 179 esp. n. 6. Hans Hottinger was the former watchman of the Augustinian monastery which served as the prison for one of the earlier imprisonments of the Zollikon Anabaptists, though we do not know whether he served in that capacity for the new prison tower where the escape of March 21, 1526, took place. See *ibid.,* 52-54, 56-57. The fact that Hottinger was released after swearing the *Urfehde* on the same day of the later March 21, 1526, escape, seems rather suspicious, especially since he had previously remained quite steadfast.

Leland Harder claims Hans Hottinger was one of the escapees of March 21, 1526. This is likely the result of confusing Hans Hottinger with Heini Hottinger (both were in prison on March 7, 1526 [*TA, Zurich,* 178-179]; the latter was one of the escapees, since he was mentioned in the account of the escape [*ibid.,* 192]) and overlooking the mention of Hans Hottinger's release during the day of March 21, 1526. See Leland Harder, ed., *The Sources of Swiss Anabaptism* (Scottdale, Pa.: Herald Press, 1985), 546.

50. *TA, Zurich,* 191-193.

51. *Ibid.,* 210-211.

52. Or December 3, 1526. *Ibid.,* 212-213, n. 4. Harder opts for December 13, 1526. *Sources of Swiss Anabaptism,* 473.

53. *TA, Zurich,* 212-213.

54. *Ibid.,* 213.

55. *Ibid.,* 216.

56. *Ibid.,* 222.

57. *Ibid.,* 223.

58. *Ibid.,* 225.

59. *Ibid.,* 227.

60. *Ibid.,* 226.

61. *Ibid.,* 227-228.

62. *Sources of Swiss Anabaptism,* 473-474. Neff and Bender claim that "Georg Blaurock refused to swear the oath [*Urfehde*] when he was to be exiled," without adding that immediately thereafter he complied, thereby leaving a false impression. At the end of the paragraph (12-13 lines later) they add, "Felix Manz swore the *Urfehde,* as did Blaurock shortly after Jan. 5, 1527," a statement that is incorrect with respect to Blaurock since Blaurock swore the *Urfehde* at the time of his beating on Jan. 5, 1527. *ME* IV, 4. In the introduction to his translation of Herman Schijn's "Concerning the Nonswearing of Oaths," *MQR* 61 (1987), 228-235, James W. Lowry merely says, "In January 1527 George Blaurock refused to swear an oath," a statement that seems to be based on the misleading statement in the *Mennonite Encyclopedia.*

63. *Sources of Swiss Anabaptism,* 483; see also Williams, *The Radical Reformation,* 145.

64. Emphasis mine. Horst W. Schraepler, *Die rechtliche Behandlung Der Täufer in Der Deutschen Schweiz, Südwestdeutschland und Hessen, 1525-1618* (Tübingen: Fabian-Verlag, 1957), 38. I would like to acknowledge Helmut Isaak for drawing my attention to this source.

65. Mantz: *TA, Zurich*, 226; Blaurock: *ibid.*, 227.

66. The full title is *In catabaptistarum strophas elenchus.*

67. *Sources of Swiss Anabaptism*, 474.

68. *TA, Zurich*, 109.

69. *Ibid.*, 108-109.

70. *Ibid.*, 261-262. A letter from Berger to the Zurich Council on September 25, 1527, apparently written in response to a request for information on the imprisonment and release of Gross in 1525 at Grüningen, which Zurich desired to pass on to Augsburg, where Gross was then imprisoned, explained that Gross (and Teck) had requested to make a promise in place of the oath, and the request had been granted. The September 28, 1527, letter from the Zurich council to Augsburg passed on this information. The council also related that while later imprisoned at Bruck in the Canton of Bern, Gross had again sought release without swearing the oath. After Bern had received a letter from Zurich, however, they required him to swear an oath, the breaking or refusal of which would result in drowning. Despite his opposition Gross eventually complied, being forced to swear both an oath of exile and the common *Urfehde. Ibid.*, 262-263.

71. *Ibid.*, 136.

72. John H. Yoder first pointed out this distinction to me in a letter dated May 9, 1988.

73. *TA, Zurich*, 144.

74. A few examples from 1525 will suffice: *ibid.*, 94-100, 134-135, 142, 149.

75. *Ibid.*, 82-83.

76. *Ibid.*, 84.

77. *Ibid.*, 84.

78. John H. Yoder gives several examples of such clauses for the Basel area. *Täufertum und Reformation im Gespräch* (Zurich: EVZ Verlag, 1968), 142-144.

79. *TA, Ostschweiz*, 608; translation from *Sources of Swiss Anabaptism*, 382.

80. Conflicting evidence on the practice of oath refusal also exists after 1527. A document presented to the Grüningen Diet on or before June 4, 1527, by the Anabaptists of the area as a summary and defense of their positions does not mention Article VII of Schleitheim, nor does it contain any other reference to the swearing of oaths. *TA, Zurich*, 234-239. On the other hand, a joint decree issued by Zurich, Bern, and St. Gall on September 9, 1527, claimed that the Anabaptists "teach and hold without any exception or distinction that no Christian nor anyone else may make or swear an oath (even to the government)." *TA, Ostschweiz*, 4; translation with minor revisions from *Sources of Swiss Anabaptism*, 509. Yet, at the same time, oath refusal itself became part of the systematic interrogations of Anabaptist prisoners by the authorities only in January of 1530. *TA, Zurich*, 318-321. Thus, at least for the government, oath refusal had crystallized as an issue by 1530--though not necessarily for the Anabaptists. One of the Anabaptists arrested in January of 1530, Hans Bruppach(er), specifically mentioned that he did not disagree with swearing oaths to governments, and stressed that one should swear, while at the same time rejecting infant baptism and refusing to recant his rebaptism. *Ibid.*, 319, 324. For further discussion of oath refusal in Zurich after 1527, see Pries, "Historical Context," 111-122.

81. For a discussion of the meaning of oath breaking, see *ibid.*, chap. 1, section D.

82. For a discussion of the religious nature of oaths in late-medieval society, see *ibid.*, chap. 1.

83. *TA, Zurich*, 234. The latter half of the statement is clearly a quote from Acts 5:29.

84. For a discussion of Carlstadt's and Müntzer's views on oaths, see Pries, "Historical Context," chap. 3.

85. See n. 80 above.

86. See, for example, the cases of Gabriel Giger, Jacob Hottinger, and Blaurock on March 25, 1525. *TA, Zurich*, 73.

87. See Pries, "Historical Context," chap. 1, section B. Releases from the oath on the basis of coercion were frequently granted by the church for political purposes. A notorious example was the release of King John's oath, after he signed the Magna Carta, on the basis that he had been coerced. No evidence has yet been found that a "heretic" was released from an oath on the basis of having been coerced into swearing the same.

88. John H. Yoder drew my attention to one additional point: If Anabaptists felt they had "sinned" by swearing the oath, and rejoined the Anabaptist conventicles, they could of course be readily forgiven by the community.

89. For an analysis of the communal oath of Zurich, see Pries, "Historical Context," chap. 2.

CHAPTER 5

The Rise of the Baptism of Adult Believers in Swiss Anabaptism[1]

Walter Klaassen

It came as a surprise to me when I realized that so far no one had taken the trouble to follow the trail of the emerging new view on baptism through the thicket of the origins of Swiss Anabaptism. People who had written on Anabaptist baptism, Rollin Armour and Christoph Windhorst, did not do it-- for good reasons. Mennonite attention to Swiss Brethren baptism has been focused totally on its theology. The numerous treatments of the rise of Swiss Anabaptism which appeared over the last fifteen years also did not give the kind of attention to baptism which they gave to tithe refusal, removal of images, and even community of goods. The most recent book on Anabaptism by a Mennonite author virtually ignores the issue of baptism.[2] It is my aim in this essay to correct this omission and at the same time to attempt an interpretation of the importance of baptism for Anabaptism. I will limit myself strictly to developments in Switzerland. It is my impression that baptism had a very similar meaning among other groups of Anabaptists.[3]

The issue of baptism as a concern of the Reformation emerged in Zurich first in December 1521, when the reformer Huldrych Zwingli, in a sermon, affirmed that unbaptized infants would not be condemned to hell.[4] This point was then also included in his sixty-seven Articles of January 1523.[5] Balthasar Hubmaier reported in 1525 that he and Zwingli had discussed the question of infant baptism while on a stroll in Zurich. He reports Zwingli to have said that children should not be baptized until they had been instructed in the faith.[6] Hubmaier's statement is supported by Zwingli himself.[7] It therefore appears certain that it was Zwingli himself who had first raised the issue of baptism of infants in Zurich. Although he did not take it further, discussion of it was continued in a lay study group of his followers under the leadership of Andreas Castelberger, a local bookdealer. Conrad Grebel, a young humanistically trained convert of Zwingli, soon became its spokesman.[8] At a certain point baptism then became the central point of contention between Zwingli and his erstwhile followers.

The introduction of a new and simplified liturgy of baptism in the summer of 1523 indicates that there was now no thought on the part of Zurich's clerical leadership of abandoning the baptism of infants. But by the winter of 1523-24 explicit criticism of "damaging superstitions" connected with the revised baptism liturgy was coming from the Castelberger group. Goeters takes this to be a reference to the continued use of exorcisms, sign of the cross, etc.[9] The group also discovered in these discussions that there was no explicit command in the New Testament to baptize infants.[10]

At the same time, there were rumblings in the rural parishes of Witikon and Zollikon. Early in 1524 some refused to have their children baptized, very likely at the urging of Wilhelm Reublin, priest in Witikon.[11] By spring Reublin was openly preaching against infant baptism. Those who had refused baptism for their children defended their action by saying that a child should not be baptized before it came of age and could make a confession of faith.[12] Thus far the discussion, and indeed the actions concerning baptism, had not gone beyond what Zwingli himself had earlier thought.

But late in 1523 the preacher Thomas Müntzer from Saxony was also thinking about baptism, and in a fire of passion wrote two small books, in the second of which he condemned infant baptism.[13] Sometime in the summer of 1524 these books came into the hands of the Castelberger group of lay persons in Zurich.[14]

But there were other things happening in Zurich at the same time. The discussion of baptism did not take place in a vacuum. When Zwingli first came to Zurich he immediately began the program of reform he had in mind by departing from the prescribed sermon texts for each Sunday, and using the Gospel of Matthew instead, and preaching about Jesus' life and teachings. That completed, he went on to the book of Acts. These Scriptures portrayed the beginnings of the church and were presented to the people of Zurich as the model to be followed in the restoration of true Christian living.[15] At Easter 1522 Zwingli publicly defended followers of his who had broken the fasting laws in Lent. He exerted pressure to make the monks conform to the Bible in their sermons. Images in the churches became a concern because they were now identified as idols. The payment of the tithe for the support of traditional church institutions became a burning issue, especially for the rural parishes, which resented having to pay money into the city. And finally, there was the mass with its doctrine of the repeated sacrifice of Christ, measured against the New Testament assertion that Christ had died once for all and that no further sacrifice was necessary. All of these issues were debated during the year 1523 with the result that the old church authorities were repudiated and the Scriptures put in their place.[16]

All the while the Great Council, which had traditionally been responsible for religious affairs in the city (this was not a Zwinglian invention), was trying to steer the ship of state in an increasingly rough political sea. Resistance to reform came from the defenders of the old order. Zwingli and his impatient followers were pushing for more progress; the council was concerned about stability, especially with respect to the continued payment of the tithe as essential to the fiscal health of the city. And so, by the autumn of 1523, the pace of reform slowed down. Thus, even though they had been judged to be unscriptural, images remained in the churches, and the mass continued for the time being in order to avoid problems for both Zurich and the Swiss Confederacy, which would be provoked to counteraction by change too rapidly carried out.

But in the minds of the Castelberger group so much remained to be done. What they found especially irksome was the argument that it was necessary to go slow to accommodate those who needed more time to accept the new order. Since the Spirit of God had spoken, should not Christians pay instant heed and obey?[17] Late in 1523 Zwingli recognized two specific dangers to the Zurich reformation: the absence of any real moral improvement, and the undermining of the civil order.[18]

The Castelberger group, however, would not have the momentum of their desire for the completion of reform interrupted. And so we return to the question of baptism, which had emerged concretely as one of the issues that had yet to be dealt with. To those who wanted the matter discussed, it must have seemed obvious that the total reform of the practice of baptism was on a par with the reform of the mass and that, as had been publicly agreed by clergy, council, and laity, the Scriptures were to be the norm for all changes.

Sometime in the summer of 1524, then, copies of Thomas Müntzer's two books, *On Fictitious Faith* and *Protestation*, came into the hands of the Zurich dissidents, who, after having read them, believed that they had found in Thomas Müntzer an ally. They wrote him a letter expressing their excitement at what they had read. Written on September 5, 1524, their letter gives us a good idea about what had been happening in their thinking since the reform had begun to slow down a year earlier.

This letter to Müntzer, writes Martin Brecht, reveals that Grebel and his group had been studying the question of baptism specifically with considerable dedication and energy. They had read the church fathers and Martin Luther. They acclaimed Jacob Strauss, who had written on the subject. They were acquainted with the new baptism liturgies that had been prepared by Luther, Leo Jud, Osiander, and the Strasbourg Reformers.[19] Finally, they knew about Müntzer's views. Even while the letter to Müntzer was being prepared, Grebel was working on a list of Bible passages against infant baptism which he was hoping to publish.[20] In this work he combined faith and baptism, which was probably the most important conclusion the Grebel group had formed thus far. It was precisely the unlinking of faith and baptism that Thomas Müntzer judged so severely in his *Protestation*. Specifically, Müntzer had stated there that by making infants into Christians, the church had turned Christians into infants, and consequently all understanding had disappeared from the church. The faith pledged by the godparents with much celebratory to-do was never kept; it disappeared as quickly as a dog ate a sausage. Hence the true baptism, the entrance to Christendom, had become a degraded monkey business. Nothing was left but ceremonies and empty form, and it all happened because of what Müntzer called the baptism of ignorance.[21] But Müntzer did not suggest the replacement of the baptism of ignorance with the baptism of understanding as one might have expected. Grebel and his friends understood that and went on to do it themselves. They explained that baptism signified that through faith and the blood of Christ, sin is washed away. It means that one has died to sin and now has a new life and spirit, and that, if faith is lived, one will certainly be saved. But they wanted it understood specifically that they did not share Luther's view that baptism was a pledge of God's grace even on one's deathbed. Nor did it secure one in God's favor simply by being performed as the old church taught. Children do not need baptism, because they are not guilty. In their letter they actually used some of Müntzer's words about baptism when they referred to the "inner baptism," "a sweet sinful Christ," the "baptism of trial and probation," and they indulged in the same excessive, disparaging words about infant baptism that Müntzer used, calling it a "senseless, blasphemous abomination." But they also had some doubts about Müntzer, and, despite the words, they certainly did not accept his interpretation of baptism. He had stimulated, perhaps even led, them to connect firmly what had earlier been severed, namely, baptism and faith. I agree therefore with Calvin Pater when he states that Müntzer's impact on Grebel "cannot be dismissed as marginal."[22]

The letter reveals another very significant aspect of their thinking which is perhaps quite as important as their words about baptism. The writers were highly conscious that they were laymen as over against their opponents, who were clergy. They knew, of course, that Müntzer, Carlstadt, and Strauss were also clergy, and they addressed the issue particularly with Müntzer as we shall see below. But in the letter they addressed Müntzer specifically, as a lay person, "without titles and as a brother." There is one master and he is Christ; all others are brothers. They dared to admonish him as a brother in the name, power, word, Spirit, and salvation which is extended to all Christians through Jesus Christ.[23] The underlying motif is that they, ordinary laymen, were conducting and anticipating more conversations on the issues that exercised people throughout Christendom, and which were normally reserved for the clergy. This motif runs through the whole letter.

The Lord's Supper is described as a supper of unity, i.e., of the unity of all Christians. It is not a clerical event as it has been for so long and continues to be in Zurich. The servant (Diener = deacon?) from the congregation is to say the words of institution. These words are not, they emphasize, words of consecration, the implication being that no priest is required for a fully valid Lord's Supper. They call for plain bread and for plain, ordinary utensils, again implying that there is nothing clerical about them that separates them from ordinary lay people. Since it is one bread, it demonstrates that Christians are one bread and body and true brothers with each other. There are no clergy-lay distinctions. Nor is there to be any individual partaking of the bread and wine, a reference to endowed masses in which only the priest took the bread and the wine since no one else was present. The Supper is not to be practiced in temples, that is, church buildings, because those are clerical places and produce false reverence for clerical surroundings rather than for God. There are to be no priestly robes, which set some Christians apart from others, because the Supper is a demonstration of unification and not a mass or sacrament.[24]

At a number of these points, especially Müntzer's own role as a priest conducting a public liturgy in clerical robes, they are very critical of Müntzer, and admonish him sharply to desist from these things. Finally, they beg him to receive their unlearned, unpolished letter. The contrast of learned-unlearned is made not between the writers and Müntzer, but rather between them as laymen and the scholarly clergy in Zurich and Wittenberg. It cannot be an accident that the letter is written in German, the language of lay people, and not in Latin, the clerical language. It was because they used common speech that they called the letter unlearned and unpolished.[25]

Near the beginning of the letter they confessed that for a long time they were lost in error because they were only listeners and readers of what the evangelical preachers said, as lay people were expected to do. But then they began to study the Scriptures themselves, as lay people, and in doing so discovered the "great and destructive deficiency of our shepherds," that is, the clerical leaders of Zurich. Major neglect in matters regarding the true faith and divine practice is due to false forbearance and indulgence, which they identified particularly as silence on important issues and as mixing God's Word with human considerations.

The rationale of Zwingli and Luther for going slow was, of course, that they did not wish to force people to change by the coercion of legalism. The shrill tone of the writers suggests the view that this was a patronizing attitude of the educated clergy towards ignorant lay people. The Word of God has been despised by those responsible for teaching it, they said, because they have continued in the Antichrist's forms of baptism and the Lord's Supper. The writers believed that they were in the company of the radical preachers Jacob Strauss, Thomas Müntzer, and Andreas Carlstadt in that as these had been cast out by the easygoing Scripture twisters and doctors at Wittenberg, so they also had been rejected by their learned shepherds, the clerical leaders of Zurich. The learned ones cannot make the distinction between God's Word and man's word, but the lay persons of Zurich, who are "poor in spirit," have been taught and strengthened by their newly discovered fellow believers. Although the evangelical leaders want laymen to read the Word of God, very few do so because people simply accept whatever the learned shepherds offer. In Zurich, they wrote, there are not more than twenty who believe the Word of God. Otherwise people run after Zwingli, Jud, and others, who are regarded as educated. The next stage, they surmised, would be persecution, but that was to be expected, for it has always been so. Meanwhile Grebel had been so encouraged by reading Müntzer that he would write against those who had knowingly or misleadingly written about baptism and who had translated the "absurd and blasphemous form of infant baptism" into German. It is important to notice at this point that one of the signatories of the letter was Johannes Brötli, the pastor of the Zollikon parish. It is therefore no longer simply the men in the city who speak. Reublin from Witikon also joined them soon after.

The conclusion of this reading of the letter is that the writers have taken a radically anticlerical stance. They see themselves as laymen, the "poor in spirit," but who, precisely because they are such, understand the Word of God and are prepared to obey it in its smallest demands regardless of the cost. The church leaders Zwingli and Jud are called the "learned shepherds" who, because they are learned, have mixed the divine Word with their own and now can no longer distinguish between the two. Still, they assume that everyone should listen to them, and if they do not, they will be persecuted, because they cannot bear the thought that lay people have caught on to their duplicity.[26]

The question of baptism must now be seen in this context. We have in this situation in Zurich an example of the old tenacious conviction held by many in earlier centuries, that ordinary lay people understand God's Word and will better than the clergy, the bishops, and the doctors. This conviction was strengthened by the view that the church is always a mixture of believers and unbelievers. This view had first been advanced by the Donatist theologian Tyconius in the fourth century and was used by Augustine in his *City of God*. In the Middle Ages one meets it frequently from the twelfth century onwards. The unbelievers in the church are virtually without exception identified as the clergy who, because of their wealth and pride, put forward their own word as God's Word. They are the servants of the Antichrist in the very holy of holies. But there are always those in the church who follow the uneducated artisan Jesus with his fishermen and tax collector disciples, and who therefore know what the truth is. With the one exception of the Waldensians, this view of the mixed church had not led to the formation of a separate church of those who believed. But by the sixteenth century things had changed. There was a ferment of freedom to think new thoughts. Grebel and his group were struggling for a truly reformed evangelical church. This letter is evidence of their disillusionment with the current leadership, and they are clearly saying that they, the lay people, know better what needs doing and how than the clergy do.

Now, if lay people are to assume responsibility for the church and take over the traditional functions of the clergy, a new model of the church is called for. This is not said in the letter, and the writers indicate no intention of moving into separatism. Nevertheless, they know that a faithful church cannot tolerate infant baptism, since it is the fundamental sign of a clerical church. It insures that lay people will be kept in ignorant dependence upon the clergy. It is a means of clerical control and the sign of lay disenfranchisement. This was the reason for the refusal of people in the rural parishes to have their children baptized, and this was the reason for the conclusion of the Grebel group in the city that infant baptism would have to be abolished and the baptism of believing adults put in its place. The baptism of faith was therefore, by contrast, an anticlerical sign. People who had knowingly, voluntarily, and publicly confessed their faith in God's salvation through Christ could legitimately be expected to live a life of obedience to Christ. Insistence upon the abolition of infant baptism was therefore much more than "a logical step in the purification of the sacraments."[27] It had to do with the desire for lay control of the church.

In the light of Calvin Pater's claim of Carlstadt's paternity of Anabaptism in Zurich, it should be pointed out that Carlstadt's tract on baptism did not reach Zurich until over a month after the letter to Müntzer was written, and could therefore not have been influential in forming the views of Grebel and his friends. The rest of Pater's case rests on the presumption that Carlstadt wrote his views on baptism to Grebel in a letter, which is an argument from silence.[28] Carlstadt's tract would certainly have encouraged them when it arrived, and it may well have helped them in later formulations of their views.[29]

After September 1524 baptism became the major point of contention between the Grebel group and Zwingli. Grebel himself continued to be concerned with it. He wrote an eight-page letter to a group of sympathizers in St. Gall in which he warned them to be on their guard against the local lay leader Kessler, who had defended infant baptism.[30] Grebel and his group must also have been speaking publicly about baptism, and also demanded public discussions with Zwingli on the subject.[31] This led to two meetings, which likely took place on December 6 and 13, 1524. Here the biblical evidence on the question of baptism was hotly debated, and the dissidents linked baptism and faith.[32] Zwingli reported that they displayed anger and hatred against him because they were defeated in the argument.[33] That they were hostile to him is well known. However, it was not because they lost the argument, but because they could not persuade him on the mutually accepted basis of *sola scriptura* of the logic of their interpretation of the biblical record on baptism.

In the Müntzer letter there was as yet only a fragmentary appeal to Scripture. But Grebel's work on Scripture passages on faith and baptism was no doubt followed by more Bible study on the subject. What we get from now on on the subject of baptism is an exclusively scriptural argument, since appeal to Scripture as the sole authority was accepted by both Zwingli and Grebel. This scriptural argument easily gives the impression that it was purely an issue of the greater biblicism of Grebel and his group. The question was really one of *how* the Bible was used as authority in the controversy over baptism.

During December, Zwingli was also writing his book *Those Who Give Cause for Rebellion*. Among the seven groups causing serious trouble for the Zwinglian reformation were the deniers of infant baptism. Zwingli's violent denunciation of this group shows that they had struck in him an exposed nerve. There had obviously been a good deal of public agitation on the part of his critics: "They contend on every street corner, in the shops and wherever else they can do it. And when they are prevented they have their own debating houses where they assemble and sit and judge people."[34] Zwingli made basically two charges against the dissidents, neither of which dealt with the point of contention. First, he accused them of being mean-spirited, self-righteous, envious, and judgmental, showing no Christian charity or patience.[35] Second, he repeatedly stated that they were concerned merely with externals in their concern for baptism.[36] He attempted a biblical justification for infant baptism which can only be called trivial,[37] but he did not engage the main point of contention that the tithe, the charging of interest, and the baptism of infants could not be defended on the basis of the New Testament, to whose authority he had committed himself.[38] What wonder, then, that his erstwhile followers doubted his sincerity and commitment, rejected him as a reliable authority, and refused to follow his leading? Appeals to exercise love and forbearance fall on deaf ears when they are used to stifle discussion. Zwingli charged his former followers with fomenting rebellion.

But Zwingli had earlier noticed something to which he did not allude in this work, perhaps in the interest of avoiding a complete break. He was aware, and rightly so, that the dissidents had a different view of churchly order, and that consequently there was real potential for an open rupture.[39] Still, the baptism of adults did not necessarily imply separatism and therefore was also not inherently sectarian. The radicals themselves did not yet have a clear idea where they were going, and the Zwinglian reform in Zurich was also by no means completed.[40] But subsequent actions by Zwingli and the council, and the growing conviction of the dissenters that Zurich was not a Christian society, pushed developments toward a break.

Following the two private discussions between Zwingli and the Grebel group, Felix Mantz, one of its members, wrote his Petition of Defense to the council in which he put forward his views on baptism, which may be regarded as those of the whole group.[41] It is important to notice that Mantz expected the council to make a decision in their favor, or at least that the council could legitimately do so, and so had not yet given up hope for an ecclesiastical order in Zurich including or based on baptism of believing adults. The Defense also reveals the agitated state of affairs in the city during December 1524. Grebel's letter to Vadian of January 14, 1525, adds a few more details.[42] The letter is evidence that Grebel was very busy with the subject of baptism, and he refers to the calling of a public disputation on baptism.[43]

This event was called for by the council for January 17. The council statement assumed that the defenders of the baptism of adults were in error. Apparently the planned proceedings were designed to prove them a public menace from their own words. The closing words "after which our lords will take whatever action is appropriate" are an unveiled threat. The rejection of infant baptism was no longer simply a matter of a faulty interpretation of the biblical record; it had become an issue of public order. Grebel and Mantz were joined by Reublin as spokesmen for the dissidents. They apparently repeated all the arguments well known by that time against infant baptism, and, *for the first time,* said that since it was not valid, one should be baptized again. So far this had not been articulated in any way.[44]

The mandate of the council which provided for action against the dissenters justified their fears.[45] All unbaptized children were to be baptized forthwith; exile awaited those who refused to comply. The internal record of the council's decision included the directive that the parish of Zollikon should immediately restore the baptismal font and find out who took it out of the church and threw it away.[46] On January 21 followed a further council decree banning the "special schools" of the dissenters, ordering Grebel and Mantz to desist from discussing baptism and any intention connected with it, and to accept the judgment of the council, and announcing a decree of banishment over Reublin, Brötli, Hätzer, and Castelberger, to be obeyed within eight days.[47] Control of baptism was now in the hands not only of the clergy but of the council as well. It was now totally clear, if it had not been previously, that Zwingli had decided not to leave these matters to the believing congregation as he had once said,[48] but to allow the council to decide on theological issues, governed to a considerable degree by the internal politics of the Confederacy. The council's action decisively rejected control of religious issues by congregational decision. They understood that the abolition of the baptism of infants would totally change the political and social order of Zurich. It must have confirmed for the dissenters the accuracy of their critique of the preceding six months. It needs to be said in the council's defense that it did not reject the vision of a Christian commonwealth in which the preachers and the Christian council would jointly guide the life of the community. However, it did reject the alternative Anabaptist model for the same thing, which was by no means clear, for which there was no precedent, and which clearly signaled immediate and grave social and political problems. The politicians of Zurich understood perhaps better than the Grebel group itself the consequences of their thinking.

The mandates against them forced the dissenters to act, although the first baptisms, which took place on January 21, do not seem to have been deliberately planned. Nor were they, as is now generally agreed, the act of founding a new church. That did not happen until two years later at the Schleitheim gathering. But after the first baptisms others took place, especially in the parish of Zollikon.

The struggle with the authorities in Zurich continued despite the decrees of the council, and it now turned virtually exclusively on the question of baptism. The same arguments were made over and over. But even after July 1525 Mantz was still offering to put his reasons for rejecting infant baptism into writing, and letting the whole church make a decision which would then be binding on all. This was likely a response to Zwingli's charge in his baptism book that this was precisely what Anabaptists would not do.[49] Two more public hearings on the matter were held in March[50] and in November of 1525,[51] but nothing new was added. The calling of two more public meetings contrary to their earlier decision was witness to the concern of the council to bring the contentious issue to a peaceful conclusion. Because they would not abandon their convictions, the judgment was that the Anabaptists were contentious, separatist, obstinate, and seditious. They were charged with despising temporal authority and with the destruction of Christian love.[52] This charge, first made in early 1525,[53] was just as often denied by the Anabaptists. They could not understand why the baptism of adults was necessarily incompatible with a Christian commonwealth in Zurich.[54]

Resistance to the government decrees continued for the very reason for which it had first begun, namely, clerical control of baptism as well as of the Lord's Supper. Every child is to be baptized *in church by a priest* without exception, reads a council decree from February 1, 1525. Infractions would be severely punished.[55] No one who was not officially authorized was allowed to preach.[56] There are clear indications that the people in the rural areas did not trust the official clergy. To provide a safety valve for unrest in the rural parishes, the council had agreed early in 1525 that assemblies of people for purposes of reading and discussing Scripture would be allowed and encouraged, but that preaching and baptizing were the sole prerogative of the clergy.[57] Such legitimate meetings seem to have been widespread during 1525. People from other areas sent to Zollikon for lay readers to read the Bible to them.[58]

This strict clerical control fueled the anticlerical sentiments among Anabaptists and confirmed them further in their conviction that only the abandonment of infant baptism with its corollary of instituting the baptism of believing adults plus a properly instructed laity would break clerical control. Some of their readers who were former priests learned a trade and earned their own living as lay people.[59] Any who preached for money, they said, were false prophets and could not speak the truth.[60] The pope, Luther, and Zwingli, and their supporters, were thieves and murderers, because they came at baptism by a door other than Christ.[61] They were shepherds who led astray,[62] and wolves who attacked the flock.[63] Hence Anabaptists were comforted that God worked his will and might among ordinary, simple people; these were admonished to help and encourage one another and to stay away from the preachers.[64]

Most of the baptized eventually gave up under the pressure of the authorities, especially after March 7, 1526, when the council, having given up its attempt to turn people away from Anabaptism, issued a decree providing for the death penalty for rebaptism.[65] This decree, and the evident readiness of some Anabaptists to ignore it and take the consequences, are witness to the serious view taken of the question of baptism by both sides. For the government the baptism of adult believers meant the breakup of an ancient Christian societal tradition, and for Anabaptists it became the test of ultimate loyalty to Christ. This is as far as I shall take the detailed story. Less than a year later followed the Schleitheim Articles, which were, among other things, a declaration of separation. All attempts at a "nonseparating congregationalism" had been abandoned.

The rejection of the baptism of infants was therefore part of a gradually dawning conviction on the part of the Zurich dissenters that clerical leaders, even the new evangelical ones, could not be trusted, because their faithfulness to *sola scriptura* was compromised by social and political considerations. This crisis called for faithfulness on the part of the lay people. But in order for lay people to be able to make decisions about Christian truth, they needed to be informed, conscious, and voluntary Christians. That called for the baptism of believing adults. Infant baptism was the sign of the disenfranchisement of ordinary Christians. It preempted their own decision and kept them in dependence on the clergy.

NOTES

1. This essay was first published in German in *Mennonitische Geschichtsblätter* 46 (1989).

2. J. Denny Weaver, *Becoming Anabaptist* (Scottdale, Pa.: Herald Press, 1987).

3. But see the treatments of Hut's baptism by Gottfried Seebass, "Das Zeichen der Erwählten: Zum Verständnis der Taufe bei Hans Hut," in *Umstrittenes Täufertum, 1525-1975: Neue Forschungen,* ed. Hans-Jürgen Goertz (Göttingen: Vandenhoeck und Ruprecht, 1975); and Werner O. Packull, *Mysticism and the Early South German-Austrian Anabaptist Movement* (Scottdale, Pa.: Herald Press, 1977).

4. J. F. G. Goeters, *Ludwig Hätzer: Spiritualist und Antitrinitarier* (Gütersloh: C. Bertelsmann Verlag, 1957), 47.

5. Emil Egli et al., eds, *Huldreich Zwinglis sämtliche Werke,* 14 vols, Corpus Reformatorum, LXXXVIII- (Berlin: Schwetschke und Sohn, 1905-), I, 168 (hereafter cited as *ZSW*).

6. Gunnar Westin and Torsten Bergsten, eds., *Balthasar Hubmaier: Schriften* (Gütersloh: Gerd Mohn, 1962), 186; H. Wayne Pipkin and John H. Yoder, trans. and eds., *Balthasar Hubmaier, Theologian of Anabaptism* (Scottdale, Pa.: Herald Press, 1989), 194.

7. Leonhard von Muralt and Walter Schmid, eds., *Quellen zur Geschichte der Täufer in der Schweiz,* I: *Zürich* (Zurich: Theologischer Verlag, 1952), 53 (hereafter cited as *TA, Zurich*); *ZSW* IV, 228, n. 21.

8. *TA, Zurich,* 388.

9. Goeters, *Ludwig Hätzer,* 48.

10. *Ibid.,* 49.

11. James M. Stayer, "Reublin and Brötli: The Revolutionary Beginnings of Swiss Anabaptism," in *Origins and Characteristics of Swiss Anabaptism,* ed. Marc Lienhard (The Hague: Martinus Nijhoff, 1977), 88.

12. *TA, Zurich,* 11.

13. Günther Franz, ed., *Thomas Müntzer: Schriften und Briefe* (Gütersloh: Gerd Mohn, 1968), 217-240. In a short discussion of baptism which Franz dates after 15 August, 1524 (see pp. 526-527), Müntzer also disputed the generally accepted metamorphosis of circumcision into baptism, and demanded scriptural proof for this teaching of Peter Lombard in the fourth book of the *Sentences.* There is no evidence, however, that the Zurich dissenters had seen this short treatise.

14. *Müntzer: Schriften und Briefe,* 217-225; trans. James M. Stayer, "Thomas Müntzer's *Protestation* and *Imaginary Faith,*" *MQR* 55 (1981), 99-130.

15. Ulrich Gäbler, *Huldrych Zwingli. Eine Einführung in sein Leben und sein Werk* (Munich: C. H. Beck, 1983), 46.

16. *Ibid.,* 62-3.

17. *ZSW* II, 784; translation in D. J. Ziegler, ed., *Great Debates of the Reformation* (New York: Random House, 1969), 50.

18. Gäbler, *Huldrych Zwingli,* 76.

19. Martin Brecht, "Herkunft und Eigenart der Taufanschauung der Zürcher Täufer," *Archiv für Reformationsgeschichte* 64 (1973), 147-165.

20. *TA, Zurich,* 12; Leland Harder, ed., *The Sources of Swiss Anabaptism* (Scottdale, Pa.: Herald Press, 1985), 283.

21. *Müntzer: Schriften und Briefe,* 228, 229, 230.

22. Calvin A. Pater, *Karlstadt as the Father of the Baptist Movments: The Emergence of Lay Protestantism* (Toronto: University of Toronto Press, 1984), 144.

23. *TA, Zurich*, 14; *Sources of Swiss Anabaptism*, 286.

24. *TA, Zurich*, 15; *Sources of Swiss Anabaptism*, 287-288.

25. *TA, Zurich*, 21; *Sources of Swiss Anabaptism*, 294.

26. I have here made the argument that anticlericalism was a major factor in the emergence and development of early Anabaptism. This argument was first made by Hans-Jürgen Goertz in his book *Die Täufer: Geschichte und Deutung* in 1980. I expressed some doubts about the pervasiveness of the motif in my review of the book (*MQR* 56 [1982], 204-205). I now say that my own study confirms Goertz's earlier judgment.

27. Stayer, "Reublin and Brötli," 88.

28. Pater, *Karlstadt*, 156.

29. *Ibid.*, 159-167.

30. Heinold Fast, ed., *Quellen zur Geschichte der Täufer in der Schweiz*, II: *Ostschweiz* (Zurich: Theologischer Verlag, 1973), 603.

31. *ZSW* VI, 36; *Sources of Swiss Anabaptism*, 300.

32. Goeters, *Ludwig Hätzer*, 51-52.

33. *Ibid.*

34. *ZSW* III, 405.

35. *Ibid.*, 403-406.

36. *Ibid.*, 404, 407, 409, 412.

37. *Ibid.*, 409-412.

38. *Ibid.*, 362-364.

39. Goeters, *Ludwig Hätzer*, 52-53; Pater, *Karlstadt*, 137, n. 109.

40. James M. Stayer, "Radical Early Zwinglianism: Balthasar Hubmaier, Faber's 'Ursach' and the Peasant Programmes," in *Huldrych Zwingli, 1484-1531: A Legacy of Radical Reform*, ed. E. J. Furcha (Montreal: Faculty of Religious Studies, McGill University, 1985), 75.

41. *TA, Zurich*, 23-28; Harder, *Sources of Swiss Anabaptism*, 311-315.

42. *TA, Zurich*, 33-34; *Sources of Swiss Anabaptism*, 331-332.

43. *TA, Zurich*, 33; *Sources of Swiss Anabaptism*, 333.

44. Heinrich Bullinger, *Reformationsgeschichte nach dem Autographon*, ed. J. J. Hottinger and H. H. Vögeli (Frauenfeld, 1838-40), 258; *Sources of Swiss Anabaptism*, 335.

45. *TA, Zurich*, 35; *Sources of Swiss Anabaptism*, 336.

46. *TA, Zurich*, 34-5.

47. *Ibid.*, 35-36.

48. S. M. Jackson, ed., *Ulrich Zwingli (1484-1531): Selected Works* (Philadelphia: University of Pennsylvania Press, 1972), 57.

49. *ZSW* IV, 78; trans. G. W. Bromiley, ed., *Zwingli and Bullinger* (Philadelphia: Westminster Press, 1953), 158.

50. *Sources of Swiss Anabaptism*, 352-356.

51. *TA, Zurich*, 132.

52. *Ibid.*

53. *Ibid.*, 51, 68, 74-75.

54. See Hans J. Hillerbrand, *Die politische Ethik des oberdeutschen Täufertums* (Leiden: E. J. Brill, 1962), 24-30, for selected references.

55. *TA, Zurich*, 44.

56. *Ibid.*, 94.
57. *Ibid.*, 82.
58. *Ibid.*, 69, 82-83, 85, 99, 105, 108, 155.
59. *Ibid.*, 45, 84.
60. *Ibid.*, 46, 123.
61. *Ibid.*, 125-126.
62. *Ibid.*, 67.
63. *Ibid.*, 75.
64. *Ibid.*, 75, 46.
65. *Ibid.*, 180-181; *Sources of Swiss Anabaptism*, 448.

CHAPTER 6

The Path to Conversion: The Controversy between Hans de Ries and Nittert Obbes

Sjouke Voolstra

The difference of opinion between, on the one hand, Nittert Obbes, preacher in the Waterland congregation in Amsterdam, and on the other hand, his fellow preachers in this congregation, Pieter Andries Hesseling, Cornelis Claes Anslo, Reinier Wybrants Wybma, and the leader of the Waterland party, Hans de Ries, culminated in a controversy fought out in pamphlets which compromised the whole Mennonite movement in the Netherlands in the years 1625-28. Until now this controversy has been illuminated primarily around the question of whether Socinian influences were involved in Nittert Obbes's over-emphasis on the written and preached Word as the only means to conversion.[1]

The course of the dispute does indeed give rise to this suspicion. His immediate colleagues accused Nittert Obbes of hiding his unorthodox ideas behind an appeal to the learned Socinus.[2] But the accused tried to counter this insinuation by pointing out that he had never read a single book by Socinus, in fact was not able to read any because he did not know Latin.[3] He based his sermons exclusively on the "straightforward words of Christ." If his colleagues permitted the rumor to spread that he was not free of Socinian stain, then Nittert Obbes in his turn could, with more justification, charge his fellow preachers with being papists, considering they loved to quote church fathers and other Catholic authors in their sermons.[4]

Where there is unorthodox smoke, there must be Socinian fire, participants and observers in the dispute thought. And with the same suspicion in their minds, the learned of other times made every effort to localize the Socinian hearth-fire in all its brightness, whether from polemical or from apologetic motives.[5] Related ideas need not, however, imply direct dependence. And when direct dependence is involved, it turns out that it is generally very selective. Recent research provides increasing support for a more balanced judgment about the supposed Socinian influences on the Anabaptist movement in the Netherlands.[6]

Also with respect to the question as to whether Socinian influences are at work in Nittert Obbes and associates, it is both useful and problematic to begin discreetly with something as vague as a general "intellectual climate," both rationalist and pietist in character, which was reflected in the internal Mennonite controversy concerning the relationship between the outer and the inner Word.

As usual, however, the need for greater clarification, arising from dissatisfaction with a term as imprecise as "intellectual climate," is always stronger than wise discretion. Therefore we want to venture an attempt to explain this controversy in terms of two streams in the spiritual climate crystallizing at the beginning of the seventeenth century in the Netherlands: (1) a reevaluation of the mysticism in the pietism of the so-called Second (*nadere*) Reformation within and outside the Reformed church; (2) the rationalism showing up particularly in Arminianism or Remonstrantism--the latter in connection with a short explanation of the (church-) political consequences brought about by the condemnation of this moderate wing of Dutch Calvinism at the National Synod of Dordrecht, 1618-19. Perhaps it is possible by this means to trace to what extent Nittert Obbes and Hans de Ries and associates were influenced by these contemporary developments and in what way both parties could appeal for their views, formed partly by their own time, to the Anabaptist tradition, which demonstrated both spiritualist and biblicist traits.

In order to identify the relationship of these particulars to the spiritual and political climate in the first quarter of the seventeenth century, it is necessary to define the *status questionis* of the dispute between Nittert Obbes and Hans de Ries in broader terms. It will become evident that we cannot reduce it to the question of the relationship between the outer and the inner Word alone, even though the opponents themselves made this point the focus of their difference of opinion. To do this, it is essential that the reason for Nittert Obbes's suspension and the pamphlet controversy which followed it, not be detached from the circumstances giving rise to the conflicts. Finally, we will give the Remonstrant Simon Episcopius, an outsider who got involved, the opportunity to set forth his view of the theological points of the conflict in a scholarly and logical fashion, thereby contributing an answer to the question to what extent he and Nittert Obbes can be said to have a relationship to Socinianism and, if this is the case, on what points. This is not the occasion to describe at length the controversy over the doctrine of predestination which underlay the conflict between the supporters of the Reformed professors Gomarus and Arminius, the Contra-Remonstrants and the Remonstrants. We refer to recent literature on this subject.[7] Only the items relevant to our subject will be touched upon.

When the Calvinist-Reformed Reformation consolidated during the revolt of the northern Netherlands against Spanish authority, two parties formed which had a different opinion about the authority of the Reformed confessions and about the relationship between church and state. The "strict" or "church" Calvinists stood for a strict commitment to the confession and opposed interference of the government in church affairs; the "moderate" or "political" group feared the compulsion of forcing a particular confession and desired the guarantee of a government tolerant in its oversight of religious matters.

This smoldering conflict came to a head during a twelve-year truce in the struggle with Spain (1609-21). Gomarus (1563-1641), professor at Leiden, presented himself as the defender of the doctrine developed in Reformed scholasticism that God had decided from eternity whom to choose or to reject and that faith is a gift of God's free grace for the elect.[8] His colleague Arminius (1560-1609), however, laid more stress on responsibility and free will. He interpreted predestination to mean that God, through grace, chooses a person for Christ's sake, taking into account the faith of the person, which God foresees.[9] The Arminians were called Remonstrants, after the *Remonstrance* submitted to the States of Holland in 1610, and their opponents, Contra-Remonstrants.

The disputes would not have reached such a crisis had political differences not played a part. Oldenbarnevelt, the Grand Pensionary, who had promoted the twelve-year truce against the wishes of the military commander Prince Maurice, was a supporter of the Remonstrants, while the latter ostentatiously chose the side of the Contra-Remonstrants. Even King James of England got involved in the controversy. Among other things, he protested against the appointment of Conrad Vorstius as successor to Arminius in Leiden, because Vorstius was suspected of Socinianism. The prince won the support of the States General and gained power through a *coup d'état*. His rival Oldenbarnevelt was executed.

Although the Contra-Remonstrants had always had an aversion to state interference in matters of faith, they suddenly appeared to be great supporters for the calling of a national synod in Dordrecht by the States General. What they had hoped for, happened: the twelve Remonstrants called to account under the leadership of the Leiden professor Simon Episcopius were ejected from the assembly after long debates, and their doctrinal statements were condemned in the five Articles against the Remonstrants.

More than two hundred Remonstrant ministers were prohibited from preaching; many of them, including Episcopius, went into exile. An unsuccessful attack on Prince Maurice in 1623 by a small group of revolutionary Remonstrants led to fresh viligance on the part of the Contra-Remonstrant governments, which, among other things, resulted in a great reduction of Remonstrant ministers.[10] Not until after Prince Maurice's death (1625) did the Remonstrants gradually receive more freedom of movement under the moderate regime of his brother and successor, Frederik Hendrik. In Amsterdam the Contra-Remonstrants remained in power until 1627 under the leadership of the influential orthodox regent Reinier Pauw. Until that time all religious minorities in this city, from Catholic to Mennonite, had to be very careful about open expressions of sympathy for the Remonstrants.

As with all other religious groups who did not follow the Calvinist line, the various Mennonite parties likely sympathized with the Remonstrants. Both placed great value on a church and a government that did not bring those of another persuasion into a crisis of conscience through compulsion to hold to a particular confession. After the condemnation of their doctrine, some Remonstrants sought refuge with the moderate Mennonites.[11] The Waterlanders in Amsterdam, who had already demonstrated their openness in 1615 by accepting into their congregation the English Puritan Baptists, followers of John Smyth,[12] had good contacts with the Remonstrants even before their condemnation.

In any case, this is hinted at by the man who was the evil genius of the conflict between Hans de Ries and Nittert Obbes, Jan Theunis, printer, publisher, polyglot, and hostelier, in one of the pamphlets in which he, as a supporter of Nittert, fights against the "pope of the Waterlanders," Hans de Ries.[13] Here it becomes evident that the Socinian ideas Nittert Obbes was supposed to have nourished probably came to him indirectly, that is, via Remonstrant writings and sermons.

According to Jan Theunis, before the Synod of Dordrecht many Arminians wanted to become disciples of Hans de Ries. The relationship was so close that the Reformed church began to be concerned about Waterland mission among the Arminians. When political consequences threatened after 1619 (for example, persecution by the government and preaching prohibitions also for Waterlanders), Hans de Ries advised that the relationship with the Arminians be allowed to cool: "Let us not bring upon ourselves an untimely cross for their [Remonstrants'] sake." But Jan Theunis remarked scoffingly that if the Calvinists obstructed the preaching of the Waterland-Mennonite teachers, De Ries would rightly protest to the government![14]

The same Hans de Ries and his supporters had warned Nittert Obbes against the writings and sermons of the Remonstrants at the beginning of the conflict.[15] Their intellectual approach to the Bible and their determination to hold to the written Word could, after all, easily lead to suspicion that Socinianism was involved, could it not? But what were the tactics of the Waterlanders in their move against Nittert Obbes? Again, according to Jan Theunis, Hans de Ries and associates had laid the Socinian stain which clung to Arminianism also upon Nittert Obbes and for this reason withdrawn his right to proclaim the Word, in order to exculpate themselves from the Reformed church's accusation that they were Arminian and, which was even worse, Socinian.

It is clear from the literary intervention of no less a person than Simon Episcopius himself that the Remonstrants did in fact demonstrate a greater affinity with Nittert Obbes's views on the matter of the relationship between the outer and the inner Word than with those of his Waterland fellow preachers, and in addition did not consider fair the lawsuit which they had begun against him. We will return to this point in more detail later.

To the warning of his colleagues not to open himself to the writings and sermons of the Remonstrants, Nittert Obbes replied with the advice that they in their turn should not allow themselves to be influenced by spiritualist writers such as Sebastian Franck, Matthias Weyer, Tauler, and Caspar Schwenckfeld.[16] Here we notice the other spiritual stream--besides Arminian rationalism--with which the Waterlanders demonstrated a relationship, namely, the pietism of the early seventeenth century. The dogmatization of the Reformation had led also in the Netherlands to a reaction in the form of active pursuit of a living, personal piety as the fruit of regeneration. Was regeneration attained through reason or through the heart? Were human beings actively engaged in the process, or need they be only passively receptive? Could the Spirit regenerate human beings also outside the Bible and biblical preaching, through direct experience? These questions form the vortices arising when the two streams, early Rationalism and early Pietism, meet and merge.

The Reformed in the Netherlands received their pietistic impulses primarily from English Puritanism. William Perkins's works were much read in this circle.[17] Gisbertus Voetius, the Reformed professor in Utrecht who wanted to unite the pietist *praxis pietatis* with dogmatic learning, frequently appealed to Bernard of Clairvaux, Bonaventura, Ruysbroek, Tauler, Thomas à Kempis, the English Puritans and their Dutch representatives such as William Ames, and the brothers Willem and Ewould Teellinck. The pietist revival among the Reformed is usually referred to as the Nearer Reformation, a term which does not imply that they considered the Calvinist Reformation as such a failure, but which gives expression to the concern that its dogmatization was at the expense of inner experience of faith and sanctification of life. The actual instigation for this revival was the growing wealth that launched the Golden Age, and the moral laxity connected with it.

It is striking that in spite of the unmistakable affinity between the Dutch Anabaptists and the Calvinists with respect to the type of piety and striving for sanctification, the former showed little evidence of having become acquainted with English-oriented Reformed pietism.[18] The predestination character of Reformed pietism, or the fact that it demonstrated a Reformed stamp on the whole, was an impediment. One can only guess that the Waterland congregation of Amsterdam became acquainted with the literary results--often translated into Dutch--of English pietism through acceptance into their congregation of the Puritan Baptists who had fled from England.

For their pietist revival the Dutch Anabaptists could simply fall back on the writings of spiritualists of their own or related traditions--writings much published at the beginning of the seventeenth century.[19] The pamphlets, which appeared as a result of the conflict between Hans de Ries and associates and Nittert Obbes, cite primarily Caspar Schwenckfeld, Sebastian Franck (and quoted in his works: Thomas Müntzer, Hans Denck, Ludwig Hätzer), Matthias Weyer, Tauler, and the *Theologia Deutsch*, but also David Joris and Hendrik Niklaes, the spiritualist authors on whom the defenders of the dual Word based their arguments.[20]

In a recent study about the Schabaelje brothers and their environment and literary work, there is a surprising, fresh view of the complex world of faith among the Waterlanders, and in particular of the pietist circle of *Vredestadsburgers* of which Jan Philips Schabaelje was a part.[21] Again Jan Theunis, the controversial supporter of Nittert Obbes named earlier, brings to light in his *chronique scandaleuse* that the general pietist revival in the Dutch churches gave evidence of extreme forms of expression.

Among other things he tells of the "new-birth séance" of Jan Philips Schabaelje's friend of later years, the poet Judith Lubberts--the most illustrative example of becoming regenerated without the outer Word.[22] He gives several additional examples of the behavior of other followers of this "spiritualist religion" who have in common the characteristic that such passionate abandonment to the immediate working of the Spirit gave evidence of something akin to moral laxity, a work ethic of no great standard, and in the worst case, fraudulent practices.

Some people from this circle had excited improper expectations with their new discoveries (new techniques for controlling the water and walking under water), which they attributed to direct inspiration of the Spirit. And, Jan Theunis concludes his insinuations, did not the Spirit-driven Hans de Ries practice alchemy, considering he hoped to make gold from the May dew which gave a red hue to the butter in early spring?[23] With the opponents of these forms of spiritualistic religion, one may perhaps conclude that the Spirit by which some people are prompted betrays more similarity to a willful irrationality than to the Holy Spirit, who in their view, after all, primarily urges people on to a right way of life. Nevertheless it is striking that rationalism and spiritualism are clearly bound up in each other here.

Earlier the observation was made that during the pietist revival the Dutch Anabaptists were oriented less toward English pietism than toward pre-Reformation ascetic and popular mystical literature beloved in their circles. The writings of Thomas à Kempis and the *Theologia Deutsch* belong to the practical ascetic writings published by the Waterlander Claes Jacobs from the Rijp and read by many.[24] Indeed, everywhere in the country people got together in conventicles to read the mystics, including the sermons of Tauler printed in Amsterdam.[25]

It cannot be denied that a leaning toward a more extreme spiritualism is traceable in the circle against whom Nittert Obbes's criticism is directed than that to be inferred from moderate popular mystical writings. The name of Matthias Weyer (?-1560) and his letters and sayings, published in Frankfurt in Dutch in 1579, came up often in the conflict.[26] His practical-mystical wisdom was to a great extent a reflection of his own life's path, which was characterized by continual illness and weakness.

Faith is for Weyer the opposite of an intellectual affair. If faith goes no further than understanding, then neither does salvation go further than understanding, and salvation together with understanding is lost at death. True faith, however, moves the soul or heart, and death cannot touch this. Becoming part of Christ and his Spirit means suffering, which is total death to one's own nature. One finds one's own perfection only in becoming nothing in oneself. The final union with God is entirely God's work; every human activity gets in the way of that experience.

Mystical interpretations of *sola gratia* such as these naturally elicited from Nittert Obbes and his supporters, who believed in a more rational-ethical way, the reproach that such a mysticism had the same disastrous consequences for good morals and human effort as the Calvinist doctrine of predestination, which made God the cause of evil and thereby excused the moral laxity of the believers. In addition, the extreme emphasis on human passivity challenged

the conviction of both Mennonites and Arminians that God's offer of grace
does not exclude human willingness to accept it. This was the central point of
dispute between Remonstrants and Contra-Remonstrants.[27] If, with the
papists, Lutherans, and Calvinists, they erroneously made faith and regeneration into such a passive affair, then immature children as well as those who had
reached the age of understanding could equally have faith and be regenerated.
But then the Anabaptist views of faith and their doctrine of baptism were put
in question.[28] This was reason enough for Nittert Obbes to call a halt to these
extreme forms of the pietist faith of his day. In this attempt he was supported
by the more rational ethical theology of the Remonstrants. But was it not
equally possible to appeal to the strong rationalistic traits linked to a moderate
biblicism in his own Dutch Anabaptist tradition?

An indication for the validity of this suspicion is to be found in the list of
authors which Nittert mentions in his *Raegh-besem*. He is very impartial in his
selection of supporters for the primacy of the outer Word. Roman Catholic as
well as Lutheran and Reformed theologians are produced as witnesses; he cites
writings of Remonstrants and Mennonites without discrimination.[29]

And what is the common sentiment that rings out in this great diversity of
voices? It is that the human being can become regenerate only by hearing the
preached Word, and that this regeneration implies that the believer is actively
involved with reason and will. And were not all orthodox Anabaptists, Menno
Simons and the moderate Frisians with their leader Lubbert Gerrits, as well as
Dirk Philips and his equally less strict Flemish followers under the leadership
of Claes Claes of Blokzijl, of the same conviction?

Nittert Obbes quotes prodigiously from the printed epistles of Lubbert
Gerrits, in particular his pronouncements showing that true regeneration
comes forth from the Word and a sincere faith, with the assistance of the Holy
Spirit, and therefore not from fanaticisms, figments of the imagination, or
sanctification by one's own works and righteousness.[30] Although in the heat of
the controversy against extreme spiritualism Nittert himself demonstrated less
balanced views, he must nevertheless have had a great affinity with this moderate representative of Mennonite orthodoxy and faithfulness to Scripture. Let
us therefore consider briefly this outstanding personality and inquire to what
extent Nittert Obbes may be related intellectually to him. At the same time,
this offers an opportunity to shed some light on Nittert Obbes's role in the
process of reconciliation between the various moderate Anabaptist parties.

In 1589 Lubbert Gerrits (1534-1612) had become leader of the so-called
Young Frisians in Amsterdam, and in 1591 had brought about the unification
of these Mennonites, who were moderate in matters of discipline, with the
High Germans. Hans de Ries's attempts to include the Waterlanders in the
process of unification at first met with resistance from the other parties. The
greatest stumbling block, along with the Waterlanders' much too open view of
the congregation, was particularly Hans de Ries's conception regarding
Christology and communion, which was less Mennonite than Reformed.

Not until 1601 did a union of these three groups begin to take form in the
so-called *Bevredigde Broederschap* (Reconciled Brotherhood), which, however,

began to show signs of splitting again immediately after the death of Lubbert Gerrits (1612). Led by the High German Lenaert Clock, a majority of Young Frisians and High Germans then went their own way as the "Separated Ones." They turned away from the Waterlanders, who had not avoided conversations with Polish Socinians, were much too open to contacts with English Puritans and Dutch Arminians, and even failed to require rebaptism of members of these two groups when they joined a Waterland congregation.[31]

The tailor Nittert Obbes was born around 1581 in Pilsum near Emden and had settled in Amsterdam in 1598. Lubbert Gerrits, who ordained him to the service of the Word on his deathbed (January 21-22, 1612) by the laying on of hands, was his patron. In 1614 he was appointed, not without opposition, as *vermaner* (preacher) in the Waterland congregation of Amsterdam on the recommendation of Reinier Wybrants, who also belonged to Lubbert Gerrits's inner circle. Nittert likely belonged to a small minority of Young Frisians who stayed with the United Waterland-High German-Frisian congregation in spite of tensions with Hans de Ries.

Unlike his younger colleagues Cornelis Claes Anslo and Pieter Andries Hesseling, Nittert was not ordained to full service; that is, he had no authority to administer baptism and communion. His good relationship with Hesseling, obviously protégé of Hans de Ries, especially suffered badly on account of this. In 1618 Nittert asked to be released from duty, a request that was not, however, granted by his fellow preachers.[32] According to his colleagues, the only reason Nittert had given for his wish to retire was that he was too busy with his daily work to travel a lot for his congregation. His colleagues had released him at that time from his task to preach in congregations outside Amsterdam. They now took over this obligation from him.[33]

P. Visser has suggested that this request for release can perhaps be explained also by the failure--partly due to Hans de Ries's opposition--of the overtures of the Remonstrants to the Waterland congregation of Amsterdam in 1617. Because of this disappointment Nittert Obbes had then wanted to turn away from his congregation, which was unfriendly to Arminianism. The beginning of the conflict with Hans de Ries could also be placed in that year.[34] This interesting interpretation deserves further investigation; however, no indications to bear this out can be found in the pamphlets published as a result of this controversy.

It is more probable that Nittert's criticism of De Ries dated from the time when he, together with Lubbert Gerrits, composed the well-known confession which was to prepare for the unification with John Smyth's congregation. In this confession Nittert could easily discern "Schwenkfeldian" characteristics, such as the distinction between inner and outer Word made repeatedly in it. Jan Theunis insisted that Hans de Ries's Schwenkfeldian ideas about the dual Word penetrated the High Germans and Young Frisians much earlier, in fact as a result of the fusion of these parties at Emden. In contrast to Hans de Ries, Lubbert Gerrits always resisted the excessive forms of spiritualist piety referred to above. But after his death Hans de Ries's views had gained ground.[35]

The understanding between Hans de Ries and Nittert Obbes had not always been strained. Nittert's wife, complaining about the ingratitude of the Waterland congregation towards him, noted the efforts he had taken (very likely only after his appointment as preacher, from which position he could derive a certain authority in faith matters) to defend Hans de Ries against all who had attacked his booklet and his opinion about the incarnation of Christ.[36] These opponents could refer to the Separated Ones, but also to the Old Frisians, who had spoken against Hans de Ries's view for a much longer time and, in the foreword to a new publication of the *Martyrs' Mirror* in 1626, had enlarged one more time on all the objections against the Waterland views. Incidentally, this once more constituted an opportunity for the Remonstrants, in that same year, to come to a written defense of Hans de Ries for his resistance to these conservative Mennonites who wanted nothing to do with closer ties with the Arminians.[37]

According to his colleagues, the latent discord between Hans de Ries and Nittert Obbes only became public in 1622 when, for the first time, Nittert spoke to the Waterland leader, during his visit to Amsterdam, and presented his objections to his teaching on the dual Word. On this occasion Hans de Ries had justified this teaching with an appeal to Schwenckfeld's ideas. Still later, in 1625, Nittert's criticism was directed at the sermons of his fellow preachers, particularly those of the "papist" Hesseling.[38] In addition he took it amiss that Anslo had used the 1610 confession of Hans de Ries and Lubbert Gerrits instead of Scripture itself as the basis for his sermons.[39] By so doing Anslo could give the impression that article XIX with its emphasis on the spiritual knowledge of Christ was an incontrovertible part of the doctrine of the Waterlanders.

These objections of Nittert Obbes provided occasion for a conversation about this matter with the full church council, on November 28, 1625. Although the majority of the deacons did not appear to be acquainted yet with the twenty-six questions Nittert asked Hans de Ries, composed in his *Raeghbesem* (*Dust-mop*), which had been printed in the intervening time, what was so objectionable in Nittert's views became perfectly clear from the criticism expressed orally by those present. His brothers feared that he put too much stress on human ability to abandon unbelief and evil works and denied that the support of the Holy Spirit was necessary to that end.[40] That is to say, Nittert was of the opinion that simply to hear, understand, and obey the call to faith and improving one's life expressed in Scripture and in scriptural preaching was sufficient for regeneration. A direct spiritual inspiration of the heart, not communicated through the outer Word, was not necessary to that end. This objection also formed the rational-ethical core of the dispute.

The oppositeness of this dispute became very clear in Nittert's refutation of these objections. He in turn reproached Hesseling for saying--in a recent address to a new baptismal candidate--too little of the human ability to come to faith and do good works. According to Nittert, the passivity tinted with mysticism required for receiving grace demonstrated, in Hesseling's position, so much similarity to the Calvinist-predestinarian rejection of human free will that it must have been difficult for his fellow preacher to support at one and the same time the first and argue against the second.[41]

This is unmistakably a partisan for the Arminians speaking. And these views remained dangerous as long as the measures against the Remonstrants continued in force and their leaders could not rush to his support. But soon that situation changed. In July 1626 Simon Episcopius returned from exile to the fatherland, and other ministers followed. As a tolerated minority the Remonstrants slowly regained their position in Dutch society and even got involved in inter-Mennonite disputes again. Now that Arminian sympathies no longer brought political repercussions, a better climate developed for bringing the Nittert Obbes affair to a good end.

As was customary in cases of conflict in a congregation, impartial preachers from outside were called in to intervene. These were Rippert Eenkes, Yeme de Ring, Hans Alenson, Engel Pieters, Gerit Jans and Jan de Pla. They drew up thirteen articles, on which Nittert Obbes and Thomas Piges, Pieter Daniels, Hans de Ries, Reinier Wybrants, Pieter Andries, and Cornelis Claes could agree respectively on September 8 and 9, 1626.[42] With his signature Nittert Obbes again embraced the teaching of the dual Word. He had to admit that besides the written Word, the gift of the Holy Spirit which enlightens us inwardly is also necessary for one to be truly regenerated (article VIII). Were his earlier views on this too extreme even for the Remonstrants, and was Nittert Obbes induced to moderation partly for this reason?

In conclusion we want to consider the Remonstrant evaluation of the conflict. Simon Episcopius returned to the Netherlands in August 1626 after five years' exile in the French city of Rouen, and settled in Rotterdam. Evidently he had informed himself in a very short time about the dispute in the Waterland congregation in Amsterdam, for with striking energy, in that same year he published anonymously a small booklet in which he ranged himself on the side of Nittert Obbes.[43]

Episcopius was an Amsterdammer by birth and was to spend the last ten years of his life there, after his appointment as professor in the Remonstrant seminary founded in this city in 1634. But in 1630 he had already been invited by his fellow believers to dedicate the just-completed Remonstrant "hidden church" in this prosperous city of commerce. Joost van den Vondel wrote jubilantly about this event in a few poems for the occasion, and attended the Remonstrant services regularly. This "prince of the poets" had become alienated from the Waterland congregation, where he had been deacon, since 1620. Vondel, with his Remonstrant sympathies, proved to be a definite supporter of Nittert Obbes, who, however, likely did not welcome the fact that his former fellow believer returned to the bosom of the Roman Catholic mother church in 1641.[44]

We can only guess at Episcopius's motives for getting involved in the conflict. Perhaps he hoped to win Nittert Obbes and his followers--incidentally a very small group--over to the idea of a Waterland-Mennonite and Remonstrant congregation, now that the possibility for establishing independent churches was opening for the Remonstrants, due to growing tolerance.[45] This small, elite congregation could use new members. Even then the saying was true that there are many Remonstrant-minded people, but very few Remonstrants. We gladly leave this unexplored research territory to the historians and turn to the question of the theological relationship between Episcopius and the Water-landers, specifically Nittert Obbes.

Episcopius gave the theology of Arminius a more definitely anthropologi-cal and rational character.[46] In his antipredestinarianism Episcopius emphasized more firmly than Arminius that it was possible for humans to resist grace. He wanted to remain faithful to the Reformed position that grace is primary, but on the other hand give free will some room within this grace. This showed a strong ethical tendency, however: one was alive to the fact that, partly through divine grace, partly through natural reason which guides the will, one must by repentance and conversion hold to the faith that works through love.

Some affinity with the teaching of Socinus on certain points cannot be denied. Episcopius, however, adhered to the doctrines of the Trinity, pre-existence and predestination (although in close association with the *prae-scientia*). He was closer to Socinus in his views as to the significance of the satisfaction theory. He considered its essence to lie in the conversion of humankind, not in satisfying God's wrath. Important for our subject, however, is their common rejection of the knowledge of God from nature. All knowl-edge of God arises from revelation. God can only be known from Scripture and through human reason which penetrates Scripture. Episcopius consistently placed the article about the Holy Scriptures at the beginning of his confession.

Can the great role Episcopius assigns to reason in his theology be stamped rationalist and Socinian? It is amazing that Episcopius's opponents found in his rational approach no cause for accusing him of Socinianism. How can this be? Hoenderdaal in the article already cited writes: "I think that this is because the role of reason in the theology of the 17th century is so self-evident that this rational element scarcely attracted notice."[47] For Episcopius reason is not, however, an independent source of knowledge, as was the case in the later Rationalism. He viewed reason as the servant of Scripture. *Recta ratio* (right reason) consists in its agreement with Scripture. Only in connec-tion with Scripture does reason actually come to true knowledge of God.

However, reason does not appear to be a humble servant. Sometimes it seems as if revelation serves only to support reason and that they are placed on equal footing. For Episcopius there is, then, no room for the *testimonium Spiritus sancti internum*, if something other is meant than divine inspiration which needs reason to understand the true meaning of Scripture. The Spirit alone, without reason, does not reveal. The inner witness of the Spirit has no independent function apart from reason.

All this is evidence of the antispiritualist, rational, and ethical tendency of the Arminian-Reformed theology. Faith directs reason, but reason has insight into revelation and in its turn bears faith. This same interaction can be seen in the relationship between reason and will, insight and ethics. The will is set in motion by right insight, but reason is directed toward truth by the will. Which one, faith or reason, will or insight, has primacy of place for Episcopius, is not easy to discern. His thinking marks the transition from sixteenth century Reformed theology, which still has a strongly experiential undertone, to the rationalism which would carry the day in the second half of the seventeenth century. "Sometimes it seems that reason has primacy, sometimes the ethical strain is in the foreground. But Scripture remains the most important factor of the three."[48]

The position of the Waterlanders can be explained against this background. Hans de Ries was right to resist Nittert Obbes's reduction of the problem of the relationship between the outer and inner Word as if it were a matter of the antithesis between the written and the unwritten Word. The expression "unwritten word" cannot be found in the Bible. Christ is meant by the Word, and this Word has two sides: the outer, written and proclaimed Word and the inner witness of the Holy Spirit. Christ as the living Word cannot be reduced to a written doctrine grasped by reason which serves only as dynamic and norm for ethical behavior.[49]

In holding to the distinction between Word and Spirit as two activities of Christ, who is the Word itself, De Ries did not deny his Calvinist-Reformed past. He appeals to Calvin,[50] but his Schwenkfeldian interpretation threatens to overemphasize the inner experience, thereby giving the immediate activity of the Spirit (the inner Word) too much independence and separating it from the outer Word. Nittert Obbes, on the other hand, wanted to bind the Spirit too much to the other Word, to the point of identification. His emphasis on the active human reason and will inevitably had to lead to a debasing of knowledge of God mediated in any other way as fanaticism and moral passivity.

This one-sidedness in Hans de Ries as well as Nittert Obbes, and the associated lack of clarity with respect to the question of how one's faith, conversion and regeneration come about, is very clearly censured in Episcopius's *Judgment*. He sympathized with Nittert Obbes's view that faith, conversion and regeneration are brought about through the outer Word. However, according to Episcopius, it still remained unclear what in his view the relationship was between Spirit and the outer Word. In their denial of this exclusive emphasis on the letter, Nittert's opponents raised other questions, however. They gave the activity of the preached Word credit for the coming to a living faith evident in deeds, working through love. But they gave a special quality to regeneration, which according to them was brought about by a direct, immediate inpouring of the Spirit in a person's heart.[51]

Episcopius quite fairly asked whether Hans de Ries and associates saw regeneration as part of justification or identified regeneration with it.[52] In other words, is a person who has come to a living faith after hearing the proclamation regenerated at the same time, or does the believer still need an additional direct, inner inspiration? Is not coming to faith and conversion in obedience to the outer Word the same thing as being regenerated? Does being regenerated not imply at the same time an active moral renewal? Is the faith evident in deeds accomplished by the outer Word not enough? Is an inner regeneration received in extreme passivity required for salvation? Is not the gospel in this way stripped of its efficacy and normativeness? To escape this individualistic, unconstrained latitude, Episcopius supported Nittert Obbes in his acceptance of the written Word as the only guideline.[53]

What is the issue in the conflict? In the words of Episcopius: "This only is the question, whether the external Word of God, preached or written, is the means or instrument by which God wants to make clear to the people his whole will, perfect and ready, necessary and of service to their eternal salvation, and by which he wants simply to inspire them to faith, love and obedience to his laws and commandments. Or whether another inner, hidden Word or meaning, apart from the meaning which is clearly expressed in the written Word, is necessary to understand God's will and to obey. On this everything turns."[54] His position is clear: the outer Word has the power to move the mind as well as the heart of humankind to faith, hope, and love. A power touching the heart directly, working outside of this Word, is a meaningless instrument without reason, working no renewal of life in morals, and makes one into nothing more than a passive object of God's grace, without will.

Does not this spiritualism, the learned Remonstrant asked himself, have the same effect as the Calvinist doctrine of predestination, in that both of them, in their striving to safeguard the sovereignty of God's grace, detract from human cooperation in receiving grace? Does not regeneration assume human activity? Or can one only pray for faith, conversion, and regeneration? Then the entire theology of the Waterland teachers could consist in the cry: "Pray, pray, pray, etc."[55] In addition Episcopius blamed the Waterlanders' manner of explaining the Bible for the lack of clarity in the dispute. In opposition to their figurative and allegorical exegesis ("allegorical labyrinth"), he argued for a logical, clear, and unambiguous biblical interpretation. In that way one avoided the lack of clarity usually found among uneducated people.[56] This observation reveals the more intellectual, academic approach to faith of the Remonstrants which has hindered until today a cooperation with the followers of Menno with their layperson's theology.

This sketch of the controversy between Nittert Obbes and his Waterland fellow preachers is dedicated to C. J. Dyck and presented to him with respect, in the hope that with this modest contribution it will be given him to complete his description of the life and work of Hans de Ries and his circle.

(Translation: Lydia Penner)

NOTES

1. The course of the conflict is described in Hermannus Schijn and Gerardus Maatschoen, *Uitvoeriger Verhandeling van de Geschiedenisse der Mennoniten*, II (Amsterdam, 1744), 490-492; and Gerardus Maatschoen, *Levensbeschryving van eenige voorname mannen, in hun leven leeraaren by de Doopsgezinden* (Amsterdam, 1750), 90-128. For biographical information about the dramatis personae, see the aforementioned book and H. F. Wijnman, "Jan Theunisz, alias Joannes Antonides (1569-1637), boekverkooper en waard in het muziekhuis 'd'Os in de Bruyloft' te Amsterdam," *Jaarboek van het Genootschap Smstelodanum*, 25 (1928), 29-123.

Regarding the influence of Socinianism in the Netherlands, see W. J. van Douwen, *Socinianen en Doopsgezinden* (Leiden, 1912; Reprint, Leeuwarden, 1980); and C. J. Dyck, "Hans de Ries en het Socinianisme," *Doopsgezinde Bijdragen*, n.s. 8 (1982), 18-32; also in *Socinianism and Its Role in the Culture of XVIth to XVIIIth Centuries*, ed. Lech Szczucki et al. (Warsaw: Polish Academy of Sciences, 1983), 85-95.

2. Reinier Wybrants, Pieter Andries and Cornelis Claes, *Apologia ofte Verantwoordinghe* (Hoorn, 1626), Djv.

3. Nittert Obbes, *Oprechtigheyd* (n.p., 1626), Cijvo.

4. *Ibid.* See also Reinier Wybrants et. al., *Apologia*, Eijvo-Eiij; and [Jan Theunis], *Redenen ende verthooninghe* (Amsterdam, 1625), Ajv.

5. Maatschoen already speaks negatively about Nittert Obbes's "wangevoelen en onrustig bedryf." *Levensbeschryving*, 90. W. J. Kühler claims that Nittert was jealous of his socially more successful fellow preachers, and attributes to him a "weak character." *Geschiedenis van de Doopsgezinden in Nederland*, II: *1600-1735* (Haarlem: H. D. Tjeenk Willink, 1940), 144.

6. P. Visser, *Broeders in de Geest: De doopsgezinde bijdragen van Dierick en Jan Philipsz. Schabaelje tot de Nederlandse stichtelijke literatuur in de zeventiende eeuw*, 2 vols. (Deventer: Uitgeverij *Sub Rosa*, 1988), I, 122. See also Dyck, "Hans de Ries en het Socinianisme," 32.

7. Historical: A. Th. van Deursen, *Bavianen en Slijkgeuzen: Kerk en kerkvolk ten tijde van Maurits en Oldenbarnevelt* (Assen: Van Gorcum, 1974); S. Groenveld and H. L. Ph. Leeuwenberg, *De bruid in de schuit; De consolidatie van de Republiek 1609-1650* (Zutphen: De Walburg Pers, 1985). Theological: C. Graafland, *Van Calvijn tot Barth: Oorsprong en ontwikkeling van de leer der verkiezing in het Gereformeerd Protestantisme* ('s-Gravenhage: Boekencentrum, 1987).

8. Franciscus Gomarus, *Twee disputátien vande goddelücke predestinatie* (Leiden, 1609), theses XIX, XXIII, XXVII and XXXI.

9. *Verclaringhe Jacobi Arminii saliger ghedachten...aengaende zijn ghevoelen, so van de Predestinatie, als van...* (Leiden, 1610), 35-38.

10. Van Deursen, *Bavianen en Slijkgeuzen*, 368, 370.

11. Little is known of the transfer of Remonstrants to the Mennonites and *vice versa*. Van Deursen provides a few facts about Remonstrants in Haarlem and Hazerswoude who made overtures to the Mennonites; further, he notes that hardly any Remonstrants could be found in areas with many Mennonites. *Ibid.*, 343-344. Visser mentions twenty Reformed believers in Amsterdam who sought connections with the Mennonites there in the period 1609-1619. *Broeders in de Geest*, I, 106; II, 53 n. 98.

12. See J. Bakker, *John Smyth: de stichter van het Baptisme* (Wageningen: H. Veenman, 1964); and Keith L. Sprunger, *Dutch Puritanism: A History of English and Scottish Churches of the Netherlands in the Sixteenth and Seventeenth Centuries* (Leiden: E. J. Brill, 1982), 80-86. To facili-

tate the unification of John Smyth's followers with the Waterland congregation of Amsterdam, Hans de Ries and Lubbert Gerrits had drawn up their *Corte Belijdenisse des Gheloofs ende der voornaemster stucken der Christelijcke leere* (40 articles) in 1610.

13. [Jan Theunis], *Der Hanssijtsch' Mennisten Socinianismus* ([Amsterdam], 1627), Aiij. See also Wijnman, "Jan Theunisz," 93.

14. Regarding the ambivalent attitude of the Waterlanders toward the Arminians and their own fellow believers, see [Jan Theunis], *Der Hanssijtsch' Mennisten Socinianismus*, Ciijvo; and Visser, *Broeders in de Geest*, I, 103-109 (and the notes in II, 52-55).

15. [Jan Theunis], *Der Hannsijtsch' Mennisten Socinianismvs*, Aiij.

16. *Ibid.*

17. See W. J. op 't Hof, *Engelse pietistische geschriften in het Nederlands, 1598-1622* (Rotterdam: Lindenberg, 1987), 299-319.

18. An exception is the Groninger Old Fleming Ucko Wallis, who had thoroughly studied Perkins's "Verklaringe van de rechte manier om te kennen Christum den gecruysten." Kühler, *Geschiedenis 1600-1735*, 135. Op 't Hof shows--incidentally, rather too summarily and generalizing too much--that there were common character traits in Pietism and Anabaptism, and asks himself whether the abundant transfers from Anabaptism to the Reformed churches in the second half of the sixteenth century could have had to do with the rise of Pietism in the Reformed church in the Netherlands. *Engelse pietistische* geschriften, 606-607.

19. In connection with the republication of the writings of, among others, Melchior Hoffman and David Joris, S. Cramer draws attention to the new revival in "Schwenkfeldian" ideas at the beginning of the seventeenth century: "dat spiritualiste, louter praktische, tolerante en verzoeningsgezinde Christendom." *Bibliotheca Reformatoria Neerlandica*, V, ('s-Gravenhage: Martinus Nijhoff, 1909), 38.

20. Nicodemus Letterknecht van Wt-gheest [Nittert Obbes], *Raegh-besem, seer bequaem om sommige Mennonijtsche schuren te reynigen vande onnutte spinnewebbens* (Amsterdam, 1625), D-E.

21. Visser, *Broeders in de Geest*, I, 82-133.

22. [Jan Theunis], *Der Hanssijtsche Menniste Gheest-drijveren Historie* ([Amsterdam], 1627), 31; Visser, *Broeders in de Geest*, I, 40-41.

23. [Jan Theunis], *Gheest-drijveren*, B.

24. P. Visser, "'Siet den Oogst is Ryp': Het fonds van de Waterlands-doopsgezinde boekverkoper Claes Jacobsz. te De Rijp," in *Geschiedenis, godsdienst, letterkunde: Opstellen aangeboden aan dr. S. B. J. Zilverberg*, ed. E. K. Grootes and J. den Haan (Roden: Nehalennia, 1989), 98-108.

25. R. B. Evenhuis, *Ook dat was Amsterdam, II: De kerk der hervorming in de gouden eeuw* (Amsterdam: W. ten Have, 1967), 254-255.

26. E. Simons, "Matthes Weyer, ein Mystiker aus der Reformationszeit," *Theologische Arbeiten aus der rhein; wissenschaftliche Predigerverein*, n.s. 9 (1907), 30-49.

27. See article IV of the "Remonstrantie": "Maer soe vele de maniere vande werckinge derselve genade aengaet, die en is niet onwederstandelijck; want daer staet van velen geschreven, dat sij den H. Geest wederstaen habben. Act. 7. ende elders, op vele plaetsen." J. N. Bakhuizen van den Brink, *De Nederlandsche Belijdenisgeschriften* (Amsterdam: Uitg.-mij. Holland, 1940), 282.

28. [Nittert Obbes], *Raegh-besem*, Cij.

29. The frequent citation of the Jesuit R. Bellarminus is striking. This theologian of the

Conter-Reformation was also quoted by Arminius, to the great indignation of the antipapist Reformed believers. See G. J. Hoenderdaal and P. M. Luca, eds., *Staat in de vrijheid: de Geschiedenis van de remonstranten* (Zutphen: De Walburg Pers, 1982), 12.

30. A summary of Lubbert Gerrits's *Zommige christelyke Zendbrieven* (Amsterdam, 1599) is taken up in Maatschoen, *Levensbeschryving*, 25-38.

31. See Visser, *Broeders in de Geest*, I, 100-103.

32. For the facts about the social status of Nittert and his fellow preachers, see Wijnman, "Jan Theunisz," 77-79.

33. Reinier Wybrants et. al., *Apologie*, Cvo.

34. Visser, *Broeders in de Geest*, I, 196-199.

35. [Jan Theunis], *Gheest-drijveren*, Ciij.

36. Nittert Obbes, *Oprechtigheyd*, C-Cvo. Probably an early edition (ca. 1600) of Hans de Ries's, *Klaer Bewys van de Euwigheydt ende Godheydt Jesu Christi* (Haarlem, 1672) is meant.

37. Lieven van Vreeland, *Cort Ondersoeck, oft noodtsaeclick zy ter saligheydt te ghelooven, dat Jesus Christus sijn vleesch heeft van 't Woord, en niet van Maria? Met een voorreden* (Haarlem, 1643). This is a reprint of the older edition of ca. 1626.

38. Reinier Wybrants et. al., *Apologia*, B; Nittert Obbes, *Oprechtigheyd*, Ciij.

39. [Liefhebber der Waerheydt], *Onbillickheyd der Proceduren, ghepleeght by Reynier Wybrantsz., Pieter Andriesz. ende Cornelis Clesz...teghen Nettert Obbes* (n.p., 1626), Ajvvo; Reinier Wybrants et. al., *Apologia*, Eijvo-Eiij.

40. Nittert Obbes, *Oprechtigheyd*, Bij-Bijvo.

41. *Ibid.*, Bijvo.

42. [Rippert Eenkes], *Derthien Artijckelen...Mitsgaders LXXII vraghen op eenige der selfder Artijckelen, nopende 't verschil tusschen Hans de Ries ende Nittert Obbes* (n.p., 1627). The text of the thirteen articles can also be found in Maatschoen, *Levensbeschryving*, 118-128. On page 128 the author gives an overview of the later editions (bound together with various confessions).

43. [S. Episcopius], *Oordeel over het Verschil van 't Ordinaris middel van 's Menschen Bekeeringhe...tusschen Nittert Obbes en Hans de Ries [c.s.]...Geschrevendoor een onpartijdigh Liefhebber der waerheydt* (Hoorn, 1626). The Latin translation of this booklet is included in the first part of Episcopius's collected works, published by Curcelleus, his successor at the Remonstrant Seminary: *M. Simonis Episcopoii, S. S. Theologiae in Academia Leydensi quondam Professoris, Opera Theologica* (Amsterdam, 1650), 372-377.

44. Joost van den Vondel wrote the following poem in connection with the conflict: *Antidotum. Tegen het vergift der Geestdryvers. Tot verdedigingh van 't beschreven woord Gods* (Amsterdam, 1626).

45. Rutger Willems was the only supporter of Nittert in the church council; see Reinier Wybrants et. al., *Apoligie*, Gjvvo. Wijnman also mentions Jan Gerrits Hooft. "Jan Theunisz," 99-100.

46. G. J. Hoenderdaal, "Arminius en Episcopius," *Nederlands Archief voor Kerkgeschiedenis*, n.s. 60 (1980), 203-235; and the biography by A. H. Haentjens, *Simon Episcopius als apologeet van het Remonstrantisme* (Leiden, 1899).

47. Hoenderdaal, "Arminius en Episcopius," 228-229.

48. *Ibid.*, 235.

49. Hans de Ries, *Ontdeckinghe der dwalingen, misduydinghen der H. Schrift ende verscheyden mis-slagen, begrepen in seecker Boeck, ghenaemt Raech-besem* (Hoorn, 1627), Ciij-Ciijvo; Hiij-Hiijvo.

50. *Ibid*, Ciij-Ciijvo. Interesting in this connection is Hans de Ries's claim that he already adhered to his teaching of the two different Words when he left the Reformed church in Antwerp. [Jan Theunis], *Gheest-drijveren*, Aij-Aijvo.

51. Cf. Hans de Ries and Lubbert Gerrits, *Corte Belijdenisse des Gheloofs*, article XXI.

52. [Episcopius], *Oordeel*, Aiij.

53. *Ibid.*, Bij.

54. *Ibid.*, Bvo.

55. *Ibid.*, Cjvvo.

56. *Ibid.*, Bij, Cjv.

CHAPTER 7

Theological Developments among Mennonites in Poland in the Sixteenth and Seventeenth Centuries

John Friesen

The history of Mennonites in Poland has long been one of the neglected areas of Mennonite history research. In the recent past practically the only major publications about this history have been made by Dr. Horst Penner in the Federal Republic of Germany, in his two volume set, *Die ost- und westpreussischen Mennoniten*. A number of other people have probed the history of the Polish/Prussian Mennonites from the perspective of family and genealogical histories. Adalbert Goertz has made significant contributions in this area.

One theme which has not been researched to any great extent is that of the theology of Mennonites in Poland. The present study is designed to begin focusing some questions, and to provide some of the outlines for an understanding of the theology of Polish Mennonites. This study will be restricted to the era from the 1530s to the end of the seventeenth century.

Two questions will be addressed: (1) "What were the theological affirmations of Polish Mennonites during this era?" (2) "What were the influences which shaped this theology?"

A comment should be made about terminology. These Mennonites will be referred to as Polish Mennonites, or Mennonites in Poland, even though it is clear that they did not originate in Poland. As Horst Penner has shown, about two-thirds of the Mennonites in Poland originated in the Low Countries, and about one-third in various German states, in Switzerland, and in Austria. Even though a common designation for this group is "Prussian Mennonites," this term will not be used. In the 1530s and 1540s Mennonites did settle in Prussia, east of Elbing and in Königsberg. They were all expelled, however, except for a few in Königsberg, who were important for the local economy. Thus, in actual fact, Mennonites in the Danzig, Elbing, and Vistula River regions found refuge in Polish regions. These regions remained Polish until 1772, when, during the first partition of Poland, a large portion of Polish Mennonites came under Prussian rule. In 1793, in the second partition, the remainder of Polish Mennonites came under Prussian rule. The designation "Prussian" is thus appropriate for the era after 1772 and 1793, but not for the earlier era.[1]

In the sixteenth century it was Poland's tradition of relative toleration of religious dissenters which made settlement in Poland possible. The first evidence of Dutch Anabaptists in the Danzig city region comes from the 1530s. In the following decades, up to the time that the seven northern Dutch provinces formed the United Provinces in 1579, numerous refugees fled the severe persecutions in the Netherlands by Emperor Charles V and King Philip II of Spain. Other Anabaptist refugees came to Poland from various South German states, from Switzerland, and from Austria/Moravia. Some Dutch Mennonites who had settled in Prussia also came to Poland when they were expelled in the 1540s. Anabaptists who came from Moravia were Hutterites fleeing persecutions. Thus the Mennonite churches which were established along the Vistula River and the lowlands (Werder) near Elbing, Tiegenhof, and Danzig included a representation from all the various Anabaptist groups in Western Europe, namely, Hutterite, German, Swiss, and Dutch. All these various backgrounds influenced the theology which eventually developed in Poland.

A survey of the writings of the Mennonites in Poland reveals that they did not concern themselves with formal theology or with traditional theological issues. They were not academic theologians. They were simple people of deep faith, who were attempting to be faithful to their convictions. This study of theology among the Mennonites in Poland is thus an attempt to make explicit a theology which was implicit. It is an attempt to understand an operative theology.

The first variant of theological influence in the Polish/Prussian regions is evident in the Prussian settlement, east of Elbing. This Dutch settlement known as *Holländer Dörfer* was founded in the 1530s, and was known as having Anabaptist characteristics. The theological influence seems to have come from the Dutch Sacramentarian movement. These Dutch Anabaptists reinterpreted Catholic sacraments symbolically, and they also replaced infant baptism with adult baptism. This whole Anabaptist settlement, as noted earlier, had to flee in 1543, and settled in the Polish regions around Danzig.[2] There is no evidence that these early Dutch Anabaptists were sympathetic to the Münsterite revolutionary theology. No violent revolution occurred in either East Prussia or in Poland. Whether any revolutionary Anabaptists, e.g., Battenburgers, were present, is not clear.

This early Dutch Anabaptism in Poland was given more definite shape principally by two people, Menno Simons and Dirk Philips. Menno Simons seems to have visited the Danzig area, and Dirk Philips lived in Danzig intermittently from 1550 until 1568.[3] Philips is remembered as the first *Ältester* of the Danzig Mennonite Church. For a number of years it was not clear whether Anabaptists in Poland would identify themselves as followers of Dirk or of Menno.[4] The issue seems to have revolved around church discipline and the ban. Dirk Philips was known as being stricter than Menno in enforcing church discipline. By the 1570s Anabaptists in the Polish regions were identifying themselves as "Mennonites."[5] This seems to suggest that Mennonites opted for a somewhat more lenient view of church discipline.

Despite having decided to be Mennonites instead of Dirkists, the Mennonites in the Danzig area still found themselves disagreeing over the issue of church discipline. From Menno they adopted an ecclesiology of a pure church, the view that the church is to be pure as Christ was pure. The church is to reflect the nature of Christ, as Christ reflects the nature of God. They thus adopted Menno's ecclesiology, which was rooted in his almost docetic Christology. In order to keep the church pure, church discipline was necessary.

Mennonites in the Netherlands had, since the 1550s, disagreed sharply over the issue of church discipline. One faction of Anabaptism in the Netherlands in the province of Holland north of Amsterdam refused to identify with Menno altogether, and formed a group known as the Waterlanders. The other Anabaptists identified themselves as "Mennonists." This Mennonist group divided in 1566 into Frisian and Flemish circles of churches. The division was over the issue of church discipline. These Dutch divisions found their way to Poland as well.

The division between Frisian and Flemish occurred in Poland in the decades following 1567. Despite valiant efforts by the Danzig *Ältester* Quirin Vermeulen and the minister Hans von Schwinden to prevent a split, the Polish Mennonite community divided into two groups in the 1580s and 1590s.[6] The larger group, the Flemish, were stricter; and the Frisians, who were joined by the Waterlanders, were more lenient. The Flemish, being stricter, experienced further divisions between more lenient and stricter factions.[7] Despite the difference in degree of strictness in exercising church discipline, theologically both groups nevertheless believed that the true church is a pure church. The Mennonites of Swiss descent who formed the congregations near Kulm and Schwetz did not join these factions until the early eighteenth century. At that time they joined the Old Flemish, the strictest of the Flemish factions.[8]

By deciding to be "Mennonists" instead of some other form of Anabaptism, Polish Anabaptists were also consciously pacifist. The reputation which had followed them from the Netherlands in the 1530s was that they were revolutionaries. Since Menno was widely known as the Dutch Anabaptist of peace, the decision to carry his name may have been an attempt to overcome the reputation that they were revolutionaries. It should be noted that the question of whether to serve in the military was not an issue at this time.

The outline of the theology of the early Polish Mennonites thus began to emerge. Their theology revolved largely around an ecclesiology which included voluntary commitment, baptism of adults, and a church whose purity was maintained through church discipline. Faith, they believed, ought to be shown in a life of faithfulness, or discipleship. The decision to be a peace church gave expression to this view. Underlying their ecclesiology was also the assumption that the true church is a minority in society and does not operate as a state church. Even though Polish Mennonites experienced no death by execution, nevertheless they felt themselves to be a persecuted church since they always had to live under some legal and financial restrictions.[9]

The basis of Polish Mennonite theology was Scripture. The issue in the sixteenth century among Dutch and Polish Mennonites was how to relate the letter and the spirit in the interpretation of Scripture. David Joris provided one option, which could be called spiritualist. He emphasized the inward Word more than the written Word.[10] A second option was that of Melchior Hoffman, the father of Dutch Anabaptism. He stood for typological and figurative interpretation of Scripture, an essentially medieval view which saw history consisting of types and their fulfillment rather than as a chronological sequence of events.[11] The third option was that of Menno Simons, who specifically rejected the interpretations of both Joris and Hoffman. In order to avoid the excesses of interpretation of Hoffmanites like Jan Matthijs and Jan van Leiden, Menno placed more emphasis on the literal interpretation of the written Word. His emphasis was, however, tempered by the principle of Christology. He advocated that all of Scripture should be interpreted christologically with 1 Corinthians 3:11 as the key. The indications are that it was Menno's more literal christological biblicism which became the operative principle for Polish Mennonites.

The views as described thus far reflect the theology of Polish Anabaptism during the early years. Of considerable importance is the question about the sources of theological influence in the subsequent years. Who influenced Polish Anabaptism? What was the effect upon Polish Mennonite theology?

During the late sixteenth and early seventeenth centuries, contact with Roman Catholic, Lutheran, and Calvinist churches in the regions in which Polish Mennonites lived was fairly minimal. Mennonites had to register their statistics of birth, death, and marriage with local churches, in addition to paying local state church levies;[12] however, there is little evidence of contact at a theological level. What then were the sources of influence?

There is not much evidence of contact with Mennonites in the South German states and in Switzerland. There is, however, evidence of some contact with Hutterites in Moravia. In the 1570s the Hutterite leader Peter Walpot came to visit the Mennonites in Poland. Upon his return he reported unfavorably about the Polish Mennonites that "they are a people who are worthless in the Church of the Lord." There seems to have been continuing communication between Hutterites and Polish Mennonites in the sixteenth century, with some Hutterites settling in Poland and joining Mennonite churches and some Polish Mennonites joining the Hutterites in Moravia.

Because of increasing persecution, Hutterites from Moravia led by Joseph Hauser settled in the Elbing region between 1603 and 1605. Most of the Hutterites were expert in the trade of ceramics. They were unable to get permission to settle near Elbing, but were reluctantly allowed to rent land so they could farm. In 1622, during the Thirty Years' War, when the persecution of Hutterites in Moravia forced all Hutterites to flee, it is evident that a number of them settled in Poland and joined Mennonite churches.[13]

The influence of these repeated contacts with Hutterites is hard to ascertain. As noted above, initially some of the contacts were not positive. Later the relationships seem to have been more so.

Even though the precise theological influence cannot be determined, it is possible that the Hutterite Mennonites made their influence felt. In the early seventeenth century there were two developments which may show some influence from the Hutterites, even though these developments also expressed beliefs which had been present among Polish Mennonites. In the 1620s Mennonites in the various lowland (Werder) regions from Danzig to Elbing established fire insurance organizations.[14] The fire insurance organizations included only church members. They were thus vehicles for expressing financial support to one another in an orderly, ongoing way. Theologically these insurances expressed the view that faith in God should result in people caring for each other. They also expressed the view that faith should be applied to economics.

A very similar conviction was expressed by Polish Mennonites when they built dwellings for their people who were destitute and could not afford their own housing. The Polish Mennonites were thus developing a discipleship theology which quite clearly involved financial and economic support within the community of believers.

During the Thirty Years' War the Danzig area of Poland suffered severe devastation, especially from the Swedish armies of Gustavus Adolphus. Danzig demanded that Mennonites provide substitutes since they themselves were unwilling to serve in the army. Other local jurisdictions made similar demands.[15] The pattern thus developed that Mennonites were excused from military service in exchange for money payments. This form of exemption was turned into extortion, and became so severe that in 1642 Mennonites negotiated a *Privilegium* with the Polish king Vladislaus IV.[16] This guaranteed that, in exchange for a regular money payment, Mennonites could be exempt from military service. It is thus evident that the peace theology continued to be important for Polish Mennonites. There was, however, a Netherlands precedent for this arrangement from the late sixteenth century.[17]

A source of theological influence which may have been of major proportions, but is one which has not been probed in great detail, is the relationship to the Polish Brethren, or Socinians as they were later known. Contacts between Mennonites and Polish Brethren began in the early 1580s and continued well into the seventeenth century.[18] Even though Mennonites and Polish Brethren had completely separate origins, they agreed in a surprising number of areas. The Polish Brethren also believed in adult baptism, church discipline, peace, and discipleship, and they too rejected the oath and service in the government.[19] However, there were differences. These were partly cultural and educational in that the Polish Brethren movement was largely drawn from the educated class and from the nobility. The most serious difference was theological. Polish Brethren were opposed to the traditional Trinitarian theology. They believed that the Bible witnesses to one God, not three persons in one God. Consequently they also rejected the divinity of Christ and the view of Christ as the second person of the Trinity. This theology clashed with the very high, almost docetic Christology the Polish Mennonites had inherited from Menno Simons.

The Flemish churches in Poland showed little interest in the Polish Brethren. The Frisians, on the other hand, especially the Frisian congregation in Danzig, were in extended dialogue with the Polish Brethren. The leader of the Danzig Frisian congregation, Adrian Pauls, himself an educated person and a teacher at the Danzig *Gymnasium*, carried on a dialogue with the Polish Brethren during the years 1610-12.[20] When the Polish Brethren were expelled from Poland later in the seventeenth century, during the reign of Johann II Kasimir (1648-68), a number of Brethren joined the Danzig Frisian church. On the whole, though, the influence of Polish Brethren, or Socinian, theology on Mennonite theology at this time seems to have been slight. Socinian views of Christology and Trinity were not acceptable to most Mennonites.

The most important theological crisis of the Polish Mennonite era occurred in the late seventeenth century. This crisis posed the greatest challenge to Mennonite theology and in the process forced Mennonites to clarify their theology, including the issues of Christology and Trinity.

The crisis arose in 1678 when the Polish king Johann Sobieski (1674-96) ordered the ministers of both Mennonite groups to appear before a Roman Catholic bishop, Stanislaus Sarnowski. Mennonites were charged with being Arians and Socinians.[21] Since Socinians had been outlawed and expelled in 1658, conviction could have led to the expulsion of the Mennonites.

The examination of Mennonite theology seems to have focused primarily on the Danzig churches. On January 17, 1678, the Frisian *Ältester* Heinrich von Dühren had to answer various questions. The examiners were not pleased with his answers on Christology and noted "hallucinatur" beside the answers.[22] Later, on January 30, the Flemish representative, the minister (*Lehrer*) George Hansen, answered forty-eight theological questions. The examiners were satisfied with his answers. Shortly after the interrogation Hansen wrote a short report of the event, and concluded with the comment, "As a result of this examination, we were freed from all suspicion; however, this time it cost us a lot of money...."[23] Hansen also republished a booklet he had written earlier, in which he now restated the orthodox theology he had defended in the interrogations.

It is evident that the theology of the two congregations in Danzig was not the same. The Flemish theology, as articulated by George Hansen, was clearly much more dogmatic, and followed orthodox Christian theology. The Frisian theology, especially the Christology, was different, even though the sources do not indicate exactly in what sense it differed. The interesting issue in this whole controversy is its source. Why did the Polish government investigate the theology of Mennonites in Danzig at this time?

The answer to this question probably lies in the Mennonite churches in the Netherlands. In 1664 the Amsterdam Mennonite (Waterlander) congregation was rent in two over the issues of Christology and the importance of dogma generally.[24] In the 1660s the doctor-minister Gelanus Abrahams de Haan led the congregation in the direction of the Collegiant movement. This movement formulated no creeds and rejected the dogmatism of the Reformed churches and other denominations. They accepted as members anyone who was spiritually-minded, and baptized as an adult. De Haan was well educated in the writings of new thinkers like Descartes and Kepler, and readily incorporated the Collegiant ideas into his Amsterdam congregation.

A large faction of the congregation rejected this new influence and separated from the church to form a new congregation called the *Zon* (Sun). They were led by Samuel Apostol, and emphasized traditional creeds and dogmatic beliefs, in particular the traditional view of the Trinity and of Christology. The main church group under De Haan's leadership took the name *Lam*. Within a short while, this theological controversy between the Amsterdam *Lam* and *Zon* congregations caused practically all churches in the Netherlands to realign themselves with the Lamist and Zonist groups.[25]

The historical question is whether this controversy was transferred to Danzig and influenced the Frisian and Flemish congregations. From the evidence available so far it seems that this may well have been the case. It is known that the contact between Amsterdam and Danzig continued to be strong during the late seventeenth century. The issues in Danzig as indicated in the interrogation before the Catholic bishop Sarnowski also seem to have been similar to those which caused the Lamists and Zonists to divide. Further research may help to illuminate this influence even more.

It is interesting to note, however, that the effect of the Dutch division on the Polish churches was not a new realignment of churches. Flemish, or Zonist, theology as articulated by George Hansen seems to have become the norm for most of the Polish Mennonites. The Danzig Frisian theology appears to have remained a minority view.

A further question is whether George Hansen in his writings expressed the traditional theology of Polish Mennonites, or whether, in his attempt to defend Mennonites against charges of Arian and Socinian heresy, he formulated Mennonite beliefs more narrowly and dogmatically. The present state of research into Polish Mennonitism does not allow these questions to be fully answered.

This theological survey concludes at the end of the seventeenth century. At the beginning of the eighteenth century, significant new developments occurred which make it possible to see the eighteenth century as quite different from the seventeenth century. The Nordic War (1700-21), the plague of 1709, and Poland's loss of military and political power changed conditions for Mennonites.[26]

However, in this early era of theological development, from the 1530s to the end of the seventeenth century, we have seen the view of Polish Mennonite theology gradually emerge. It appears that there was also a gradual shift of emphasis. In the early years the emphasis seems to have been more on ecclesiology and ethics. In both of these areas the concerns were rather practical. In the later part of this era we see the emphasis shift to theological issues, Christology and Trinity. Their concern on both of these issues was to be seen as "orthodoxy." There seems to be an attempt by late seventeenth-century Polish Mennonites to define themselves as fitting into the mainstream of Christianity. As part of the attempt to be more orthodox, they were thus moving to a more dogmatic self-understanding.

NOTES

1. John Friesen, "Mennonites in Poland: An Expanded Historical View," *Journal of Mennonite Studies* 4 (1986), 94-108.

2. Horst Penner, *Die ost- und westpreussischen Mennoniten*, I: *1526 bis 1772* (Weierhof: Mennonitischer Geschichtsverein, 1978), 49.

3. George H. Williams, *The Radical Reformation* (Philadelphia: Westminster Press, 1962), 416. See also J. Ten Doornkaat Koolman, *Dirk Philips 1504-1568* (Haarlem: H. D. Tjeenk Willink, 1964), 111-130.

4. Wilhelm Mannhardt, *Die Wehrfreiheit der Altpreussischen Mennoniten* (Marienburg: Selbstverlag der Altpreussischen Mennonitengemeinden, 1863), 24.

5. Penner, *Die ost- und westpreussischen Mennoniten*, I, 61.

6. H. G. Mannhardt, *Die Danziger Mennonitengemeinden: Ihre Entstehung und Ihre Geschichte von 1568-1919* (Danzig: Selbstverlag der Danziger Mennonitengemeinden, 1919), 44; Penner, *Die ost- und westpreussischen Mennoniten*, I, 67f.

7. *Ibid.*, 70f.

8. *Ibid.*, 71f.; Herbert Wiebe, *Das Siedlungswerk Niederländischer Mennoniten im Weishseltal* (Marburg: Johann Gottfried Herder Institut, 1952), 29, 84.

9. Gottfried Lengnich, *Ius Publicum Civitatis Gedanensis* oder *Der Stadt Danzig Verfassung und Rechte* (Danzig: Th. Bertling, 1900).

10. Williams, *The Radical Reformation*, 383.

11. Klaus Deppermann, *Melchior Hoffman: Soziale Unruhen und apokalyptische Visionen im Zeitalter der Reformation* (Göttingen: Vandenhoeck und Ruprecht, 1979), 214-226.

12. Penner, *Die ost- und westpreussischen Mennoniten*, I, 181.

13. For this recital of facts, see *ibid.*, 72-79; R. Wolkan, ed., *Geschicht-Buch der Hutterischen Brüder* (MacLeod, Alta.: Hutterian Brethren, 1923), 470f.; and A. Hartwich, *Geographisch-histor. Landesbeschreibung der drei im polm. Preussen liegenden Werder* (Danzig, 1722), 279.

14. Penner, *Die ost- und westpreussischen Mennoniten*, I, 166.

15. *Ibid.*, 111.

16. W. Mannhardt, Die Wehrfreiheit, 80, 81.

17. Peter Brock, *Pacifism in Europe* (Princeton: Princeton University Press, 1972), 167-169, 185.

18. Kazimierz Mezynski, *From the History of Mennonites in Poland* (Warsaw: Akademia Rolnicza W. Warszawie, 1975), 53; Penner, *Die ost- und westpreussischen Mennoniten*, 78f.

19. *Ibid.*, 77; Williams, *The Radical Reformation*, 733f.

20. Penner, *Die ost- und westpreussischen Mennoniten*, I, 78-79.

21. H. G. Mannhardt, *Die Danziger Mennonitengemeinden*, 76f.

22. *Ibid.*, 77.

23. *Ibid.*, 78.

24. W. J. Kühler, *Geschiedenis van de Doopsgezinden in Nederland*, II: *1600-1735* (Haarlem: H. D. Tjeenk Willink, 1940), 195.

25. N. van der Zijpp, *Geschiedenis der Doopsgezinden in Nederland* (Arnhem: Slaterus, 1952), 101-106.

26. Penner, *Die ost- und westpreussischen Mennoniten*, I, 159; H. G. Mannhardt, *Die Danziger Mennonitengemeinden*, 828.

CHAPTER 8

Spiritual Reformer versus City Reformer: The Baptismal Debate between Schwenckfeld and Zwingli

H. Wayne Pipkin

In May of 1529 Wolfgang Capito wrote to Huldrych Zwingli to report the arrival of a new refugee in Strassburg, one whom Capito described as "vir vere nobilis. Totus Christum spirat" [a truly noble man; he wholly breathes Christ]."[1] This perfect Christian was none other than the Silesian nobleman Caspar Schwenckfeld, now in Strasbourg in "voluntary exile" as a result of his identification with the reformed movement. It looked like the auspicious beginning of a close working relationship. The Silesian was accepted as one who had joined forces with the Reformed theologians not only against the traditional enemy Rome, but also one who had proven his mettle in writing against the eucharistic fallacies of Wittenberg. The happy relationship, however, was not to endure.

Born in November or December 1489, three hundred miles east of Strasbourg in Silesia, Caspar Schwenckfeld von Ossig was apparently destined not for the role of radical reformer, but for that of courtier.[2] Educated in at least two universities and exposed to the humanistic currents of his age, Schwenckfeld found himself attached to the court first of Georg of Brieg, and later of Friedrich II of Liegnitz, *Oberlandeshauptmann* of Lower Silesia.[3] As Schwenckfeld became disaffected with life at court,[4] he found himself turning to the revolutionary theology of Martin Luther. This occasioned the first of perhaps three "divine visitations."[5] At first a devoted follower of Luther, the nobleman moved gradually in the decade of the 1520s to a decisive break with Luther. Disenchanted with an overemphasis on justification by faith, he became increasingly uneasy with the lack of ethical renewal in the Reformation movement.[6] In October 1526 the nobleman wrote an urgent letter to Paul Speratus concerning the failure of the reform totally to affect the lives of individuals:

> Not once, but often I was violently agitated and assaulted with something like pain because at that time still so few of those who heard the present preaching of the gospel showed any improvement. And if we should admit the truth (and I speak here of our people), the longer it was preached, the worse they were, God help us.[7]

Before long, Schwenckfeld found himself departing from Luther. The public break came with the publication by Oecolampadius in May 1527 of *De cursu verbi dei*, originally a privately circulated letter of the nobleman to Conrad Cordatus.[8] In it he ". . . rejected Luther's conception of the spoken word as a vehicle for the spirit, not least because it condemned so many who had no opportunity to hear or read the word, and because it stripped God of his freedom."[9] A short time later, another writing, the *Anwysung* was published--also without his consent--by Zwingli at Zurich, largely because Schwenckfeld criticized Luther's eucharistic views as being ". . . contrary to the Word of God of the New and Old Testaments, the institution of Christ, and the original church."[10] This publication provided the excuse for Ferdinand of Austria to attack Friedrich of Liegnitz for tolerating the renowned heretic in his realm. As a result, Schwenckfeld found it necessary to leave, albeit "voluntarily," his beloved Silesia, heading west, eventually for Strasbourg. It may well be that Schwenckfeld never quite forgave the Reformed camp for publishing his *Anwysung* without his permission, thereby necessitating his exile.[11]

Meanwhile Strasbourg had become a haven for religious expatriates and would offer hospitality to many radical reformers, including Ludwig Hätzer, Jakob Kautz, Andreas Carlstadt, Michael Sattler, Pilgram Marpeck, Melchior Hoffman, Hans Denck, Wilhelm Reublin, Sebastian Franck, and others. Yet the tolerant leadership under its chief reformer, Martin Bucer, was already in the process of change when Schwenckfeld arrived, though Wolfgang Capito still maintained a measure of toleration.[12] Although Schwenckfeld at first found congenial companionship with the apparently irenic Bucer and Capito, he soon became involved with the separatists in the city. There was a strong affinity for these Anabaptists and spiritualists, especially with their stress on the fruits of justification in concrete Christian living.[13] Soon disagreement with the official reformers led to estrangement and disaffection. Schwenckfeld's recent biographer, R. Emmet McLaughlin, suggests that "the real cause of Schwenckfeld's alienation was Martin Bucer's drive for order, uniformity, and concord."[14] This may well be part of the ultimate cause, but one must look elsewhere for the more practical, efficient cause of the separation, more specifically to the issue of baptism. As long as Schwenckfeld's theological and reforming concerns centered on the eucharist and Luther's interpretation thereof, there was little difficulty in maintaining close collegial relations with the Reformed camp.[15]

As soon as the question of baptism came to the front, however, the collegial relationship between Schwenckfeld and Bucer and Zwingli was brought into jeopardy. Ironically enough, it is likely that Schwenckfeld was first encouraged by Bucer to address the problem of baptism, perhaps partly in relation to the theological and pastoral problem of what to do with the Anabaptists.[16] Whatever he may have wished to do, Schwenckfeld could no longer remain silent. He had to address the question of baptism, which he did with a treatise on infant baptism[17] and with a series of propositions that he sent to Leonard Brunner, pastor at Worms.[18] Apparently Bucer had warned Brunner beforehand about Schwenckfeld, for Brunner noted in a letter to Bucer on

November 18, 1530:

Your brief suggestions in regard to Schwenckfeld are good and appreciated. For I have a feeling of something in that man that is destructive of Christian love. This I tell you in confidence. He has sent me forty-six questions directed against the baptism of little children, which are calculated to make an impression upon persons untaught in the Scriptures and without the special judgment bestowed by the Spirit. I can say that I have never run across sweeter poison.[19]

Apparently Bucer, perhaps deciding that the questions were weighty enough to deserve an expert theological answer, had them sent on to Zwingli for his analysis and response.[20]

The rejoinder of Zwingli to the questions of Schwenckfeld, written in the Zurich reformer's last year of life, has been scarcely noticed by scholars. The reply by Zwingli, at this late stage, and with this strong reaction, suggests that the question of order and disorder was still very much a lively and important question for him. The challenge of Schwenckfeld is essentially the fourth encounter which Zwingli had to face concerning the baptismal issue in his career. Earlier he had had to deal with the Swiss Brethren in Zollikon in early 1525; later that year he had to confront Hubmaier; and in 1527 he found himself answering the "Brotherly Union" of Michael Sattler.[21] Clearly, the issue was one that was often facing him and would not go away. Now, in the time of grave confrontation with the Catholic forces throughout the Confederation, and in the face of Zwingli's attempts to construct a European evangelical alliance,[22] he met again the doctrine of baptism and the many challenges that accompanied this issue. It is little wonder that he met the inquiry with vigor and anger. An analysis of the propositions of Schwenckfeld and the response of Zwingli will allow us to see what the issues were which divided the two similar but different colleagues. It will also suggest that the question of order was ever a continuing and dominant concern in the Zurich reformation.

The Forty-Six Propositions regarding Baptism

Schwenckfeld organized his forty-six questions into four parts: the first part (questions 1-14) addresses baptism in the narrow sense; the second part (questions 15-17), the children of God; part three (questions 18-29), the comparison between the Old Testament practice of circumcision and Christian baptism; and the fourth part, the ministry of the Old and New Testaments and the gathering together of the church of the Gentiles.

Schwenckfeld's concern in the first part is with the meaning of true baptism. Only incidentally does he argue polemically against infant baptism. He consistently contrasts true baptism with mere external baptism. Baptism is a mystery, not an external ceremony [question 1].[23] If there is not repentance, examination of conscience, faith, and a certain maturity of person and age, then true baptism does not exist [2-3, 13-14]. Contrary to Zwingli, "baptism is not an initiation, but a confession and proclamation of the benefits of Christ, and of the blessing received through Christ" [7]. In summary, Schwenckfeld is clearly drawing a contrast between the inner and the outer Word, between the law and the gospel, noting that "external symbols occupy a secondary place" [9]. It profits little "to have received baptism without the Holy Spirit and faith" [14].

In part two Schwenckfeld classes among the children of God those who intentionally express faith. It is the children of promise, that is, of faith, who are the reborn, not those who are children of Christian parents. This affirmation of Schwenckfeld potentially undercuts the religious and social structures of Zurich, for "there is no promise that the children of the flesh belong to the church of Christ. . . . The child of Christian parents clearly has no prerogative in the sight of God over the one born of the Gentiles" [17].

In part three the Silesian clearly reaches to the heart of the matter in discounting an essential touchstone of Zwinglian thinking about baptism. In short, there is no justification for the comparison of circumcision with baptism, for "circumcision was altered rather than perfected" [18]. If one wants to keep circumcision as the basis for the entrance into the church, then one begins with Judaism rather than with Christ. "Are not the mysteries of circumcision and baptism distinct from each other? Are they not signs of different covenants?" [21]. Furthermore, "if anyone says that Christian baptism, that is, the baptism through which one attains the church of Christ, is equivalent to the baptism of John, he is in error by the whole width of the heavens" [26]--which is to say, Zwingli is in error.

The fourth section on the ministry of the Old and New Testaments and the gathering in of the church of the Gentiles treats basic theological concepts of Schwenckfeld. He discusses questions of letter and spirit,[24] the inner and outer Word, the inner and outer person, and especially the role of the Spirit in the experience of divine grace. A typically Schwenkfeldian assertion is that the Old Testament has little to do with the church of Christ.[25] Whoever baptizes children is guilty of false order. "Does not the one run beyond Christ and get before Christ who imparts the divine mysteries to the infants of the flesh before Christ is fashioned in them, and who, by the baptism of circumcision, prematurely enrolls in the church the Gentiles to be blessed in the seed of Abraham, perverting the regular order of the apostle's ministry of which we learn in Romans 10?" [39].[26] Finally, he concludes that advocating pedobaptism completely nullifies the preaching of repentance. Nor should one use arguments of Christian order and charity in order to justify the continued practice of the baptism of infants. Indeed the practice leads to the destruction of the church.[27] He concludes, "In short I hold that the baptism of the little ones is the beginning of papalism and the foundation of all errors and ignorance in the church of God, even the destruction of all piety and at the same time of the apostles' ministry. I cannot without violence to my conscience hold otherwise until I am taught better from the Scriptures."[28]

Summary of the Concerns of Schwenckfeld
With this summary of his propositions in hand, what appear to be the fundamental concerns of Schwenckfeld?

1. There is a *soteriological* concern. The emphasis on the external rite neglects the work of the Spirit. Pedobaptism rests on the action of the creature

rather than on that of the *Creator* and on an action of the human being rather than on Christ. It is faith which saves, not the action of an individual, and false baptism leaves no room for faith. For this reason pedobaptism is dangerous to the individual's quest for salvation and cannot be simply ignored.[29]

2. There is an *ecclesiological* preoccupation. The true church is founded by faith and by the work of the Spirit, not by the accident of birth. Infant baptism destroys the church, and by perverting the divine order, annihilates the sacraments. The sacrament of baptism is a divine mystery, not a human activity.[30] It is for this reason that he criticizes not only Zwingli, but also the Anabaptists, whom he accuses of observing only the outward symbol and not the inward baptism of the Spirit.[31]

3. There is a *hermeneutical* concern. The Old Testament simply does not have the same authority as the New. The old covenant, the way of Moses, has been surpassed. Any attempt to read the Old Testament as still valid is not only liable to misunderstanding but subverts the gospel.[32]

4. There is an *ethical* concern. For some time Schwenckfeld was concerned about the quality of Christian living. It was this concern which led him to leave the Lutheran fold and to question the eucharistic doctrines of Luther. In fact, it was in large part the concern over morality that had led Schwenckfeld to his unique doctrine of the *Stillstand* of the sacrament, in which he suspended observation of and participation in the eucharist.[33] Now he sees infant baptism as "destructive of Christian piety" and a practice which simply prevents true Christian living.

5. Finally, there is a *concern for Christian freedom.* One ought not force an individual into belief, and one should not persecute one who believes differently. Schwenckfeld was one of the strongest advocates of religious freedom in the sixteenth century. He wrote in his *Commentary on the Augsburg Confession*, ". . . even in those things which Christ Himself instituted, such as preaching, baptism, communion, etc., freedom must still remain. . . . Christ did not . . . . establish any coercion of conscience. . . ."[34] Obviously this calls into question the fundamental alliance of church and state.

These interests of Schwenckfeld reflect long-term concerns of the Silesian nobleman. They do not surface here for the first time, and they are completely understandable in the context of his life story to 1530, and, indeed, afterwards. Let us now turn to Zwingli's treatise to see how he responds to these questions.

Zwingli's Response to Schwenckfeld's Questions

Zwingli begins his answer to Schwenckfeld with a fundamental theological analysis, not of baptism, or even ecclesiology as such, but of election. It is a theme that had become increasingly important to Zwingli himself as noted in the sermon *De Providentia.* Originally preached at Marburg, it was then published in August of 1530, that is, basically at the same time he was responding to Schwenckfeld.[35] Zwingli accuses Schwenckfeld of going "astray in externals" and not knowing "the election, providence, grace, and kindness of God," which, if he ". . . had read my book upon Providence would ere this, I believe, be sailing in smooth water" [217v].[36]

Zwingli begins with election so that he can justify the inclusion of both the elect and the nonelect within the visible church. It is not faith, but election, which saves through Christ [axiom 4, 217v], "for no one believes save the one who has been destined and ordained to eternal life beforehand" [axiom 5, 217v]. The church, then, is composed of both elect and nonelect and "the catabaptists are wrong in driving out of the society of the church the infant children of Christians" [axiom 18, 219v]. It is clear that those who do not have faith are not necessarily damned. Faith comes only after election. The church ". . . embraces spurious members, not infants only but grown persons also, as well as elect, both children and adults, and embraces also unbelievers, some of whom will one day become believers, but some of whom will never have faith" [axiom 18, 219v]. Therefore, it is right to baptize children even though some of them will not come to faith.

With this theological foundation, Zwingli next turns to the four parts of Schwenckfeld's questions and sets about to answer them. First he addresses the issue of baptism in the narrow sense.

Zwingli does not question that baptism as such is an external ceremony, but it is one that symbolizes the baptism of the Holy Spirit and fire which Christ brings [answer 5, 220r].[37] It does not guarantee it,[38] but it is still baptism, even if the recipient is a spurious member such as Judas [6, 220v]. For ". . . in the church which is called the church by us, are included elect, unbelievers, and traitors" [6, 220v]. Zwingli stresses the communal element rather than the individualistic one. There must be a confession at the time of baptism, but it is not the confession of the one being baptized, but of the parents, that is, of the church [9, 221r]. "Baptism is a symbol of the truth, not of that which is at the time manifested in the person baptized, but of the fact that Christ truly washed the church with his blood. . . " [12 and 13, 221r]. Certainly this might mean that an individual could receive the sacrament unworthily, but this is also true of the Supper, so why not of baptism? [12 and 13, 221v]. Thus, the true meaning of baptism is community dependent.

In the second part, on the children of God, Zwingli begins with what is for him a fundamental assertion: "Those who are in the church are not outside" [15, 221v]. It is the concern to be inclusive in regard to the whole community. The sacrament belongs to the visible church and to the children of promise who are in the church [16, 221v]. Baptism is a symbol of rebirth, which does not mean that all the baptized are reborn, nor that one ought to be baptized only if born again with personal faith [17, 221v].

Part three turns to the question of the comparison of circumcision and Christian baptism. Not surprisingly, Zwingli turns in a different direction than Schwenckfeld. He agrees that baptism has abrogated circumcision, but only because both worked the same way, that is, for the reception into the people of God [18, 221v]. Circumcision and baptism are both one and the same mystery,

for both sacraments mean that those who are circumcised or baptized form the people or church of God. Both require that the initiated circumcise their hearts, and become washed and clean as new beings. . . . The church is the same and one, because there is one faith, as well of those who have been circumcised as of those who have been washed with baptism [21, 222r].

There is no distinction in terms of the fundamental content between the old and the new covenants. Both sacraments perform the same essential function: "They are signs of holy union and interaction *(commercium)* between God and humanity and among human beings themselves" [24, 223r]. At this point Zwingli returns to a familiar theme: the baptism of John,[39] which he affirms ".. . is no less the baptism of Christ than the baptism of Paul" [27, 223v]. In some ways, in exegetical terms, there is a problem in maintaining the identity of the two baptisms, but in terms of Zwingli's hermeneutic it makes sense: there is no essential difference between the two covenants, nor between the baptisms of John and Christ.

In part four Zwingli turns to the letter and the spirit. Although the letter sometimes represents the law and sometimes externals, it is not without continuing value, for "the gospel also has a law and externals, namely, the sacraments. . . " [30, 224v]. The externals are not an end in themselves; one does not trust in them. That is saved only for the mercy of God. He sees a problem with the emphasis of Schwenckfeld on faith before baptism, as putting too much trust in human beings. "By your heresy the kingdom of God would come with observation" [37, 225v]. Not only this, it is based on another error, namely, the assumption that everyone who confesses faith is in fact a true member of the elect. The mistake of the Anabaptists, and herein he includes Schwenckfeld, is that they ". . . trust in their own righteousness, not in the election and grace of God" [43, 226r]. Finally, Zwingli concludes that the baptism of infants is both a continuation of the old covenant and a guarantee that children will be brought up in the essentials of the faith, for if the teachings of the church were not there, ". . . many would fail to put their children under the public teaching of the church and many schisms would arise. . . " [45, 226v]. In other words, infant baptism is a guarantee of order within the church and society.

Summary of the Concerns of Zwingli

What are the fundamental considerations of Zwingli in his response to Schwenckfeld?

1. There is a *theological* concern expressed, especially in the doctrine of election. There has been a consistent theocentric emphasis in Zwingli's thought from the beginning. Early on, it emerged more in a concern for true religion, which meant that he was preoccupied with the matter of ceremonial religion, much as Schwenckfeld. Now he has turned to express his theocentrism in terms of predestination. Clearly, in this document it is for other than theological reasons as such.

2. There is an *ecclesiological* emphasis. Zwingli clearly stresses the notion of the territorial or inclusive church. The doctrine of election serves him here. He downplays the role of faith and emphasizes the divine activity in salvation rather than the human response. This means that the visible church contains both believers and nonbelievers, both elect and reprobate. Con-

sequently, baptism is for all infants born within the territory.

3. There is attention to the *hermeneutical* dimension. Zwingli has a "flat Bible." The Old Testament and the New Testament are of equal authority. The old covenant and the new covenant are in the final analysis one covenant, which one enters by the initiatory rite of circumcision-now-become-baptism.

4. There is a *sociopolitical* focus. Quite simply, Zwingli reveals a concern for order in church and society that one might call "typically Swiss." The strongest emphasis one sees in Zwingli's baptismal thought is on the social dimension. By baptism one enters into the people of God, which in sixteenth-century Zurich means into the "warp and woof" of Zurich society. One need only think of Zwingli's stress on baptism as being concerned with the symbolic expression of *commercium*, between human beings and God and among human beings themselves. It is a wholly social expression of the sacrament. This is, in fact, not surprising, and is possible to understand as an extension of his sacramental thinking as revealed in his eucharistic doctrine.[40]

Conclusion: The Issues at Stake in the Debate Between Zwingli and Schwenckfeld

With this analysis of the document in hand, what can be said about the issues at stake in the debate between Zwingli and Schwenckfeld?

To begin with, there is little theological necessity for disagreement between Zwingli and Schwenckfeld. Both reformers are theocentric and pneumatic, though Zwingli tended to limit the freedom of the Spirit in his later writing.[41] Likewise, Schwenckfeld's attention to the inner and outer, the inward and the external, are not equally matched in Zwingli at this later stage, though they were characteristic of the early Zwingli.[42] Both had concern for looking to the Creator and for not misdirecting worship to creatures so as to end up in idolatry.[43] Both felt that ceremonies could interfere with true godliness. One might suggest that where Zwingli tends to emphasize the grace of God in salvation, Schwenckfeld tends to stress faith in God without intentionally depreciating grace.

There is a clear disagreement between the two reformers in their views of the Old and New Testaments and the applicability of the law to the present life of the Christian. The abrogation of the Old Testament is far more radical in the Silesian and is reminiscent of Luther's distinction of law and gospel. It is certainly true that Zwingli's tendency to turn to the Old Testament is understandable in terms of his justification for the city church, whether or not one wants to call it a theocracy.

Obviously there is a disagreement over baptism and the role it plays in the Christian community or church. Zwingli's own understanding has developed and changed. In his earlier treatments on baptism he was concerned with faith. As he said to his teacher Thomas Wyttenbach in 1523, "You can wash an unbeliever a thousand times in the water of baptism, but unless he believes, it is in vain. It is faith that is required in this matter."[44] His earlier doubts over infant baptism were clearly done away with during the course of the conflict with the Anabaptists and, especially, with Hubmaier.[45] An element in

Zwingli's baptismal theology has been strengthened at this stage, namely, the use of election to justify the state church and infant baptism. In his treatise *On Baptism* Zwingli mentioned election, but only after having made his arguments for infant baptism and against rebaptism. In the response to Schwenckfeld, election is the foundation on which the arguments for infant baptism are built.

One can only wonder at the appearance of election at this late stage of Zwingli's theological development. Although it has always been there to a degree, his radical turning to predestination at the time that he was involved in planning for extending his influence throughout the evangelical forces in Europe and in fighting the emerging Swiss Catholic Counter-Reformation leads one to surmise that there are fundamental social and political implications for Zwingli in the doctrine of election.[46] If election was an affirmation of grace in Luther, and the freedom of God in Calvin, in Zwingli it came to justify the existing social order.

It is obvious that the concern for order is very much a recurring issue in Zwingli and Zurich. For the Zurich reformer, convergence is to be sought; divergence is not possible. The baptismal alternative of the Anabaptists and Schwenckfeld represents a clear threat to the order and structure of the Zurich church.[47] The concern of Schwenckfeld for the quality of Christian behavior could not be fully met by Zwingli. The Zurich church, for all its development of an ethics police which was to oversee the moral life of the city, would not accommodate the rigorist's wish to eliminate the nominal Christian from the church. Fundamentally, Zwingli was more committed to the larger community than Schwenckfeld. He was always so concerned, a point which was not grasped by his radical friends-become-enemies in 1524-25 or later.

Consequently, the demand of Schwenckfeld for religious freedom could not be accommodated in Zurich. In his earlier career Zwingli asserted that one cannot force another to believe. As he developed into the city reformer, however, this was not to remain. He could not extend to others who disagreed with him the freedom he had originally demanded for himself. Not only this, but one must also recognize that Zwingli was precisely at this time under fire both within the Confederacy and without. John Eck had only just published a scathing attack on Zwingli that was being widely circulated. In it he blamed Zwingli for the very existence of the Anabaptists: "I laugh at the empty boasting of Zwingli that he was the first to teach and write against the Anabaptists, since I am aware that it was Zwingli who by his counsel and advice really founded this lost sect, and was goaded more by jealousy than love of the truth in his pursuit of Balthasar the Catabaptist, as all his neighbors testify."[48] With this kind of attack being made, it is not surprising that Zwingli felt it was necessary to prove his commitment to order and stability and to disassociate himself as thoroughly as possible from all forms of radicalism.

One can conveniently say that the concerns of Zwingli in his reforming work can be understood in terms of a quest for both true religion and civic religion. These two elements, so understandable in the person of the Swiss humanist pastor in Zurich, were a lifelong commitment. Caspar Schwenckfeld, the Silesian nobleman, never at home in the city, could affirm the one, while at the same time undercutting the other.

NOTES

1. Emil Egli et al., eds., *Huldreich Zwinglis sämtliche Werke*, 14 vols., Corpus Reformatorum, LXXXVIII- (Berlin: Schwetschke und Sohn, 1905-), X, 124 (hereafter cited as *ZSW*). The modern edition of Schwenckfeld's works is *Corpus Schwenckfeldianorum*, 19 vols., ed. Chester David Hartranft et. al. (Leipzig: Breitkopf, 1907-1936; Göttingen: Hubert, 1960-1961) (hereafter cited as *CS*). A somewhat different version of this article was given at the spring meeting of the American Society of Church History, Louisville, Kentucky, April 28, 1989.

2. The best studies on Schwenckfeld's context and development are Peter Erb, *Schwenckfeld in His Reformation Setting* (Valley Forge, Pa.: Judson Press, 1978); Selina Gerhard Schultz, *Caspar Schwenckfeld von Ossig (1489-1561)* (Norristown, Pa.: Board of Publication of the Schwenkfelder Church, 1947); Edward J. Furcha, *Schwenckfeld's Concept of the New Man* (Pennsburg, Pa.: Board of Publication of the Schwenkfelder Church, 1970); and esp. R. Emmet McLaughlin, *Caspar Schwenckfeld, Reluctant Radical: His Life to 1540* (New Haven: Yale University Press, 1986).

3. McLaughlin spells out the implications of this appointment for Schwenckfeld. *Ibid.*, 16ff.

4. Furcha, *Concept*, 13.

5. The date for this was likely 1518 (Schultz, *Caspar Schwenckfeld*, 6ff.) or 1519 (McLaughlin, *Reluctant Radical*, 14).

6. At first, Schwenckfeld did not blame Luther, noting that even Jesus had no success in and around Jerusalem during his three years of ministry. See *CS* I, 270. He gradually came to the conclusion that there was something in the doctrine of Luther itself that was responsible for the problem. Horst Weigelt, *Spiritualistische Tradition im Protestantismus: die Geschichte des Schwenckfeldertums in Schlesien* (Berlin: Walter de Gruyter, 1973), 33; R. Emmet McLaughlin, "Schwenckfeld and the South German Eucharistic Controversy, 1526-1529," in *Schwenckfeld and Early Schwenkfeldianism: Papers Presented at the Colloquium on Schwenckfeld and the Schwenkfelders*, ed. Peter Erb (Pennsburg, Pa.: Schwenkfelder Library, 1986), 182.

7. *CS* II, 368; trans. McLaughlin, *Reluctant Radical*, 61-62.

8. *CS* II, 581-599.

9. McLaughlin, *Reluctant Radical*, 96-97.

10. *ZSW* VI/2, 258. Unless specifically noted otherwise, the translations are the present author's.

11. In his *Protestation* to the City Council in Strasbourg, June 12, 1533, Schwenckfeld reminded his opponents that he had suffered for his faith and had been forced to leave his homeland because of his religious position. *CS* IV, 789.

12. For a brief description of the situation in Strasbourg for the radicals with references to other studies, see James M. Kittelson, *Wolfgang Capito: From Humanist to Reformer* (Leiden: E. J. Brill, 1975), 172f.

13. George Williams, "Caspar Schwenckfeld and the Royal Way," in *Schwenckfeld and Early Schwenkfeldianism*, 21.

14. McLaughlin, *Reluctant Radical*, 129.

15. Among the Reformed theologians at first supportive of Schwenckfeld was Wolfgang Capito, who published, in May 1529, a preface in praise of the Silesian's eucharistic teachings. See Kittelson, *Capito*, 152-153.

16. In 1531 Schwenckfeld wrote to Johann Bader: "Bucer himself began to speak with me about [baptism] and entreated me to confer with him on it." *CS* IV, 243. See also Weigelt, *Tradition*, 218. The influence of Valentine Crautwald was possibly also a factor. *Ibid.*, 122.

17. *Von dem Kindertauf*, in *CS* III, 813-824.

18. *Quaestiones de baptismi sacramento, CS* III, 846-858.

19. Manfred Krebs and Hans Georg Rott, eds, *Quellen zur Geschichte der Täufer*, VII: *Elsass, I. Teil: Stadt Strassburg 1522-1532* (Gütersloh: Gerd Mohn, 1959), 281.

20. Schultz, *Caspar Schwenckfeld*, 194.

21. Zwingli's three major treatises on baptism directed against the Anabaptists were as follows: "Von der Taufe, von der Wiedertaufe und von der Kindertaufe" (May 1525), in *ZSW* IV, 206-337; "Antwort über Balthasar Hubmaiers Taufbüchlein" (Nov. 1525), *ZSW* IV, 585-642; "In catabaptistarum strophas elenchus" (July 1527), in *ZSW* VI/1, 21-196.

22. On January 5, 1530, Zurich, Bern and Basel concluded an alliance with Strasbourg that was the culmination of twelve prior alliances over the previous five years. One can only understand the later reforming work of Zwingli if one takes seriously his continuing attention to the formation of such alliances as calculated to maintain, defend and preserve the Reformed gospel as realized in Zurich. After 1528 such alliances were designated as Christian, "das christliche Burgrecht." G. R. Potter, *Zwingli* (Cambridge: Cambridge University Press, 1976), 353 n. 4.

23. The text of Schwenckfeld's propositions which the editors of the Zwingli critical edition utilize in the forthcoming volume is from *D D Joannis Oecolampadii et Huldrichi Zvinglii epistolarum libri quatuor...opus...nunc denique primum in lucern editum*, ed. Theodor Bibliander (Basel, 1536), 69v-76v. The wording of this edition corresponds to that which Zwingli cites in his response. There are differences between this text and the one produced by *CS* IV, 848-858, which has only forty-four propositions. The latter also omits considerable portions of the material in Bibliander. In this paper the questions of Schwenckfeld will be cited in the text by numbers within brackets. The present translations are based on the manuscript of Henry Preble that was prepared for Samuel Jackson's multivolume translation of Zwingli. The typescript of Preble's unpublished translations was prepared by the present author and may be found in the H. Henry Meeter Center for Calvin Studies at Calvin College.

24. "Is the ministry of the New Testament a ministry of the letter or of the spirit? If of the spirit, certainly it ought to begin with the spirit and not with externals" [30].

25. "There is a very great difference between the house of Moses and the house of Christ" [32].

26. See also question 45: "Since Paul enjoined that in the Church all things be done decently and in order and at the same time unto edification, it is asked, who was ever edified in the sight of God by the baptism of the little ones, or is even today so edified in the Lord. For this is to glory in the flesh, not in the cross of Christ."

27. "These and countless other considerations, however much others make a pretence of Christian love or liberty, influence me to hold distinctly that the works of the pedobaptists are a detestable abomination and the destruction of the Church of Christ, the extinction of the mystery of baptism as well as of the calling to mind of the confession of Christ, the extinguishing from among us of Christ and of the truth which is in Christ, the restoration of Moses and the old order, the confounding of the gospel and the Law, of the shadow and the substance, the utter weakening of the promises of God, the obscuring of grace and of the origin of the people of God, the increase of the curse under which children are born, the putting aside of the Christian catechism, the utter weakening of the ordinances of Christ (Matt. 28:19), the perversion of the

order of God in the sacraments, the extinction of brotherly correction, excommunication, and all true edification in Christ, the encouragement of rebaptism (just as much as in the time of Augustine), the thrusting down of the Holy Ghost from his office" [46].

28. This passage is omitted from the Bibliander text but is included in *CS* III, 858.

29. "Had infant baptism stood alone, Schwenckfeld might well have remained silent. But the arguments which Zwingli, Bucer, and others used to defend the practice threatened, in Schwenckfeld's opinion, to corrupt the very nature of the church and robbed Christ of his unique role in salvation." McLaughlin, *Reluctant Radical*, 134.

30. "According to Schwenckfeld only the chosen people to whom eternal life is granted belong to the church. 'No one comes to Christ if the Father does not draw him.' Therefore, worldly, contrived faith is useless. The Christian church is founded on freedom from worldly influences and on the equality of all its members. The criteria for eternal life is [sic] 'the new creation and the faith which are put into effect through love.' [*CS* IV, 753-754]." Klaus Deppermann, "Schwenckfeld and Leo Jud on the Advantages and Disadvantages of the State Church," in *Schwenckfeld and Early Schwenkfeldianism*, 219.

31. Naturally enough, Schwenckfeld and his followers were often taken to be Anabaptists. There are similarities, but, in the final analysis, the nobleman did not so identify himself. About the time of this exchange with Zwingli, the Silesian wrote a mild criticism of the Anabaptists: *Judicium de Anabaptistis, CS* IV, 831-834. The conflict between Schwenckfeld and Pilgram Marpeck led to growing disillusionment and eventually to hostility toward the Anabaptists. For a helpful study on this topic, see Walter Klaassen, "Schwenckfeld and the Anabaptists," in *Schwenckfeld and Early Schwenkfeldianism*, 389-400. The judgment of Erich Seeberg that Schwenckfeld "sharply criticized the Anabaptists though he did not exactly know them" is indefensible. "Der Gegensatz zwischen Zwingli, Schwenckfeld und Luther," in *Reinhold-Seeberg-Festschrift*, ed. Wilhelm Koepp (Leipzig: A. Deichertsche Verlagsbuchhandlung, 1929), 62. He may have taken too literally the nobleman's opening sentence from his *Judicium*, wherein he says that he does not know all the doctrines and opinions of the Anabaptists. See *CS* IV, 831. It is certainly clear that Schwenckfeld defended the Anabaptists from their persecutors over the years. See *ibid.*, 257-259.

32. According to Gottfried Seebass, "Schwenckfeld...considered the relationship between the Old and New Testament as the most important topic which he treated during his Strassburg period." "Caspar Schwenckfeld's Understanding of the Old Testament," in *Schwenckfeld and Early Schwenkfeldianism*, 87. Schwenckfeld wrote an open letter in June 1531 to develop his assertions that the New Testament sacraments are independent of the Old Testament. See *Der dritte Sendbrief*, in *CS* IV, 150-197.

33. In defending the suspension of the eucharist rather than in reforming it, Schwenckfeld wrote: "I hear you with many others saying: Why wasn't the true use of the supper instituted after the truth was perceived? I answer: Why aren't there yet any true Christians? Why aren't the dinner guests as yet gathered? Why aren't there yet any of the cleansed, who might eat worthily?" *CS* II, 359; trans. McLaughlin, *Reluctant Radical*, 75. Elsewhere Schwenckfeld noted the general shortcomings of the church as reasons for the *Stillstand*, though still emphasizing moral impurity as a reason: "I see here no true worship, no earnestness, no better order, no true love, no fruit of the Spirit, no brotherly admonition. Therefore I am inclined to doubt with some justification whether or not this is the Lord's Supper." *CS* III, 383; trans. Edward J. Furcha, *The Piety of Caspar Schwenckfeld* (Pittsburg, Pa.: Pittsburgh Theological Seminary, 1969), 105. There is no clear evidence in the *Forty-Six Propositions* that Schwenckfeld is advocating a similar

Stillstand in regard to baptism, though it might be implied. He is concerned about the impact of infant baptism on moral behavior.

34. Fred Grater, *Caspar Schwenckfeld: Commentary on the Augsburg Confession* (Pennsburg, Pa.: Schwenkfelder Library, 1982), 35.

35. *ZSW* VI/3, 64-230. For an English translation of Zwingli's sermon, see William John Hinke, ed., *The Latin Works of Huldreich Zwingli*, II (Philadelphia: Heidelberg Press, 1922), 128-234. For an analysis of the doctrine of predestination in Zwingli, see Gottfried Locher, "Huldrych Zwingli's Doctrine of Predestination," *Zwingli's Thought: New Perspectives* (Leiden: E. J. Brill, 1981), 121-141.

36. The modern critical text of Zwingli's writing has not yet been published, but is scheduled to appear within the year as vol. VI/4 of *Zwinglis sämtliche Werke* edited by the Institut für schweizerische Reformationsgeschichte under Professor Fritz Büsser, with Chief Assistant Heinz Stücki and Assistant Christof Weichert. I have been graciously supplied with a photocopy of the manuscript prior to publication and wish to express my appreciation to Professor Büsser and Mr. Weichert for facilitating my access. Since the pagination of the critical text has not yet been determined, the citations of the work of Zwingli in this paper will be to the folio pages of the best available manuscript, which lies in the City Archives of Strasbourg, as cited in the typescript of the forthcoming edition. The original autograph of Zwingli has been lost. Zwingli begins his remarks with twenty axioms before answering the questions of Schwenckfeld. The axiom numbers will be noted along with the folio page numbers. The translations are again based on the manuscripts of Henry Preble but edited to conform to the modern Zwingli edition and current English.

37. After developing his twenty axioms, Zwingli then turns to answer each of the forty-six questions of Schwenckfeld. The answer and folio page numbers will again be cited.

38. "Therefore baptism is an external ceremony which symbolizes but does not guarantee the thing" [question 5, 220v].

39. The baptism of John was a familiar concern of Zwingli in his debates with Hubmaier. For the response of Hubmaier, see H. Wayne Pipkin and John Howard Yoder, trans. and eds., *Balthasar Hubmaier, Theologian of Anabaptism* (Scottdale, Pa.: Herald Press, 1989), 98-111, 184-185, 196-197, 202-205. For a study of the debate between Zwingli and Hubmaier, see David Steinmetz, "The Baptism of John and the Baptism of Jesus in Huldrych Zwingli, Balthasar Hubmaier and Late Medieval Theology," in *Continuity and Discontinuity in Church History: Essays Presented to George Hunston Williams on the Occasion of his 65th Birthday*, ed. F. F. Church and Timothy George (Leiden: E. J. Brill, 1979), 169-181.

40. For a summary statement of the social dimension of Zwingli's eucharistic thinking, see H. Wayne Pipkin, "The Positive Religious Values of Zwingli's Eucharistic Writings," in *Huldrych Zwingli, 1484-1531: A Legacy of Radical Reform*, ed. E. J. Furcha (Montreal: Faculty of Religious Studies, McGill University, 1985), 129f.

41. For example, in his 1527 treatise *Friendly Exegesis*, Zwingli affirmed the centrality of the Spirit while limiting it: "The superior thing, I frankly acknowledge, is the spirit, but unless it be restrained by the reins and ropes of Scripture...it will become headstrong and violent." *ZSW* V, 734; trans. H. Wayne Pipkin, *Huldrych Zwingli: Writings* II: *In Search of True Religion: Reformation, Pastoral and Eucharistic Writings* (Allison Park, Pa.: Pickwick Publications, 1984), 354. For Zwingli, the Spirit "is one of harmony and unanimity, not one of contention and discord." *ZSW* V, 735; *Writings*, 355.

42. An illustration of the close manner of referring to the inner working of the Spirit in

Zwingli is found, for example, in his 1525 treatise *On Baptism*: "The inner baptism of the Spirit is nothing other than the teaching which God has done in our hearts and the calling by which he comforts and secures our hearts in Christ. No one other than God can give this baptism. Without it no one can be saved, though without the other baptism of outward teaching and dipping in water one can be saved. The proof of this is that the thief on the cross was neither outwardly taught nor baptized, but was saved." *ZSW* IV, 225-226. For an analysis of the spiritual concerns of the early Zwingli, see H. Wayne Pipkin, "In Search of True Religion: The Spirituality of Zwingli as Seen in Key Writings of 1523/24," in *Prophet, Pastor, Protestant*, ed. E. J. Furcha and H. Wayne Pipkin (Allison Park, Pa.: Pickwick Publications, 1984), 117-135.

43. "These are the real, true anti-Christs. Everything they should ascribe to and attribute to Jesus Christ, our savior, they take away from him and give it wrongly and falsely to another creature--without any scriptural foundation, against the clear word of God." *ZSW* II, 646; *Writings*, 61. This early statement by Zwingli could well have been uttered by Schwenckfeld.

44. *ZSW* VIII, 85; trans. in G. R. Potter, ed., *Huldrych Zwingli* (New York: St. Martin's Press, 1977), 37.

45. Much has been made of the flirtation of Zwingli with the idea of believers' baptism. Although it does not appear to have been more than a passing concern, he did himself comment on it in *On Baptism*: "Just as some have so rashly supposed that signs strengthen faith, so some have felt obliged to oppose child baptism, for faith cannot be strengthened in children who cannot yet believe. This mistake had misled me some years ago so that I thought it was much better that children should have their first baptism when they reached an appropriate age, although I did not act so presumptuously that I put myself arrogantly forward, as some now do who are much too young and inexperienced to be able to understand the matter, maintaining that child baptism comes from the pope and the devil, and such unseemly phrases. I see Christian manliness and fortitude with pleasure, but crazy madness without love and order and Christian discipline can suit no one except hooligans and creators of disturbances." *ZSW* IV, 228-229; translation in Potter, *Huldrych Zwingli*, 37.

46. One might note as well that the sermon *On Providence*, which was preached at Marburg, was dedicated to Philip of Hesse. See *ZSW* VI/3, 64; *Latin Works*, II, 128-130.

47. Schwenckfeld was perceived widely in the Reformed camp as being a threat to the given order. It is for this reason he was said by Brunner to be "destructive of Christian love." See n. 19 above. We began by citing the laudatory welcome of Capito for the Silesian. By 1533, there was a different report as Capito wrote Jacob Truchsess: "I do not want to burden you with how much he has damaged.... He considers that no one else is a Christian...and that he alone has the truth." Quoted in Kittelson, *Capito*, 165.

48. John Eck, *Refutation of the Articles of Zwingli*, in *Latin Works*, II, 83.

PART II: MENNONITES TODAY

CHAPTER 9

The One and the Many:
The Recovery of Mennonite Pluralism

Rodney J. Sawatsky

I

The category "Mennonite" typically conjures up for the uninitiated a unitary entity based on limited data. Perhaps a brief encounter with the Mennonite Central Committee or a passing picture of an Old Order horse and buggy or a chance reading of a short story by a Mennonite author premises such a unified perspective. Such naiveté is impossible for the initiated. For those who know Mennonite reality, pluralism is, if not *the*, at least *a* central reality.

The large assortment of ecclesiastical subgroupings is only one evidence of this pluralism. The variety of theological and sociopolitical orientations, worship forms, organizational structures, and other expressions of faith and faithfulness--both individual and corporate--add further substance to this pluralistic fact. Any attempt to define a unitary "Mennonite" in the *Mennonite Encyclopedia*, for example, is an exercise in frustration, given that "Mennonite" embraces the many as much as the one.[1]

Despite this variety, the Mennonite community also evidences a commonality which gives substance to the common "Mennonite" designation. Scholars of the Mennonite experience have pursued unity both descriptively and prescriptively with a particular focus on Mennonite history, in the process sometimes confusing their analytical and normative tasks. Such a normative construct emerged in the World War II era as "the Anabaptist vision." Premised upon a differentiation of sixteenth-century Anabaptists deemed "evangelical" from those considered less worthy ancestors for the Mennonites, an historically based norm resulted against which all contemporary and successive Anabaptist and Mennonite reality was tested. A unitary vision thus sought to be the normative one, amidst the pluralistic many.

In recent decades the unitary, normative Anabaptism so defined has become increasingly problematical. Scholars of Anabaptism, for example, are identifying considerable pluralism even among the so-called "evangelical" Anabaptists. Even those Mennonites committed to Anabaptist normativity in some form evidence significant variety in their translation of that normativity.

And, finally, Mennonites within modernity have, alongside other Christians, learned to recognize and appreciate the various gifts and understandings evidenced by different individuals and communities.

The many is once again challenging the one. A recovery of Mennonite pluralism is occurring even as Mennonites are becoming increasingly ecumenical. These two dynamics need not be incongruent. A normative unity can, and in the case of Mennonites probably must, embrace considerable variety. The challenge now is to do justice to the many in the definition of the one. To this end this chapter focuses primarily on the recovery of Mennonite pluralism in Mennonite scholarship, and concludes with only brief reflections on the one beyond the many.

II

James Stayer, one of today's preeminent historians of the sixteenth-century Radical Reformation, recently expressed surprise at the ease with which Mennonites accepted his Anabaptist revisionism.[2] His *Anabaptists and the Sword* published in 1972, followed in 1975 by "From Monogenesis to Polygenesis: The Historical Discussion of Anabaptist Origins," written together with Klaus Deppermann and Werner Packull, strongly reasserted the reality of Anabaptist pluralism.[3] This pluralist proposal challenged the isolation of the so-called "evangelical Anabaptists" on theological bases which premised the Goshen College-based "Anabaptist vision" school in the mid-twentieth century. Stayer's book recognized the variety of Anabaptist attitudes towards the sword not only beyond, but also within so-called "evangelical Anabaptism," and his co-authored article identified the varying origins of Anabaptists in various regions of Europe. Rather than uniform outrage at these pluralizing challenges to the established normative vision, Stayer received strong support at least from some segments of the Mennonite community. Why?

The explanation, Stayer believed, may well be found in the thesis of "Mennonite bipolarity" proposed by James Juhnke, a Bethel College-based historian of the North American Mennonites. Said Juhnke: "The self-understanding of Mennonites in North America, from the latter 19th century until the mid-20th and beyond, has been foundationally conditioned by a two-fold European heritage." These two--the Swiss-South German and the Dutch-North German--are distinct on the bases of "definably different historical memories, cultural characteristics, and theological preferences."[4] Said Stayer: "Specifically, I infer from Juhnke's analysis that a major reason for the easy abandonment of Bender's 'Anabaptist vision' had been the discomfort of Dutch-Russian "Low German" Mennonites with Bender's variety of Mennonite ecumenism, which assumed the precedence of the Swiss-South German Mennonites and of the (Old) Mennonite Church."[5]

Not only is Stayer correct that contemporary Mennonite pluralists were not threatened by his reassertion of Anabaptism pluralism, but also a recovery of Anabaptist pluralism may well be serving as a legitimation of modern Mennonite pluralism. Whatever the precise relationship between Anabaptist and modern Mennonite historiography, pluralism is now a primary theme in twentieth-century North American Mennonite history.

As Stayer rightly suggested, Mennonite pluralism is championed primarily, although definitely not exclusively, by persons from the Dutch-North German tradition and/or the General Conference Mennonite churches. All those Stayer identified by name as responding positively to his Anabaptist pluralism writings are thus embraced.[6] Similarly, the authors of the papers delivered at the Conference on Mennonite Pluralism in Fresno, California, in October 1982, fall into these two categories except for one, and his paper did not explore the pluralism theme.[7] Although these modest indices may well be explained by coincidence, a broader pattern does seem to emerge. Recognition of Mennonite pluralism is the concern, it seems, particularly of one wing of the Mennonite community. Why is this?

Before going any further, however, pluralism requires further definition. The term "pluralism" can be employed both descriptively and prescriptively. This distinction is central to this discussion. When historians such as James Stayer identify the variety and complexity of sixteenth-century Anabaptism, their purpose is primarily *descriptive*. To describe Anabaptist pluralism is not to suggest that the Anabaptists were pluralists. In fact, the opposite would be more accurate, though with notable exceptions. To speak of Anabaptist pluralism need be no more than cataloguing all the various subgroups over time that label themselves as Mennonite. When, however, various Anabaptist or Mennonite personalities or groups are recognized as alike struggling to attain Christian faithfulness, then pluralism in a more *prescriptive* sense is being affirmed. Pluralism as a prescriptive category is relatively relaxed about variety and is relatively hesitant to judge others as inferior in understanding God's will.

The "relatively" qualifier here is most important. No pluralist posture is absolute unless it is promulgated on the basis of an absence of principles and beliefs. No Mennonite could be an absolute pluralist! Rather the term is used to reflect relative inclusiveness in contrast to greater exclusiveness.

In this more normative sense, the pluralist perspective among Mennonites is essentially a phenomenon of modernity. It begins, first, with the recognition of the variety of Mennonitisms alongside all the other Christian denominations which populate the North American religious landscape in particular. Second, it requires a shift from a sectarian self-confidence to a more humble acknowledgment that others may have equal claim to truth, or more specifically, to Anabaptist faithfulness. At this point, of course, Anabaptist pluralism moves beyond description to prescription.

III

Returning to the earlier question regarding the relatively greater openness to pluralism, in the prescriptive sense, in the Dutch-North German tradition, some historical sampling may point towards an answer. A history of Mennonite pluralism might well go back to the likes of Hans Denck and perhaps Pilgram Marpeck. The more tolerant Dutch and North Germans who found Menno Simons too legalistic would surely be embraced. The *Kirchliche*

Mennonites in Russia who reacted so vehemently against the nascent *Brüdergemeinde* would have difficulty being included. The *Brüdergemeinde*, in turn, had rather an exclusivist view of their righteousness over against all the *Kirchliche*. They too were less than pluralist.

In North America the Dutch Mennonite-Quakers of Germantown surely evidenced a pluralist orientation. And, for that matter, the general mood of most Pennsylvania Mennonites prior to the French-Indian Wars was relatively ecumenical in comparison to the following century. But in the nineteenth century the General Conference Mennonite Church evidenced the most sustained pluralism.

The General Conference began in Iowa in 1860 under the leadership of recent South German immigrants. These more acculturated South Germans felt the "old" church lacked the organization and vitality necessary for the church's missionary task. The Eastern Pennsylvania Conference led by John H. Oberholzer quickly found fellowship among these more progressive and less traditional fellow believers. Others, including some Amish, similarly joined this new united and uniting Mennonite body. Most important, the majority of the 1870s *Kirchliche* immigrants from Russia chose the General Conference over the (Old) Mennonite Church despite the courting of John F. Funk, a leader in the (Old) Mennonite Church. Indeed, as symbolized in the move of its headquarters from the East to Newton, Kansas, the General Conference recognized these immigrants as increasingly formative of its work and vision.

Pluralism characterized both the experience and ideology of the General Conference. As Edmund G. Kaufman, president of Bethel College, liked to document, the General Conference embraced a much greater variety of Mennonites than the (Old) Mennonite Church or than the Mennonite Brethren.[8] It is not surprising that leaders of the General Conference claimed the motto: "In essentials unity, in non-essentials liberty, in all things love." The reality of pluralism required an ideology of tolerance. Or did a tolerant ideology encourage this variety of Mennonites to join? Probably both were operative.

General Conference historiography supported this pluralist perspective but awaited the coming of the Mennonites from Russia. Cornelius H. Wedel, the first president of Bethel College--a college established on the Kansas prairies little more than a decade after the Russian Mennonite settlers built their first homes and churches--served also as the first historian for the General Conference. His historiography is now being rediscovered, especially at Bethel College, as part of the recovery of the pluralist vision.[9] Historians there are finding that Wedel criticized the Anabaptists for being "excessively legalistic and literalistic" and separatist, and the (Old) Mennonite Church for not differentiating "between primary and secondary issues, between essentials and nonessentials."[10] While being rooted in Anabaptism, Wedel also learned from Pietism and found much in common with Baptists, Methodists, Reformed, and the like. This kind of expansiveness provided a ready historical correlate to the General Conference's pluralistic experience and ecumenical tolerance.

C. Henry Smith, an Amish convert to the General Conference cause and the first academically trained American Mennonite historian, continued the pluralist tone of Wedel even if not consciously building on Wedel. Unfortunately, Smith has not yet experienced a rediscovery equal to that of Wedel's. Perhaps this awaits someone from Bluffton College, where Smith taught much of his life after a brief stint at Goshen. Such a reappropriation would surely discover a scholar who, long before Stayer's work on Anabaptist pluralism, attempted to objectively describe the variety of Anabaptisms. To be sure, he found common norms within the variety in Anabaptism, or at least brought norms to Anabaptism, namely, individualism, congregationalism, religious freedom and tolerance. Such norms both assumed and legitimated pluralism in both the sixteenth and twentieth centuries. The tolerant liberalism he learned at the University of Chicago influenced both his theology and his history. Because of this commitment to tolerance, he was drawn to the General Conference and managed to be amazingly fair to the great variety characteristic of the Mennonite community.[11]

This more pluralist orientation was continued into the post-World War II era by such historians as Cornelius Krahn and Cornelius J. Dyck. But for a time it became a rather muted counterpoint to the powerful normative vision defined by Dean Harold S. Bender and his colleagues at Goshen. In this normative construct, in typical restitutionist fashion, purity rested at the source of the stream which, according to these Swiss-South Germans, was located in Zurich and environs from 1523 to 1527. As the movement spread northward, the original purity became increasingly muddied. Not only did Bender raise questions about Menno Simons, not to speak of the Münsterites, but he also could, according to this model, find explanation for the liberal compromises of Dutch and North German Mennonites in succeeding centuries.[12] The (Old) Mennonite Church, in turn, also the purported continuing community of the original, most pure Anabaptists, could claim to be the true bearer of the faithful tradition.

The reasons that this perspective gained dominance in virtually the entire North American Mennonite academic community during and following World War II are several. Stayer's proposal that the "prominence of fundamentalism among Dutch-Russian Mennonites...probably interfered with the General Conference and Mennonite Brethren developing any clear alternative to the Goshen school's outlook on Anabaptism" is not too compelling for the General Conference, although it may be more true for the Mennonite Brethren.[13] Juhnke is closer to the issue when he notes the "prolonged eclipse" in General Conference historiography following C. H. Wedel's premature death, until Edmund G. Kaufman assumed the Bethel presidency and brought in Cornelius Krahn--a recent immigrant from Russia via various German universities.[14] Besides, Wedel wrote in a language and idiom--German--which was rapidly losing its place even among the recent immigrants. Juhnke, however, does not adequately acknowledge the importance of C. Henry Smith, and for that matter, E. G. Kaufman himself--pluralists both. Indeed a theory opposite to Stayer's deserves consideration. Because General Conference pluralism as articulated by Smith and others was closely correlated with a somewhat diffuse

pietist-liberal theology and an optimistic liberal pacifism, neither of these were
equal to the challenges the Mennonite community faced in World War II.

The Goshen school, in marked contrast, responded brilliantly to the
World War II era. The "Anabaptist vision" as formulated by Dean Bender, his
colleagues, and students, and published in the *Mennonite Quarterly Review*,
provided an historically and theologically sophisticated ideology well suited to
those troubled times. Minimally this ideology challenged centuries of distorted
Anabaptist historiography, offered a third way beyond fundamentalist-liberal
polarities, legitimated the tradition of biblical nonresistance anew, and encouraged a new, more aggressive attitude of service in the world. In summary, "the
Anabaptist vision" was much more than historical revisionism. It was a
theological construct anchored in an (idealized) past but with the present and
future as its primary considerations. Psychologically, sociologically, and
ecclesiologically it served the Mennonite churches most powerfully. Students
of this era cannot help but be amazed and impressed with the accomplishments
and contributions of Harold S. Bender and company.

The "Anabaptist vision," however, had little room for pluralism. The
Swiss-South German historical experience and its Mennonite Church
ecclesiastical incarnation provided the norm against which all other Mennonites were measured.[15] The pluralist historiography of the General Conference could not, or at least did not, match this new normative construct.
Cornelius Krahn, Cornelius J. Dyck, William Keeney, and others sometimes
had to fight to include the Dutch and North German Anabaptists and implicitly
thereby their offspring in the company of the normative or "evangelical"
Anabaptists.[16] They were thus pluralizers, yet the normative categories, such
as "evangelical" Anabaptist, were being defined by the Goshen school. The
pluralist tradition had an uphill battle in the 1940s and 1950s.

The hegemony of Swiss-South German normativity began to break in the
late 1960s and 1970s. Many factors contributed. The civil rights and Viet Nam
era raised new questions about the appropriate response of Mennonites to the
social and political issues of the day. A new breed of students of American
Mennonite history were asking new questions. Social history was complement-
ing intellectual and church history. A relativizing of earlier history resulted.
Canadian Mennonites and Mennonite Brethren were newly finding their
academic voices. General Conference and Mennonite Brethren historians
became increasingly unhappy about being implicitly considered second-class
citizens. Anabaptist historiography was undergoing major changes. As
Umstrittenes Täufertum evidenced, Mennonites joined non-Mennonite scholars
in this revisionism.[17] And the pluralistic realities of modernity surrounded and
imbued all this to result in a recognition that at least the Mennonite reality,
and likely also Mennonite visions, were many rather than only one.

Only through the recovery of pluralism can historical sense be made of
recent decades of Mennonite history. But by extension, as James Juhnke
demonstrated so well, how can less than a pluralist perspective be employed to
do justice to all of Mennonite history? With a little historical reconnaissance,
an historical ancestry for contemporary pluralism is readily identifiable. This

pluralist tradition, as James Juhnke and James Stayer rightly note, is the Dutch-North German alternative to the Swiss-South German normative vision.

Unfortunately, when hegemonies are challenged, battle lines tend to be drawn. Juhnke's pluralism, for example, does not challenge the legitimacy of the Swiss-South German vision, but argues that equal recognition and value be ascribed to other visions. This, of course, is easier for Juhnke and other pluralists to accept than for those who subscribe to a single normative vision.

IV

New, more pluralistic models are imperative both to describe Mennonites and also to envision normative Mennonitism. If description and prescription could be separated even briefly in the process of devising such more pluralistic models, the task would be significantly simplified. But this is virtually impossible as long as a unitary normative standard labeled "Anabaptist" stands in judgment over all deviations. Consider just one example which reflects the problem of a unitary normative Anabaptism. The Church Member Profile survey of the attitudes, beliefs, and practices of North American Mennonites conducted in the early 1970s and reported in *Anabaptists Four Centuries Later*[18] assumed the appropriateness of a unitary Anabaptist norm. As legitimate as that standard may or may not have been two decades ago, it is being questioned as appropriate today as a repetition of that study is anticipated in the near future.[19]

The central question of the original study was: "to what extent do twentieth-century Anabaptists still evidence the essential ingredients of the faith of the sixteenth-century Anabaptists?"[20] "Anabaptism" in the study is defined exclusively in terms of "evangelical" Anabaptism as formulated by the "Goshen school." Two Swiss-South German scholars, Harold S. Bender and/or John Howard Yoder, are quoted in almost every chapter as the authoritative interpreters of this Anabaptist norm. Each Anabaptist index might well be challenged on the basis of a more pluralistic reading of Anabaptism, but one example will need to suffice. This one is chosen because "the discrepancy between the normative Anabaptist vision and the present attitudes of church members appears to be greater in this area than in any other covered in the study so far."[21] The issue involves leadership, and the norm posited is a shared ministry of all members. An ordained professional leadership is at least implicitly if not explicitly deemed un-Anabaptist. But does a more pluralistic reading of Anabaptism, which includes the bishop Menno Simons, for example, justify the imposition of this kind of norm on twentieth-century Mennonites in the name of sixteenth-century Anabaptism?

The problems with this unitary Anabaptist norm become especially evident when the authors sketch out their concluding "Summary and Implications for the Churches." They raise two questions which are particularly revealing. For one, noting the "negative association between Anabaptism and ecumenism," they wonder: "Is it possible for a people to have a strong commitment to a particularistic faith and still be open to full fellowship with those Christians whose faith is different in certain ways?" Kauffman and Harder answer their own question: "The continuing agenda for contemporary Anabaptists is to find ways of working cooperatively with each other and with other Christian denominations, and to put the goal of organic unity into the larger perspective of the Anabaptist vision."[22] Second, they note the negative correlation between Anabaptism and participation in the political process and ask: "Are modern Anabaptists a political cop out, refusing to lend their interest and support to the development and maintenance of enlightened and responsible (if not Christian) government?" Their own bias is evident in the question, yet they are forced to conclude that on the basis of their unitary definition of Anabaptism and "on the basis of the data, nonparticipation appears to be the most Anabaptist."[23]

Their conclusions placed Kauffman and Harder in a dilemma. As academically trained, ecumenically oriented, and politically concerned modern Mennonites, they did not fully share the sectarian and apolitical position of the Swiss-South German "evangelical" Anabaptism they assumed as normative. Yet they considered themselves strong Anabaptist advocates. In the last paragraphs of the book they challenged "the leadership of the denominations that participated in this study" to "more rigorously promote the principles of Anabaptism as an essential part of the larger Christian gospel and witness."[24] But does not Anabaptism as defined by them include sectarianism and non-involvement in politics with which they are not comfortable? What is the answer to their dilemma?

The answer is clear! As long as sixteenth-century Anabaptism is considered normative for twentieth-century Mennonites, then a more pluralistic perception of Anabaptism is imperative. The alternative is for a Swiss-South German definition of "evangelical" Anabaptism to remain hegemonic.

Translation of the typologies differentiating sixteenth-century Anabaptism to the twentieth-century Mennonite community would be one approach to developing a more pluralistic perspective. While George H. Williams' and James Stayer's subtypes would clearly signal pluralism, the applicability of categories such as apocalyptic, spiritualistic, or mystical to the present day is debatable.[25] Types that more closely reflect twentieth-century emphases or language usage would be more descriptive of Mennonite reality.

Furthermore, full justice to such a desired pluralistic perspective cannot be one-dimensional. Williams' categories are primarily theological; Stayer's are more sociopolitical. Greater comprehensiveness and nuance can be attained through a multidimensional approach to developing a taxonomy of twentieth-century Mennonite options. While distinct typologies are needed to differentiate among the various theological and sociopolitical positions, worship forms, and organizational structures, the interrelationships between these sub-categories of Mennonite thought and practice need to be recognized. A great variety of combinations are possible, each contributing further to the Mennonite pluralistic reality. For example, a Mennonite congregation might be persuaded that Anabaptism requires of them a neo-evangelical theology, a transformationist sociopolitical posture, a liturgical worship form, and a house church organization. A multidimensional taxonomy would capture the many other ways Mennonites endeavor to capture their particular reading of Anabaptist normativity or at least what they believe is most appropriate for them.

No attempt can be made here to develop a comprehensive taxonomy. At best, brief explorations in the formulation of a typology of sociopolitical positions might serve to exemplify a more pluralistic approach.

In the following chart and diagram, four sociopolitical positions are identified.[26] The differentiation is based upon emphasis rather than on which position is more or less Anabaptist. All the emphases will be recognized as Anabaptist, and hence each type is so labeled to indicate that no one of these groups is considered more authoritative than the other. Each adjectival qualifier might be considered pejorative by some, but they were purposefully chosen to avoid negative connotations to the individuals or groups holding to that position.

Type	*Emphasis*
Separationist Anabaptist	Social/cultural nonconformity to the world
Establishment Anabaptist	Biblical nonresistance/personal holiness
Reformist Anabaptist	Discipleship of Christ/service to the world
Transformationist Anabaptist	Political/ideological nonconformity to the political powers

The diagram which follows seeks a further differentiation on the social and political dimension. The horizontal plane divides political postures between conservative and liberal. In terms of voting behavior in the United States, the conservative would correlate roughly with a Republican vote and the liberal with a Democratic vote. In Canada the two extremes would be Social Credit on the conservative end and the New Democratic Party on the liberal end of the spectrum. The Progressive Conservatives would tend towards the conservative side and the Liberals to the liberal side. The vertical plane divides social orientations between the sectarian/separatist on one end and the denominational/integrationist on the other. The former stance suggests relative discontinuity with North American society, while the latter relative harmony and commonality with North American society.

Social
Sectarian/
Separatist

	Separationist		Transformationist
P			
o			
l	Conservative		Liberal
i			
t			
i	Establishment		Reformist
c			
a			
l			

Denominational/
Integrationist

Characterizing each of these four options in a little more detail:

Separationist Anabaptist--The emphasis is on a two-kingdom theology which requires separation of the church from a fallen world primarily in the social and cultural realms. Separation is symbolized in dress and/or technological nonconformity and/or limited political involvement. Key words are: nonconformity and nonresistance. The Schleitheim Confession would be important to proponents of this posture.

Establishment Anabaptism--While the two-kingdom theology remains here, it primarily calls for separation from worldliness to holy living, including nonresistance, particularly on the personal level, and to political activity against liberalizing trends such as abortion and governmental centralization. Key words are: conversion and obedience. Menno Simons might be considered a sixteenth-century parallel to this posture.

Reformist Anabaptism--The two-kingdom perspective is here modified considerably away from separation and towards Christian responsibility for the world. The emphasis in turn is on following the way of Jesus by serving the world vocationally and avocationally and responding to social problems in various ways, including the political process. Key words are: love and peace. Perhaps Pilgram Marpeck is the patron saint of the reformists.

Transformationist Anabaptism--Premised on a "radical" vision of the gospel and of the Anabaptists, the emphasis here is on liberating men, women, and children from social, political, economic, and ideological structures which limit their human potentiality. Sometimes impatient with normal political processes, proponents may advocate confrontation, nonpayment of taxes, or other means. Even violence in the name of liberation may not always be considered wrong. Key words are: justice and freedom. Hans Hut and other more apocalyptically-oriented sixteenth-century Anabaptists have most in common with this posture.

Critics will challenge the adequacy of this typology for many good and legitimate reasons. To anticipate just one criticism, there are those Mennonites who are seeking a recovery of more classical understandings of theology and social order for whom none of these four categories would be appropriate. Better models may emerge. But in the process of critique and reconceptualization, Mennonite pluralism both descriptively and prescriptively will be recognized.

V

Recovering a pluralistic perspective of Mennonite reality requires challenging the unitary, normative perspective which gained preeminence in this century in North America. The question still remains: can a perspective be both pluralistic and normative?

The answer is yes, though with important qualifications. Alternative traditions in and interpretations of Anabaptist-Mennonite history have already been noted. These more pluralistic orientations do not thereby necessarily abandon normativity. But pluralism does complicate normativity. Pluralism requires openness, tolerance, and humility. It is an ecumenical stance. Normativity by definition places limits on pluralism. But where in the Mennonite world are the limits, or conversely, what are the definitive norms? Alongside a recovery of Mennonite pluralism is the correlative task of redefining the one in terms that recognize the many.[27]

Rather than here pursuing the normative one embracing the pluralistic many in the abstract, an example of one among the many is the more typical Mennonite approach. C. J. Dyck, a child of the Dutch-North German tradition, became a member of the General Conference Mennonite Church at his baptism as a teenager in Saskatchewan. He graduated from Bethel College and the University of Chicago. Serving as the historian of his denomination's only seminary, he taught church history generally and Anabaptist and Mennonite history more specifically through much of his adult career.

Despite his heritage and denominational affiliation, Dyck rarely publicly challenged the unitary norm of "evangelical Anabaptism" authored by his colleagues down the hall. Indeed he might well say with Walter Klaassen: "Up to 1975 that [the evangelical Anabaptist] model was taken for granted, as indeed virtually all of us who were taught by Harold Bender and George Williams did."[28] Yet indirectly and probably with more profound consequences, he articulated and lived a much more pluralistic vision of Mennonite normativity.

Pluralism is an implicit theme in much of Dyck's work as an historian and churchman. His *Introduction to Mennonite History*,[29] as just one example, is both the only comprehensive history of Mennonites written in this generation and the most embracing of Mennonite pluralism. It was particularly as a churchman-scholar, however, that Dyck incarnated his ecumenical, pluralistic Mennonite vision. His work for the Mennonite Central Committee, the Mennonite World Conference, and most recently on the *Mennonite Encyclopedia* revision symbolize the expansiveness characteristic of his tradition and denomination. But despite all the many evidenced in the MCC, MWC, the new *ME* V, and by C. J., there is an essential and powerful one that draws the Mennonite variety together and that serves as a common norm. It is hard to articulate, but no doubt it is real. What is it? Ask C. J., or you might do as he does, live for the one while embracing the many.

Time here too brings changes. The one becomes more tenuous amidst the many of modernity. Yet reasserting old or redefining new normative unity in the face of the acids of modernity will be premature and unacceptable if it does not first recover the richness of Mennonite pluralism.

NOTES

1. This paper reflects, in part, the author's struggle to write the article "Mennonite" for the *Mennonite Encyclopedia*, vol. V, edited by C. J. Dyck. It also continues the dialogue on Mennonite historiography between James Juhnke, James Stayer, and the author in *Mennonite Identity: Historical and Contemporary Perspectives*, ed. by Calvin W. Redekop and Samuel Steiner (Waterloo, Ont.: Institute of Anabaptist and Mennonite Studies, 1988), 83-116.

2. James Stayer, "The Easy Demise of a Normative Vision of Anabaptism," in *Mennonite Identity*, 109.

3. *Anabaptists and the Sword* (Lawrence, Kans.: Coronado Press, 1972); "From Monogenesis to Polygenesis: The Historical Discussion of Anabaptist Origins," *MQR* 49 (1975), 83-121.

4. James C. Juhnke, "Mennonite History and Self Understanding: North American Mennonitism as a Bipolar Mosaic," in *Mennonite Identity*, 84.

5. Stayer, "The Easy Demise," 111.

6. Note, as examples, Walter Klaassen, Winfield Fretz and Rodney Sawatsky.

7. The papers are reproduced in the *MQR* 57 (1983), with Paul Toews as guest editor. The exception is Theron Schlabach, who wrote on "Mennonites and Pietism in America, 1740-1880: Some Thoughts on the Friedmann Thesis."

8. See, for example, Edmund G. Kaufman, "The General Conference Mennonites and the Biblical Church," in *Proceedings of the Study Conference on the Believers' Church* (Newton, Kans.: General Conference Mennonite Church, 1955), 102-103.

9. Keith Sprunger, "Cornelius H. Wedel and Oswald H. Wedel: Two Generations of Mennonite Historians," *Mennonite Life* 36 (Dec. 1981), 16-22; James C. Juhnke, "*Gemeinde Christentum* and Bible Doctrine: Two Mennonite Visions of the Early Twentieth Century," *MQR* 57 (1983), 206-221; and James C. Juhnke, *Dialogue with a Heritage: Cornelius H. Wedel and the Beginnings of Bethel College* (North Newton, Kans.: Bethel College, 1987).

10. Juhnke, "*Gemeinde Christentum* and Bible Doctrine," 212.

11. For more on Smith, see Rodney J. Sawatsky, *Authority and Identity: The Dynamics of the General Conference Mennonite Church* (North Newton, Kans.: Bethel College, 1987), 38-56.

12. Juhnke, "Mennonite History and Self Understanding," 87-88.

13. Stayer, "The Easy Demise," 112.

14. Juhnke, "*Gemeinde Christentum* and Bible Doctrine," 214.

15. Juhnke, "Mennonite History and Self Understanding," 86-88.

16. Reference need only be made here to Krahn's struggles to gain equality for the Dutch-North German tradition in the *Mennonite Encyclopedia*.

17. Hans-Jürgen Goertz, *Umstrittenes Täufertum, 1528-1975: Neue Forschungen* (Göttingen: Vandenhoeck und Ruprecht, 1975; 2nd ed., 1976).

18. J. Howard Kauffman and Leland Harder, *Anabaptists Four Centuries Later* (Scottdale, Pa.: Herald Press, 1975).

19. Consultation on Church Member Profile II, sponsored by the Institute of Mennonite Studies, Associated Mennonite Biblical Seminaries, Elkhart, Ind., Nov. 11-12, 1988.

20. Kauffman and Harder, *Anabaptists Four Centuries Later*, 22.

21. *Ibid.*, 198.

22. *Ibid.*, 338-339.

23. *Ibid.*, 339-340.

24. *Ibid.*, 343.

25. See especially the threefold Radical Reformation typology with Anabaptism further subdivided into three types in George H. Williams and Angel M. Mergal, eds., *Spiritual and Anabaptist Writers* (Philadelphia: Westminster Press, 1957), 19-38; and the various types identified by Stayer in *Anabaptists and the Sword.*

26. I wish to recognize Paul Toews of Fresno Pacific College for his role in formulating this typology.

27. An excellent recent contribution to this task is a paper by Walter Klaassen, "Sixteenth Century Anabaptism: A Vision Valid for the Twentieth Century?" presented to the Consultation on Church Member Profile II, Associated Mennonite Biblical Seminaries, Nov. 12, 1988.

28. *Ibid.*, 1.

29. Dyck did more than edit this work. He wrote major sections of the first edition (Scottdale, Pa.: Herald Press, 1967) and did significant revising of the revised edition.

CHAPTER 10

Differing Historical Imaginations and the Changing Identity of the Mennonite Brethren

Paul Toews

In 1886 on a midsummer Sunday evening, Johann Johann Wieler visited Peter Martin Friesen to inform him that the Rückenau, Russia, Mennonite Brethren (MB) congregation was commissioning him to write a history of the first twenty-five years of the Mennonite Brethren Church. As part of discharging his obligation, Wieler gave Friesen some historical documents, authorized him to interview the older people, and presented him with fifty rubles to cover the research costs and reimburse the time.[1]

Twenty-five years later, Raduga, the Mennonite publishing house in Halbstadt, published Friesen's great work, *Die Alt-Evangelische Mennonitische Brüderschaft in Russland (1789-1910) im Rahmen der mennonitischen Gesamtgeschichte.* The twenty-five-year lag stood in sharp contrast to the comment of one member of the Rückenau congregation who remarked when the decision was made, "That is a nice piece of work exactly suited for Friesen. But he will earn handsomely from it, for he will complete it in fourteen days!"

The 1886 call for a history of the Brethren was repeated in 1951 when the Board of Reference and Counsel (the highest governing board of the denomination) urged the North American conference to authorize publication of four denominational books, including a new history. This new call was fully completed twenty-four years later with the 1975 publication of John A. Toews's *History of the Mennonite Brethren Church: Pilgrims and Pioneers.*[2]

The needs of the fledgling Mennonite Brethren group in Russia in 1886 and those of the North American conference in 1951 were surely as different as the gap in time and place suggest. Yet they also shared a profound similarity. They were both important moments in the Mennonite Brethren search for a historical identity. Equally revealing is the time lag in both instances between the realization that history could speak to the moment and the ability to fashion a usable historical interpretation. In both moments the precariousness of a people's identity precluded the immediate writing of the history.

The Mennonite Brethren were born in 1860 in Russia, the same year that the General Conference Mennonite Church (GC) emerged as a distinct communion in the United States. What was happening in the nineteenth century, in both Russia and the United States, is clear. Modernity was creeping to the outer reaches of most Western societies, and peoples heretofore largely isolated were brought into greater contact with their respective host societies. The nineteenth century was the period of schisms in the Mennonite worlds of both Russia and the United States. The greater cultural contact brought into focus a series of new issues. Decisions were required about the preservation of inherited patterns forged in relative isolation compared to the pluralism of the increasingly integrated national cultures. Questions of what was to be normative, what was to be the pattern of isolation or integration into the dominant culture, what would preserve the best of the Mennonite traditions, were common to Mennonites in both countries.

The responses given were seldom equivocal. In American society, with its freer religious climate, schisms were easier to sustain and a differentiation among Mennonites was more readily secured. What emerged was a spectrum from those seeking to remain on the fringes of society, to those that began the movement which resulted in their becoming involved in the central institutions of North American society. There was a particularity to the groups that emerged in North America: Old Mennonites (MC), New Mennonites (GC), Old Order Amish, Progressive Amish, and numerous other well defined groups. The freedom and religious pluralism of America permitted a degree of internal coherence to the emerging groups.

The Russian story was different. The terms of the *Privilegium* and the integrated nature of the Mennonite commonwealth made religious schism threatening to political authority and cultural solidarity. The political structure contained the schismatic tendencies inherent in an unstable religious environment. The *Kleine Gemeinde* of 1812 and the Mennonite Brethren of 1860 were the only two substantial divisions before the new pressures introduced by Russification policies in the 1870s.

The writings of David G. Rempel, James Urry, Harvey Dyck, and John B. Toews, while offering different interpretations, all point to a complex religious and social environment. The Ukraine was undergoing sweeping economic, political, and cultural changes. Mennonites were increasingly affected by the changes. The isolation sought in the migration to Russia was breaking down, as "New Russia" experienced the early processes of transformation into a modern industrial economy. The environmental changes were accompanied by an enlargement of the intellectual landscape. New religious ideas coming from Moravians, Lutherans, Baptists, Pietists, and others gained entrance into the mid-nineteenth-century Russian Mennonite world.[3]

The beginning of the Mennonite Brethren movement reflects the pluralism of forces seeking change, yet hinged together by the constricted opportunity for reform. The year 1860 was a moment when divergent religious and cultural traditions operating throughout the Russian Mennonite world converged to create a new religious community. Cultural progressives seeking greater liberation from the constraints of a closed community, and cultural conservatives seeking a tighter morality, worked together to fashion an alternative to the existing community. Some of the early Mennonite Brethren reached back into history--to Menno Simons--to shape a new ideal; others reached out beyond the boundaries of the existing community to the religious currents of neighboring traditions. Anabaptism, Pietism, and Evangelicalism were present at the creation of the Mennonite Brethren. Mennonites, Baptists, Moravians, and Lutherans mediated reforming ideas and dispositions.

The continuing MB debate as to whether they were born of Anabaptist, Pietist, or Baptist influences may imply historical confusion, but it also points to the plurality of forces seeking change and needing to join together. Was the birth of the Mennonite Brethren progressive or conservative, expansive or narrow, cosmopolitan or provincial? The answer now is surely that it was both. Those contradictions made the Mennonite Brethren diverse rather than singular, fragmented rather than integrated, and their historical identity precarious.[4]

The interpreters of the Mennonite Brethren story have not always understood these conflicting realities. There are six histories of the Mennonite Brethren Church. Five were authorized by the denomination and received varying forms of official support: P. M. Friesen (1911); J. F. Harms, *Geschichte der Mennoniten Brüdergemeinde* (1925); J. H. Lohrenz, *The Mennonite Brethren Church* (1950); A. H. Unruh, *Die Geschichte der Mennoniten-Brüdergemeinde* (1955); and John A. Toews (1975). The sixth one, Peter Regier's *Kurzgefasste Geschichte der Mennoniten Brüder-Gemeinde* (1901), is the shortest and privately authored. All have nurtured the memory of the church and selectively shaped its identity.[5]

The interpretative frameworks utilized by the six historians in assessing the origins of the movement have had ideological consequences. Two issues in particular have been important. First, was the renewal impulse to be attributed largely to the revitalization of historic Mennonite understandings, or did it derive from newer religious movements? Related is the role of the social, economic, and political changes in the emergence of the Mennonite Brethren. Was 1860 to be defined only in religious terms, or could it also be related to changes in the sociopolitical environment?[6] The degree to which the memory dismissed social causes and attributed the renewal impulse to Pietism or other newer ideologies had theological and ecumenical consequences. If the birth of the church was the result of divergent theological streams working in a complementary fashion, then surely an openness to recurring currents coming from outside the tradition might offer subsequent replenishment for diminished religiosity. Only later would it become clear that imbibing divergent renewal currents could offer confusion as well as revitalization.

The authoritarian structure of Russian colony life presented the second issue important to the emergence and historical identity of the Mennonite Brethren. The appearance of the new group was part of a larger fracturing of the economic, educational, political, and religious control that had been practiced in these colonies. The repression experienced by the Mennonite Brethren group was common to various groups diverging from and challenging the established leadership. The degree to which the repression was highlighted as an important part of the story would influence the continuing relationships between the new group and the parent body. Insofar as the early historians found this hostility central, their histories had the net effect of widening the gap and imprinting a strong measure of inter-Mennonite hostility into the emerging MB consciousness.

The debate about the origins is more than historical speculation. The birthing process does provide a trajectory for the future. The origins of the Mennonite Brethren insured multiple and conflictual trajectories. It surely is the experience of all movements born in the modern world to be fated by pluralism. Yet the nature of the birth and the degree of integration achieved at the beginning does give a cast to the subsequent story. The history of North American political societies illustrates the imprint of the birthing process. Various commentators suggest that the United States was born out of a democratic revolution, and hence for at least the next hundred years the left generally triumphed in American politics. The left was the inheritor of the legacy of the founding fathers; they were the perpetrators of the original design. Canada, on the other hand, was born out of a counterrevolutionary movement. The forces of conservatism, of tradition, won out during the first hundred years. Those forces, stimulated in part by the refugees from the American Revolution, also made anti-American sentiments critical in the birthing process of Canadian identity. In the same way, it is plausible to suggest that the understandings of the MB birth substantially shaped the subsequent identity of the church.[7]

P. M. Friesen and J. A. Toews are the two premier historians of the Mennonite Brethren story. Friesen established the interpretative framework that was largely adopted by his successors. Toews fashioned a differing interpretation. Like others who wrote between 1911 and 1975, their interpretations of the beginnings became central to an understanding of the subsequent story and the appropriate role that the past could play for the church facing issues in their respective times. Both Friesen and Toews, as well as the intermediary historians, were trained in theology before coming to history. In each case their foremost contribution to fashioning a "theology" for the Mennonite Brethren was to render an interpretation of the past.[8]

I

One contemporary historian has suggested that Peter Martin Friesen's *Die Alt-Evangelische Mennonitische Brüdershaft in Russland (1789-1910)* belongs in the singular category of Anabaptist-Mennonite writings shared only by *The Chronicle of the Hutterian Brethren* and the *Martyrs' Mirror.*[9] They are the indispensable symbols of and guides to Anabaptist-Mennonite history. Friesen, like these other works, preserved the documentary material that permitted the subsequent telling of the story. The upheaval and destruction of Russian Mennonites in the twentieth century, all too reminiscent of the sixteenth century fate of Anabaptists and Hutterites, destroyed many of the records necessary to an understanding of the history. By publishing them in his massive history, Friesen preserved at least the rudiments necessary for historical reconstruction.

Friesen, born in the Ukraine in 1849, was educated in Switzerland, Odessa, and Moscow. From 1873 to 1886 he taught in the *Zentralschule* in Halbstadt. He spent most of the following years, till his death in 1914, in the non-Mennonite communities of Odessa, Sevastopol, and Moscow. Friesen joined the Mennonite Brethren Church in 1866 at age sixteen, was ordained as an MB minister in 1884, and subsequently became one of its leading theologians. He authored the 1902 MB Confession of Faith written in Russia. Although he was intimately involved in the Russian Mennonite world he was simultaneously on its boundary. His last twenty-eight years, lived largely in the context of other Russian peoples, helped to shape a perspective on his own smaller world. He brought to the writing of history the perspectives of both the insider and outsider, a viewpoint that was both separatist and ecumenical, laudatory and critical.[10]

Friesen's twenty-five-year effort to write the commemorative history of the Mennonite Brethren became much more. It became the definitive Russian interpretation of the entire northern European Mennonite story. Taking the events of 1860 as the centerpiece, it ranged back to Menno Simons and forward to 1910.

Friesen brought to his task a high degree of self-consciousness about the problem of constructing a written narrative and interpretation of his people. The expressive lament in the introduction suggests the degree to which selectivity is always a problem for the historian, and the way that is compounded when constructing the narrative for a small and conflictual group: "Emotions and historical conscience came into severe conflict. Time and again I listened to dozens of honorable men and women from the various factions and read and reread their documents--and a great sorrow overcame me! I could impossibly present loving old men of this or that faction in all their nakedness in a cold-blooded fashion during their lifetime, a nakedness of which they had themselves been unaware."[11]

For Friesen, the MB movement, while sharing a continuity with the larger Mennonite tradition, also clearly drew from new sources to fashion a necessary revitalization of Russian Mennonite society. He began with Menno and continued the Mennonite story from Holland through northern Europe, Prussia, and into South Russia. Yet "the good house of Menno had become practically desolate and empty and was about to collapse."[12] The history of "narrow interpretations, differences over small things, and numerous divisions"; the triumph of "externally 'correct doctrine' and morality" over "true faith and its inevitable fruits of sanctification in most hearts"; "rationalism" and "indifferentism" was now arrested by the "brotherhood" piety of the Moravian Brethren, evangelical Pietists, and Hernhutters.[13]

"Brotherhood" was a "warmhearted Christian fellowship, something that is now found in the M.B. Church as well as in all truly vital Christian circles...."[14] This "vital air and warmth, food and drink brought into the impoverished house" permitted the renewal of the tradition "according to the old plan, on the old foundation." Just as Mennonitism was both a "critique and complement of Lutheranism," so Pietism "in its wholesome essence has...a harmonious effect on Mennonitism." It was, in this interpretation, a necessary dialectic. During the Reformation, Lutheranism and Anabaptism had seemed mutually exclusive, but in the end they had formed "a whole when balanced in an apostolic arrangement." Together they had purified the "impoverished Christianity of the West." By implication this new union of Pietism and Mennonitism would purify not only the Russian Mennonite world, but extend itself far beyond those parochial boundaries.[15]

A second element in Friesen's temperament that shaped both his work and the subsequent understanding of MB history was his sympathy with the rights of religious dissenters, whether Jews, Mennonites, or Russian Stundists. In his later years he was an outspoken defender of the weak and oppressed, even to the point of endangering his own political freedom. He resisted any form of state intrusion into religious practice. He was concerned that the Mennonites clearly differentiate between civil and ecclesiastical authority.[16]

The intrusion of colony civic leadership into the religious questions and the attempt to deny legitimacy to the emerging MB group was precisely the kind of issue that engaged Friesen's sense of justice. The avoidance ban placed on MB members resulted in oppression, incarceration, floggings, impoverishment, and threats of banishment to Siberia. Family members suffered exclusion from other family members as households were divided against themselves.[17]

The Chortitza Area Administrative Office circular of February 28, 1862, was all too typical, in Friesen's mind, of the shortsightedness of the political leadership. Referring to the new converts, the memo declared:

Admonition and persuasion have no effect upon them, since they have become totally taken up with the idea that they are born again and consequently possess the Spirit of God, who makes no mistakes. Police authority must therefore be put to use to keep these dangerous people within bounds...the application of law enforcement by police may serve to bring these deluded people back to their senses. Should all of this prove fruitless and these people persist in their heresies, then they must, according to the law, be handed over to the higher authorities as harmful sectarians so that they might be banned from the colonies and sent into exile.[18]

Friesen would himself overcome the animosity of these early years. As he moved into the Alliance fellowship, he sought a more ecumenical posture that could heal the breaches of the past. His MB coreligionists, however, steeped in the conflict of the early years, maintained "a certain reluctance to acknowledge the good aspects, both old and new, in the Mennonite churches."[19] That reluctance, growing out of the circumstances and the interpretation of the early years, would remain a detriment far beyond 1911. Even to this day an unwillingness to acknowledge the good in the larger Mennonite fellowship remains in the recesses of the MB imagination.

II

The P. M. Friesen interpretations defined the North American Mennonite Brethren historical tradition for fifty years following the publication of his magisterial work in 1911. The first American history, Peter Regier's *Kurzgefasste Geschichte der Mennoniten Brüder-gemeinde*, was published in 1901 and predated Friesen by a decade. His history was more the publication of letters and documents surrounding the beginnings of the Mennonite Brethren than an interpretative narrative.

Regier, born in 1847 in Hierschau, Russia, migrated to America in 1876 and successively settled in Mountain Lake, Minnesota; Henderson, Nebraska; and Enid, Oklahoma. He was one of the founders of the Henderson MB congregation and became the presiding minister and elder of the Enid congregation. His pamphlet, published largely without commentary or citation, was designed to distribute more widely some of the sources surrounding the early years.[20]

The first serious interpretative work in North America belongs to John F. Harms. *Die Geschichte der Mennoniten Brüdergemeinde, 1860-1924* was commissioned as part of the sixty-fifth anniversary celebrations of the Mennonite Brethren Church. It appeared in 1924-25 as a series of installments in the *Zionsbote* and was then published in book form in 1925. P. C. Hiebert, secretary of the Jubilee Committee and author of the foreword, expressed the hope that the book would "awaken and nurture the unity and loyalty of the brotherhood."[21]

Harms was well suited to write a "unitive" interpretation. Born in Kleefeld, Russia, in 1855, he migrated to the United States in 1878. His subsequent career as a minister, itinerant preacher, educator, editor, and publisher took him to many parts of the fledgling and scattered MB churches across both Canada and the United States. The Mennonite Brethren, consisting of approximately 200 families among the 18,000 Russian Mennonites who immigrated during the 1870s and early 1880s, were located in communities from Minnesota to Kansas. Soon after this initial settlement they scattered south into Oklahoma, north into Canada, and by the turn of the century to Oregon, Washington, and California. Harms's own wanderings were illustrative of the unsettled quality of many Russian immigrant families. Between 1878 and 1921 he lived in Mountain Lake, Minnesota; Elkhart, Indiana; Naperville, Illinois; McPherson, Kansas; Medford, Oklahoma; Canada, Kansas; Hillsboro, Kansas, on several different occasions; Edmonton, Alberta; Herbert, Saskatchewan; Seattle, Washington; and Reedley, California. In most of the central states he was an editor and publisher of either the *Mennonitische Rundschau* or *Zionsbote*. In Canada and California he either farmed or pastored congregations.[22]

As resident in so many scattered communities and as editor of the churchly press that prominently featured reports from local communities, Harms brought to his task an intimate knowledge of the fifty-year MB sojourn in America. He also knew the frailty of small denominational groups living in widely divergent places and subject to the Americanization pressures of the 1920s. A history that would more closely bond the churches to each other was an appropriate aspiration for the sixty-five-year story.

The approach Harms utilized was to compile the reports submitted by local congregations to the *Zionsbote*. Together with a concluding section reporting on the work of various conference agencies, these local and institutional reports constituted 270 pages out of the 342 total. Sharing the stories of local congregations and communities scattered over half a continent was an important means of increasing the sense of unity.

His preface to these local glimpses was another means. The first seventy pages described the beginnings and early history of the church in Russia. Here Harms repeated the P. M. Friesen perspective. He began with the degenerating state of Russian Mennonite religiosity in the mid-nineteenth century and the infusion of vitality from Eduard Wuest. Any genetic connection to the entire Mennonite story was omitted. The MB Church of 1860, by this account, was born out of the Russian environment. Its continuity with earlier Mennonite concerns were not understood or were deemed insignificant. Readers hoping to understand the religious renaissance represented by the MB movement were implicitly encouraged to find the stimulus in external sources. That unity that P. C. Hiebert wished for could be nurtured by remembering the heroic struggles of the first generation. But the paradox of that unity being found amidst a diversity of new religious emphases was not reconciled.

The first English history, John H. Lohrenz's *The Mennonite Brethren Church*, was published in 1950 under the auspices of the Board of Foreign Missions of the MB conference. An English history of the church was clearly needed to meet the demands of a denomination where the U.S. churches had largely navigated the shift to the English language and the Canadians would follow suit in the next two decades.

Like Harms, Lohrenz came to the writing of history from other churchly vocations. Born in 1893 in North Dakota, he grew up in the Ebenfeld church near Hillsboro, Kansas. Graduating from Tabor Academy and College, he took a one-year master's degree program at Witmarsum Theological Seminary in Bluffton, Ohio. His thesis, "A History of the Mennonite Brethren Church of North America," became the basis for the 1950 publication. The thesis, predating Harms by more than six years, broke new ground in providing a narrative of the North American MB experience. Presumably written with the counsel of C. Henry Smith, it provided analysis of the migration of Mennonite peoples, described the beginnings of various institutions, and offered a more sociological set of descriptors than previous accounts.[23]

Lohrenz, in recounting the origins of the church in Russia and the relationship of the MB Church to the other Mennonites, relied almost exclusively upon P. M. Friesen's work and thus did not advance the understanding of the issues surrounding the origins. Between the writing of the 1918 thesis and the 1950 publication, the degeneracy of the Russian Mennonite world increased; the role of Eduard Wuest as the catalyst for the renewal stirrings and the animosity between the Mennonite groups intensified. By enlarging these perspectives Lohrenz perfected a denominational apology, but hardly addressed the identity needs of a denomination increasingly troubled about its Americanizing process.

III

Those identity needs surfaced at the 1951 sessions of the General Conference of the Mennonite Brethren meeting in Winkler, Manitoba. The Board of Reference and Counsel (the conference in interim) brought a lengthy document assessing the state of the church and the requirements to shape a future hospitable to the continuation of Mennonite Brethren distinctives. At issue were the "revolutionary changes" of the previous decades. Those changes reflected the cultural transition occurring among the Russian Mennonite immigrants of the 1870s and 1920s. For the first years of their settlement in Canada and the United States, the interaction with the host society was bounded by the isolation of the rural village, ethnic seclusion, cultural traditionalism, and a distinctive language. By the 1940s and 1950s the cumulative impact of the North American experience was obvious. The pressures for conformity during two world wars, the reality of cultural pluralism, and the easy trafficking with other religious traditions now threatened the continuing unity and coherence of Mennonite Brethren people.[24]

By the 1950s Mennonite Brethren, particularly in the United States, were full participants in the political and commercial life of many small towns. They were increasingly active in community affairs. Election to city councils, school boards, and county administrative positions were common. Other Mennonite Brethren were drawn to civic clubs, service clubs, and institutional auxiliary associations. The ease of association is also suggested at the same 1951 conference by a report noting that people working in the church had received training at Lutheran, Baptist, Pentecostal, Presbyterian, and interdenominational schools. Between the early 1940s and 1950 twelve MB graduates from Central Baptist Seminary alone moved into pastorates.[25]

The Board of Reference and Counsel issued a series of proposals to deal with the fracturing theological and cultural identity of the conference. Among the suggestions for recentering the denomination was the recognition of the need for a new history. What was needed was not another retelling of the same story, but a different angle of vision for interpreting the story, an angle that might utilize the past to refashion the present and future. It was the search for a usable past. Lohrenz had just recently provided a past. A. H. Unruh's *Die Geschichte der Mennoniten-Brüdergemeinde, 1860-1954*, published in 1954, was the immediate response to the 1951 need. But its impact was limited, since it was mostly a reprinting of sections from P. M. Friesen and John F. Harms. By 1954 both Friesen and Harms were out of print, and another version was needed for the German Bible schools in Canada. But neither the Lohrenz nor Unruh volume told the story in a way that provided the necessary connectors to arrest the fraying identity of the denomination.

That task was left undone until John A. Toews's history in 1975. The introduction to his volume made explicit the relationship of the new history to the needs of the church. Editor A. J. Klassen wrote, "The need for an up-to-date history was born in the crisis of the search for identity that has become so apparent in the life of the church during the last decade or two."[26] Toews himself was concerned for several decades with the identity of the church. His most explicit warning began with the assertion that the "Mennonite Brethren are experiencing an identity crisis unprecedented in their history." It was a position echoed by others.

For Toews the precarious identity was the consequence of three factors: first were the pluralistic influences and the unresolved and conflictual trajectory since 1860. The historic pluralism had been reinforced by a continuing indiscriminate "exposure to every wind of doctrine from various theological schools of thought." Second was the polarization between the "left wing" and "right wing." Toews differentiated between those favoring relief and service, and those interested only in missions--between those who would align with the National Association of Evangelicals, the Billy Graham Evangelistic Association, and Campus Crusade, and those whose allegiances ran to inter-Mennonite alliances. Third was a lack of historic self-consciousness: "In our circles there is a woeful ignorance with respect to our past history, as Mennonite Brethren and as a part of the larger Anabaptist movement. Our emphasis on 'existential Christianity' is cutting us off from our historic roots. Such willful ignorance and deliberate rejection of our past leads to spiritual impoverishment and complete loss of identity."[27]

Toews was convinced that the necessary corrective to this identity confusion was a rediscovery of the Anabaptist roots of the church and closer relationships with other Mennonite groups. Insofar as the Mennonite Brethren could reclaim the Mennonite part of their story, they might be able to both recenter themselves and reposition the church for more effective work and witness. Toews, in articulating this "recovery" theme, was both a leading voice and a collaborator with others who in the 1960s and 1970s defined the needs of the church in similar fashion.[28]

Toews was an immigrant of the 1920s. Born in Rückenau, Russia, in 1912, he attended the *Zentralschule* in Alexanderkrone before migrating to Alberta in 1927. His educational training began in Canada at Coaldale Bible School and continued at Tabor College. His tenure at Tabor coincided with the few years that Cornelius Krahn taught Mennonite history at Tabor. In 1950 he completed a graduate degree in divinity at United College in Winnipeg. His thesis topic, "The Anabaptist Concept of the Church," showed his inclination to the themes of the broader Mennonite story. His subsequent 1964 Ph.D. dissertation at the University of Minnesota, "Sebastian Franck: Friend and Critic of Early Anabaptism," confirmed his approach to Mennonite Brethren history. Much of his remaining scholarly work in history would be devoted to understanding the specific MB experience as part of the larger Anabaptist-Mennonite story.[29]

In coming to nineteenth- and twentieth-century Mennonite history from this background in sixteenth-century Anabaptist scholarship, Toews's *A History of the Mennonite Brethren Church: Pilgrims and Pioneers* was able to reassess the relationship between the renewal moves in Russia and those of the sixteenth century. He was also the first historian to bring professional training to the writing of the denominational story.

Working in Winnipeg, the intellectual center of the 1920s Russian Mennonite Brethren immigrants, John A. Toews participated in an environment that nourished greater Mennonite historical and ecumenical understandings than was the case for the Mennonite Brethren in the United States. The difficult aftermath of the Russian Revolution had helped to transcend the distance of 1860. Mennonites of all kinds could ill afford to separate themselves from each other amidst the survival pressures of the post-Revolution period. Mennonite Brethren in the States, bereft of any such moment to heal the breach, continued their aloofness towards both Mennonite history and inter-Mennonite relationships.

Nonetheless, a reclamation of Mennonite history and identity did take place among the U.S. Mennonite Brethren, albeit from an unexpected source. That Pacific Bible Institute and the Mennonite Brethren Biblical Seminary would become a catalyst for the recovery of Mennonite history and relationships was paradoxical indeed. The 1944 opening of Pacific Bible Institute (PBI) showed fundamentalist influences.[30] When the Mennonite Brethren Biblical Seminary opened in 1955, it was a miniature Dallas Theological Seminary. Indiscriminate theological borrowing permitted both institutions to begin with little self-conscious Anabaptist-Mennonite reflection.

That was to change in the early and mid-1960s when Arthur J. Wiebe became president of PBI in 1960 and transformed it into a liberal arts college instead of a Bible school. He recruited a young faculty, for the most part still pursuing graduate degrees. Among them was Peter J. Klassen, having recently earned his doctorate in Radical Reformation studies. His coming to the college in 1962 was the first time since Cornelius Krahn had left Tabor College in 1945 that an MB school in the United States had a faculty member trained in Anabaptist-Mennonite history. Other young faculty members--Dalton Reimer, John E. Toews, John H. Redekop--participated in the Mennonite graduate student network and were familiar with the Goshen school of scholarship. Henry Krahn, also a Reformation scholar, joined the faculty in 1967. The determination to give the fledgling college an Anabaptist cast resulted in "The Pacific College Idea," a remarkable institutional mission statement. College buildings carried names--Sattler, Marpeck, Witmarsum, Strasbourg--previously unknown to the MB religious lexicon. Largely because of Klassen's initiative, in the early 1960s both the West Coast Mennonite Brethren Historical Society and a Mennonite historical library were established.[31]

The refashioning of the Mennonite Brethren Biblical Seminary from a fundamentalist to an Anabaptist institution began in 1964 with the ascension of J. B. Toews to the presidency. Toews was Russian-born, younger than, but nevertheless a close associate to, the previous-generation leaders like A. H. Unruh, B. B. Janz, H. W. Lohrenz, and P. C. Hiebert, who mediated more of the Mennonite past than many of Toews's contemporaries. A document prepared in 1964--"A Mennonite Brethren Seminary"--committed the school to a clear Anabaptist orientation: "The Seminary holds to the Anabaptist view of the church.... The Seminary is committed to teach, live and exemplify the life of the true New Testament Church."[32]

Within the first four years of Toews's presidency there was an almost complete turnover in the seminary faculty. The first addition, A. J. Klassen, had been a student of H. S. Bender and was a graduate of Goshen Biblical Seminary. As academic dean from 1968 to 1974, he was instrumental in reshaping the curriculum to reflect Mennonite theological concerns. Courses in Anabaptist theology were introduced as requirements.[33]

During the first decade of reorientation, the new seminary faculty became involved in varied activities that both moved the denomination towards a reconsideration of its Anabaptist roots and became directly interrelated with the writing of the J. A. Toews history. The 1965 establishment of a General Conference Board of Christian Literature (BCL) and the establishment of the Historical Commission (1969), while done under the auspices of the conference, were initiated and energized by the new seminary faculty. A. J. Klassen and Elmer A. Martens (who joined the seminary faculty in 1969) provided the leadership for the Board of Christian Literature. The first publication of the new board, *The Church in Mission* (1967), edited by Klassen, sought to understand the MB mission impulse within the context of the "Anabaptist vision of discipleship and mission in the life of the church."[34] At the 1969 triennial conference the BCL received authorization to proceed with a two-volume history of missions, a new history of the MB Church, a series of biographical pamphlets, and the establishment of a commission to work with the BCL in "coordinating the work of historical research, establishing archives, gathering oral materials...on a conference-wide basis."[35] It was the most far-reaching set of commitments to nurturing memory ever made by an MB conference.

The work of the Historical Commission became particularly significant during the decade of the 1970s. Charged with preserving the historical materials of the denomination and "revitalizing the historical consciousness," it moved under the energetic leadership of J. B. Toews, the former seminary president. Archival and research centers were established as affiliates of the denominational schools in Winnipeg, Fresno, and Hillsboro, Kansas. These Centers for Mennonite Brethren Studies began the systematic locating, gathering, and classifying of archival materials.[36]

The 1978 publication of the English translation of P. M. Friesen's monumental work was a joint project by the Board of Christian Literature and the Historical Commission. Its availability became a popular symbol of the growing hunger for memory among Mennonite Brethren. It was both a history of the Russian past and a tangible artifact whose presence seemed to link people into the past.

It was in the early stage of this renewed climate of MB historical activism that J. A. Toews began working towards his 1975 history of the Mennonite Brethren. He spent the 1971-72 academic year in research at the seminary in Fresno, where his presence symbolized the collaboration that had emerged between Winnipeg and Fresno. His salary was funded through the joint efforts of the seminary, the Board of Christian Literature, and the Historical Commission.

Toews completely understood that the moment required more than an update of the past histories. In "The Story behind the History" he explicitly identified both the needs of his people and the temperament he brought to the task. Invoking Eugene Rice, he observed that "historical writing is in constant flux because historians ask their sources questions newly shaped by changing social and cultural needs."[37] Those changing needs required a reassessment of the role of Anabaptism in the 1860 renewal movement and the possibility for using the past to alter the MB aloofness from the Mennonite family.

Toews found the inspiration for the reform movements in mid-nineteenth-century Russia in the Anabaptist-Mennonite story. Chapter 1, "Spiritual Heirs of the Early Anabaptists," suggested the genetic connections. The search for an authentic witness of freely chosen and disciplined religious commitments was at the center of the story. The awakenings in the Russian Mennonite church during the nineteenth century were to be understood as attempts to regain something of the original impulse now muted by the paradoxes of time and isolation. The emergence of the *Kleine Gemeinde* in 1812; the religious ferment at Ohrloff and Gnadenfeld in the midcentury decades; the organization of the *Vereinsschule, Missionsstunden,* and *Leseverein*; the impact of Eduard Wuest in the 1840s and 1850s; and the secession of the Mennonite Brethren in 1860 were all pieces in the same movement of revitalization. These stirrings were responses to the paradox of a believers' church having succumbed, because of its history of spatial isolation, to a "parish" church system. The renewal movements, in seeking to recover the high degree of personal religiosity incumbent in the believers' church story, were reenacting the dynamic of the sixteenth century.[38]

For Toews the impact of the external inspirations were important, "but in their confessional documents the early Brethren repeatedly identify with the teachings of Menno Simons." He would readily invoke the quotable lines of Cornelius Krahn: "This renewal did not want to be Pietistic, nor Baptist, but rather Mennonite. It wanted to be and remain historical, consistent Mennonitism, a pure Mennonitism that was based not upon birth, but upon rebirth."[39] Precisely because the renewal grew out of the historic tradition, it was able to flavor the entire Mennonite community. Earlier apologists who had limited the search for "new life" to those joining the Brethren were provincial in their understandings. This reading of the wider influence of the reform movement also suggested the need for greater MB generosity towards the existing church in Russia: "the charges made by the Brethren in the Document of Secession were too sweeping and too severe."[40]

The relationship between Pietism and Anabaptism, so balanced and nurturing to P. M. Friesen, seemed different to Toews. He was impressed, not by complementarity, but by the distance between the two. If Pietism had "revived the early Anabaptist emphasis on personal faith and commitment," it simultaneously was deficient in its "concept of *ecclesiola in ecclesia*." Its place in the Russian Mennonite world was not among those recovering the concept of the believers' church. Rather, "the believers who remained in the old church were probably more in conformity with pietistic tradition than those who seceded."[41]

The J. A. Toews interpretation together with the renaissance in historical activity and the recovery of memory in the MB imagination provided new ways of interpreting the past and facing the future. While recognizing the plurality of theological influences present at the MB creation in 1860, Toews provided a different and more definitive answer to the MB debate about their ideological parentage. The year 1860 saw the rebirth of Anabaptism. The taproot of the MB Church was to be found in the convictions of Conrad Grebel and Menno Simons rather than Eduard Wuest. The rediscovery of a beginning nourished by Mennonite traditions encouraged a more self-conscious embrace of the Anabaptist tradition.

Confirmation for this analysis of the relationship between the early MB leaders and the Anabaptists came in Cornelius J. Dyck's important essay "1525 Revisited? A Comparison of Anabaptist and Mennonite Brethren Origins," delivered at a Symposium on Mennonite Brethren History held in Fresno in May 1975 to celebrate the publication of Toews's *A History of the Mennonite Brethren Church*. It suggested the importance of the restitutionist theme for 1525, 1526, and 1860. The renewal movements in nineteenth-century Russia, bereft of substantial formal knowledge of the sixteenth-century, were nevertheless the bearers of similar aspirations. The center of Dyck's paper was to suggest the numerous parallels between the Swiss Brethren, the early Dutch Anabaptists, and the impulses of the early MB movement. The obvious presence of the Pietist and Baptist influences had not smothered the replication of emphases historic to the Anabaptist and Mennonite traditions.[42]

IV

The MB historical activism of the 1960s and 1970s is reminiscent of the "Anabaptist recovery" that took place in the Mennonite Church under the leadership of Harold S. Bender and associates.[43] Bender also came to history because of the identity needs of his people. History became a way to navigate between the tensions introduced by fundamentalist and liberal controversies and the changes required of a people undergoing accelerating social change. For the Mennonite Church, history became a way to fix an ideological center precisely when the spatial and cultural identity markers of the past were giving way.

The Mennonite Brethren historical renaissance, beginning four decades later, came to a people more urbanized, occupationally diversified, and theologically fractured than the Mennonite Church of the 1920s. The pluralism of most religious groups has increased geometrically during the twentieth century. Memory, tradition, and history are casualties of accelerating informational, ideational, and cultural change. The scholarly milieu is also different. Bender could provide a more singular interpretation for his people. There was a purity of religious idealism to his Swiss Brethren. The scholarship on the nineteenth-century Russian Mennonite world recognizes the plurality of forces at work. The dynamism and the conflictual aspirations, now understood as part of the 1860 movement, mitigate against the heroic quality that an earlier generation could impart to its founders.

Even so, Toews and the other scholars active in this renaissance refashioned the past, and enabled a different future. By linking the MB story more closely to the cultural nonconforming themes of Anabaptism, they nourished the historic continuity of a denomination increasingly tempted with cultural assimilation; by reaffirming the ethical imperatives of Anabaptism, they provided renewal for service and benevolence in a denomination increasingly tempted by the adequacy of verbal witness; and by their more ecumenical history, they nurtured a growing participation in the associational networks that link together Mennonite peoples. The historical renaissance in the Mennonite Church provided for the recentering of that denomination. Whether the rediscovery of the Anabaptist past will do the same for the Mennonite Brethren remains unclear.

NOTES

1. Peter M. Friesen, *The Mennonite Brotherhood in Russia (1789-1910)*, J. B. Toews, Abraham Friesen, Peter J. Klassen, and Harry Loewen, Translation and Editorial Committee (Fresno, Calif.: Board of Christian Literature, General Conference of Mennonite Brethren Churches, 1978), xxvii.

2. John A. Toews, *A History of the Mennonite Brethren Church: Pilgrims and Pioneers*, ed. A. J. Klassen (Fresno, Calif.: Board of Christian Literature, General Conference of Mennonite Brethren Churches, 1975).

3. See David G. Rempel, "The Mennonite Colonies in New Russia: A Study of their Settlement and Economic Development from 1789-1914" (Ph.D. diss., Stanford University, 1933); and "The Mennonite Commonwealth in Russia: A Sketch of its Founding and Endurance, 1789-1919," *MQR* 47 (1973), 259-308; and 48 (1974), 5-54. Among the many writings of John B. Toews, see "The Russian Mennonite Intellect of the Nineteenth Century," *MQR* 53 (1979), 137-159; *Czars, Soviets and Mennonites* (Newton, Kans.: Faith and Life Press, 1982); and *Perilous Journey: The Mennonite Brethren in Russia, 1860-1910* (Hillsboro, Kans.: Kindred Press, 1988). Contributions from James Urry include *None but Saints: The Transformation of Mennonite Life in Russia, 1789-1889* (Winnipeg: McPherson Press United, 1989); "The Social Background to the Emergence of the Mennonite Brethren in Nineteenth Century Russia," *Journal of Mennonite Studies* 6 (1988), 8-35; and "Through the Eye of the Needle: Wealth and the Mennonite Experience in Imperial Russia," *Journal of Mennonite Studies* 3 (1985), 7-35. Harvey L. Dyck analyzes the changes in "Russian Mennonitism and the Challenge of Russian Nationalism, 1889," *MQR* 52 (1982), 307-341; and "Russian Servitor and Mennonite Hero: Light and Shadow in Images of Johann Cornies," *Journal of Mennonite Studies* 2 (1984), 9-28.

4. See Frank C. Peters, "The Early Mennonite Brethren Church: Baptist or Anabaptist?" *Mennonite Life* 25 (1959), 176-178, and Victor Adrian, "Born of Anabaptism and Pietism," *Mennonite Brethren Herald*, March 26, 1965, special insert.

5. John F. Harms, *Geschichte der Mennoniten Brüdergemeinde* (Hillsboro, Kans.: Mennonite Brethren Publishing House, 1925); John H. Lohrenz, *The Mennonite Brethren Church* (Hillsboro, Kans.: Board of Foreign Missions of the General Conference of the Mennonite Brethren Churches of North America, 1950); A. H. Unruh, *Die Geschichte der Mennoniten-Brüdergemeinde, 1860-1954* (Hillsboro, Kans.: General Conference of the Mennonite Brethren Church of North America, 1955); Peter Regier, *Kurzgefasste Geschichte der Mennoniten Brüder-Gemeinde* (Berne, Ind.: Light and Hope Publishing Company, 1901).

6. For insight into the issues surrounding 1860, see Peter J. Klassen, "The Historiography of the Birth of the Mennonite Brethren Church: An Introduction," in *P. M. Friesen and His History: Understanding Mennonite Brethren Beginnings*, ed. Abraham Friesen (Fresno, Calif.: Center for Mennonite Brethren Studies, 1979), 115-127.

7. See Seymour Martin Lipset, *The First New Nation: The United States in Historical and Comparative Perspective* (New York: Basic Books, 1963); Carl Berger, ed., *Approaches to Canadian History* (Toronto: University of Toronto Press, 1967); and Louis Hartz et al., *The Founding of New Societies: Studies in the History of the United States, Latin America, South Africa, Canada and Australia* (New York: Harcourt, Brace, Jovanovich, 1969).

8. Rodney Sawatsky traces the role of history in the formation of Mennonite identity and the close relationship between historical writing and theologizing. "History and Ideology:

American Mennonite Identity Definition through History" (Ph.D. diss., Princeton University, 1977).

9. *P. M. Friesen and His History*, vii.

10. For biographical detail, see Franz C. Thiessen, *P. M. Friesen, 1849-1914: Personal Recollections* (Fresno, Calif.: Board of Christian Literature, General Conference of Mennonite Brethren Churches, 1974); "Peter Martin Friesen," *ME* II, 405.

11. Friesen, *Mennonite Brotherhood*, xxix.

12. *Ibid.*, 212.

13. *Ibid.*, 212-213.

14. *Ibid.*, 97.

15. *Ibid.*, 212.

16. Thiessen, *P. M. Friesen.*

17. Friesen, *Mennonite Brotherhood*, 244-262.

18. *Ibid.*, 312-313.

19. *Ibid.*, 977.

20. For biographical details, see Lohrenz, *The Mennonite Brethren Church*, 317.

21. P. C. Hiebert, "Forward," in Harms, *Geschichte der Mennoniten Brüdergemeinde*, iii.

22. Lohrenz provides the estimate of Mennonite Brethren immigrants. *The Mennonite Brethren Church*, 64. See also Orlando Harms, *Pioneer Publishers: The Life and Times of John F. Harms* (Hillsboro, Kans.: Kindred Press, 1984).

23. John H. Lohrenz, "History of the Mennonite Brethren Church of North America" (M.A. thesis, Bluffton College, 1919). For biographical information, see Mrs. John H. Lohrenz, "John H. Lohrenz: A Missionary Educator" (privately mimeographed, n.d.); and John H. Lohrenz, *A Life for Christ in India: Mrs. Maria Lohrenz, 1892-1962* (Hillsboro, Kans.: Board of Missions, General Conference of the Mennonite Brethren Church, 1963).

24. *Yearbook of the 45th General Conference of the Mennonite Brethren Church of North America* (Winkler, Man., 1951), 124-144.

25. Paul Toews explores more fully some of these transitions. "Faith in Culture and Culture in Faith: The Mennonite Brethren in North America," *Journal of Mennonite Studies* 6 (1988), 36-50.

26. Toews, *A History of the Mennonite Brethren Church*, vii.

27. John A. Toews, "In Search of Identity," *Mennonite Brethren Herald*, Mar. 10, 1975, pp. 2-4, 25; reprinted in *People of the Way: Selected Essays and Addresses by John A. Toews*, ed. Abe J. Dueck, Herbert Giesbrecht, and Allen R. Guenther (Winnipeg, Man.: Historical Committee, Canadian Conference of Mennonite Brethren Churches, 1981).

28. *Ibid.*, 114.

29. John A. Toews, "The Anabaptist Concept of the Church" (B.D. thesis, United College, 1950); John A. Toews, "Sebastian Franck: Friend and Critic of Early Anabaptism" (Ph.D. diss., University of Minnesota, 1964).

30. The background to the emergence of PBI is explored in Paul Toews, "A Shelter in a Time of Storm': The Establishment of Schools in the Pacific District," in *75 Years of Fellowship: Pacific District Conference of the Mennonite Brethren Churches, 1912-1987*, ed. Esther Jost (Fresno, Calif.: Pacific District Conference of the Mennonite Brethren Churches, 1987).

31. This transition at the college is explored more fully in an unpublished essay, "From Pietism to Secularism via Anabaptism: An Informal History of Fresno Pacific College and Its Changing Relationship to the Pacific District Conference," 1985.

32. A. J. Klassen, ed., *The Seminary Story: Twenty Years of Education in Ministry, 1955-75* (Fresno, Calif.: Mennonite Brethren Biblical Seminary, 1975), 21-22.

33. *Ibid.*, 25-34.

34. *Yearbook of the General Conference of the Mennonite Brethren Church of North America* (Reedley, Calif., 1972), 94-100.

35. *Ibid.*

36. *Ibid.*

37. Rice was quoted from Mortimer Chambers, *The Western Experience* (New York: Knopf, 1974), xvi, in John A. Toews, "The Story behind the History," *Mennonite Brethren Herald*, Apr. 4, 1975, p. 1; also reprinted in *People of the Way*.

38. Toews, *A History of the Mennonite Brethren Church*, chaps. 1-3. On the paradoxical transition in Russia from a believers' to a parish church, see Robert Kreider, "The Anabaptist Conception of the Church in the Russian Mennonite Environment, 1789-1870," *MQR* 25 (1951), 17-33.

39. Toews, "The Story behind the History," 122. Krahn is quoted from "Some Social Attitudes of the Mennonites of Russia," *MQR* 9 (1935), 173.

40. Toews, "The Story behind the History," 117.

41. *Ibid.*, 122.

42. Cornelius J. Dyck, "1525 Revisited? A Comparision of Anabaptist and Mennonite Brethren Origins," in *Pilgrims and Strangers: Essays in Mennonite Brethren History*, ed. Paul Toews (Fresno, Calif.: Center for Mennonite Brethren Studies, 1977), 55-77.

43. Harold S. Bender, "The Anabaptist Vision," *MQR* 18 (1944), 67-88.

CHAPTER 11

THE "FREE CHURCH?": A TIME WHOSE IDEA HAS NOT COME

Paul Peachey

Fritz Blanke, church historian at the University of Zurich in the early 1950s, defined sixteenth-century Anabaptism as the first modern "free church." The concept of the free church, of course, was formulated in contrast to the state and folk Christianity that had prevailed in Europe for more than a millennium. Reviewing the price paid by the radical reformers for abandoning that tradition, Blanke ended his Anabaptist research seminar with the comment, "Their only error was that, historically speaking, they embraced the free church prematurely." The unspoken implications: first, the radical proposition was valid; and second, though premature then, the "free church" was destined nonetheless to be the wave of the future.

In this essay I offer some reflections on Blanke's free church thesis. These reflections, however, will be my own, and thus are not intended as speculations as to what may have been in my esteemed teacher's mind. For the purpose of this essay I accept the notion of sixteenth-century prematurity as a descriptive tool; that is, the sixteenth-century was not ready to listen to the "free church" project, and thus all but crushed it. Our own century, to the contrary, is cupping its ears, but, I shall argue, the churches, now free, are stuttering.

In part the mission of the "free church" has been realized, and this fact alone can give rise to uncertainty. Church and state have been separated, Christianity has been disestablished, states have become "secular," and freedom of religion has come to be recognized as a basic human right. In any event, the ecclesiological idioms available in the religious marketplace are mostly establishment and sectarian vestiges from the past, and these have relatively little to offer to this age. The task of this essay is to critique these idioms, and then to address our current situation. It will be necessary thus to recall rapidly some salient though familiar facets of salvation history.

Biblical Faith as an Aporia
Biblical faith, beginning with the call of Abraham and climaxing in the (New Testament) age of the Spirit, entails a conundrum, perhaps in the end an

aporia, a set of contradictions for which there is no logical solution. On the one hand, Old Testament people encountered God in a qualitatively new mode, and with this came a new definition of humanity. At the same time, however, this Creator God, Yahweh, disclosed himself through a specially chosen people, the Israelites, and eventually through Jesus and his followers, the Christians. Something had gone wrong--the "Fall," "original sin," or whatever--so that action, supplementary to the creation covenant, became necessary.

Thereafter things seem to move on two tracks, one for all humanity, the other for the chosen people (Hebrews, later Christians). There seem to be two orders, one of creation, the other of salvation, one of nature, the other of grace. The chosen people, however, move on both tracks, and matters become rather complicated in all directions. At times the chosen people appear as the center or end of all things, and thus as recipients of special blessing. At other times, however, and fundamentally, they appear as means to a larger end, the salvation of all humanity. They are called apart, with a special identity but only as a means to a larger end, an end beyond themselves. They are constituted an "eschatological" community, rooted in a reality beyond time and space. They are yeast destined to "leaven" the entire "lump" of all humanity. Two impulses, one centripetal, the other centrifugal, stand in unrelieved tension, always shifting in the flux of history, never at rest.

We thus face a series of quandaries. How are the sociabilities of "nature" and of "grace" related among the people of the covenant? How are the covenantally chosen people related to the rest of humankind? And growing from these two questions, how is an eschatological community, a manifestation of a kingdom that "is not of this world" (John 18:36), to express itself historically? Thus far, over the course of more than three millennia of "salvation" history, this problem has been manifest as an aporia. A faith community that is merely "spiritual" possesses no reality. A faith community, organized historically, as other groups are organized, perpetually tends to debase itself. This aporia is the subject of the present essay.

Israel and Christendom

The problem arises with the Israelite exodus, the Sinai covenant, and the formation of the nation Israel. The interplay of theocratic vision and primitive (elementary) tribalism in the emerging Israelite social organization is not readily decipherable. Did the covenant in fact contain a blueprint for decentralized self-sufficiency without a central state? Was the monarchy simply the result of the lack of faith or a loss of nerve? Or did the subsequent assimilation of the royal motif in the figure of the Messiah imply a more positive dimension as well? Whatever the answer, we know that the uniquely Hebrew prophetic tradition emerged in juxtaposition to the monarchy (monarchies). The covenant became an ellipse with two foci: the royal institutions, with their corrupting tragedy of power, in ever-heightening tension with the prophet-championed theocratic vision. There are cycles of apostasy and partial repentance, but the general direction is down, leading eventually to the captivity and collapse of the monarchy. In the end, only Diaspora remains, a phenomenon to which I will return.

Remarkably enough, a parallel mutation occurred in early Christianity, specifically in the fourth century, when the new faith was first recognized and tolerated by the Roman Empire (Constantine) and then late in the same century was made the exclusive state religion (Theodosius). This mutation, however, was not limited to the empire. From Armenia and Georgia in the East to Britain in the West, Christianity "triumphed" in nation after nation as princes embraced the faith and harnessed its energies to state-building. A mutation of this sort, moreover, has not been limited to Judaism and Christianity. Other "founded" religions,[1] notably Islam and Buddhism, have been similarly employed. It may also be noted in passing that in modern times Christian missions have gained hearing mostly where other "founded" religions have not entered previously.

Here, then, an acute question arises. What does it signify that historically Christianity has been a civilizing energy, that it has afforded the spiritual resources for state- and society-building? Roland Bainton, in effect, addresses our above aporia when he distinguishes the two methods by which the Christian faith can be (has been) promulgated. One is "the way of individual conversion with a goodly period of instruction prior to baptism.... The disadvantage of this method is that the Christian converts in a pagan culture become, by reason of their change in faith, deracinated from their own culture and compelled to move into an alien conclave. The other method is mass conversion, and it was this method which converted Europe. Kings like Clovis (early 6th century) embraced the faith." The disadvantage of this method was that it "entailed the paganizing of Christianity."[2] The former method, Bainton observes, was characteristic of the nineteenth-century Protestant missionary movement.

George Mendenhall, an Old Testament scholar, notes the parallel between the rise of the Israelite monarchy and the Constantinian turning point in Christianity. Describing King David as the "Old Testament Constantine," he extends the canvass to include a similar mutation of the original message of Zarathustra by the later Achaemenids (7th, 6th centuries, B.C.). He writes, "All three cases are entirely analogous, illustrating (to put it as provocatively as possible) *the dissolution of religion into politics.* At the same time, the basis of solidarity was no longer the covenant, but the myth of descent from a common ancestor."[3]

More than politics was involved, or rather, this "dissolution" itself was a multidimensional process. Apparently princes espoused the founded religion when it demonstrated sufficient power to appear politically useful. On the other hand, in both the Israelite and the Christian instance, the faithful had "good" reason to accept a political embodiment of the faith. The Israelites thought they needed a king to enable them to cope with surrounding hostile powers. Christians, for their part, had suffered under persecution. A reversal of imperial policy was understandably welcome.

These externally triggered anxieties, however, had deeper roots as well.

Though our common human life is materially rooted and determined, our very humanity consists in our capacity and vocation to transcend those determinisms in thought, in choice and action. We construct tools, buildings, and spaceships first in our minds, and then translate our mental pictures into material constructs. Similarly our perception-based actions give rise to the social cultural order that shapes our existence.[4] But we also visualize possibilities and realities that cannot be thus materialized. We espouse visions and ideals that spur us forward even when they are not directly attainable. Religious faith pertains to the unseen, the "otherworldly"; and the faith experience is profoundly personal, never fully communicable. But religious prehensions are mediated and validated intersubjectively, and this brings them into the world of symbolic culture.

By their very nature, however, religious prehensions are highly precarious. Unexpressed or unembodied, they tend to evaporate. Once culturally embodied, however, they are exposed to other energies and readily assume a life of their own. In any event, authentic "otherworldly" quests have profound "this-worldly" consequences. Christian monasticism, for example, is an example of withdrawal and otherworldliness. At its best it has profoundly impacted events in the world. On the other hand, monasticism has often been corrupted by the very historical processes which it set in motion. This, in the end, may be the root problem. Both the Hebrew and the Christian prophetic visions were so powerful that in effect they generated entire civilizations. Once institutionalized, however, and subjected to the vitalities of nature, they assumed a life of their own, thereby losing contact with the originating vision. It was as if the burning bush which Moses saw was in fact consumed.

If the emergence of Christendom may be viewed as analogous to the rise of the Hebrew monarchy, the rise of Christian monasticism and of medieval sects, by the same token, may be seen as analogous to the rise of Hebrew prophecy. Just as there were false prophets, there were monastic and sectarian perversions. Similarly instructive parallels can be drawn between the decline of the Hebrew monarchies and the decline of Christendom, though these parallels may be less direct. More particularly, the resulting Jewish dispersion (Diaspora), as we shall see, has ecclesiological significance.

Ancient Israel and medieval Christendom both succumbed to the illusion that their respective covenants could be, and in fact were, historically embodied and secured. In the former instance the cult and the temple seemed to make this explicit. The subsequent establishment of the monarchy reinforced this notion. Nonetheless, from the outset these material embodiments tended to suborn the covenant. With advancing apostasy, tension between the prophetic vision and both cult and monarchy mounted. Finally the full truth dawned. The word of the Lord came to the prophet, "For I desire steadfast love and not sacrifice, the knowledge of God, rather than burnt offerings" (Hos. 6:6). Once the prophetic vision climaxes in Jesus, the veil in the temple is rent, and all doubt is removed (Mark 15:38). The kingdom is simply not of this world (John 18:36). On the material plane it employs neither altar nor throne! Altar and throne were provisional didactic measures, leading to Christ (Gal. 3:24). Not

Moses (though he, too, had his prophetic side), but Abraham is the prototypical figure!

Given the historical and cultural context of ancient Israel, and the vulnerability of its tribal polity to surrounding military intrigue, the materialization of the covenant in Hebrew history is at least understandable. But how, without fundamentally misreading the gospel, does one get to imperial Christianity, whether of the Roman or of the Byzantine variety? The path traveled was doubtless complex and cannot be pursued here. Obviously the same human impulses and needs asserted themselves in both instances, the Hebrew and the Christian. Political rule and religious establishment would reduce the insecurities and risks inherent in faith. But there were important differences as well. Whereas the Hebrew state was organized from within the faith community, in the Christian case the state came from the outside. While for that reason one might view the fourth-century establishment of Christianity as the rape of the church by the empire, church life had already become diluted by that time. In the ensuing era many churchmen were only too ready to invoke imperial power in support of their cause.

Less than a century after embracing Christianity, however, the empire, inwardly decadent, collapsed under invasions from the North (476 CE). For more than a millennium thereafter, the notion of empire as a spiritual entity was to haunt European rulers, as one after the other vainly pursued the imperial purple. The problem was to surmount a chaotic tribalism with wider, more stable political configurations. Christendom, the civilization that arose thereby, was a dazzling, though ruthless, achievement. Meanwhile, the struggle to surmount intertribal chaos and conflict that dominated Europe during the Middle Ages has gone worldwide, and in our era is far from resolution. The brutality of society- and state-building processes, of course, is not to be blamed directly on Judaism or Christianity, or for that matter, on any of the founded religions that energized the building of civilization. The scandal is rather that these religions all have been prostituted in the process.

Reformation: Freeing the Church?

The medieval vision of a universal church, united under one head, admittedly has enormous aesthetic appeal. But it rested on premises, both at the point of departure and of subsequent development, that are far from explicit in the Gospels. Moreover, historical evidence, both in the biblical era and since, speaks against such a project. But if not by such organizational and hierarchical means, how is the covenant or faith community to become historically real and manifest?

This question arose acutely in the Protestant Reformation. The "magisterial reformers,"[5] for their part, presupposed the unity of the church universal as they embarked on their journey. Luther in particular remained thoroughly medieval in his mystical conception of human unity, a conception later known as the *corpus christianum*. He, and others like him, wished to reform, not to divide, the church.

That, however, was not to be. The controversy with the papacy that followed, as we know, ended in a complete break between Rome and the Reformers. Once out of fellowship with Rome, the latter acutely faced the problem, theologically as well as practically: Where in the church is authority vested? Indeed, what and where is "the church"? Luther, it has long been noted, toyed with the vision of a believers' church, a gathering of people who wished to be Christian in earnest.[6] But for this, Luther opined, he did not have the people. In any case, concerned as he was for civic order and for the fate of the whole society, such a church was hardly an option.

Zwingli's brush with the free church idea was more serious. Not only was that conception beginning to dawn among his associates, but on precipitating the first disputation in Zurich in early 1523, he found himself on the defensive. Zurich belonged to the diocese of Constance, and obviously, according to church law, only the bishop could convene the clergy. But in the early 1520s, as reform ferment in Zurich mounted, the city council, at Zwingli's prompting, convened a public disputation to consider the first reforms. Zwingli, needing to justify the procedure, invoked the promise of Christ's presence where two or three gather (Matt. 18). The logic, of course, was strained. A meeting of a city council is hardly a meeting "in my name." Lamely he appealed to the fact that council members were Christians, doubtless a claim nominally true, but malapropos. In any case the meeting was not an ecclesial gathering.

For both Luther and Zwingli, given their assumptions, the "free church" was not an option. In the sixteenth century, social and political cohesion was seen generally as dependent on religious uniformity. Moreover, had Luther been seriously tempted by the "free church" model, the Peasants' Revolt would quickly have disabused him of the notion. In the end, he divided the temporal and spiritual spheres, ceding the public activity of the church to the temporal sphere, thus to the jurisdiction of the territorial prince, and retaining matters of faith for the church. While this was intended as an emergency measure, German kings were to carry the title *Notbischof* for four centuries. Swiss reformers, though with different reasoning, followed the same course. In their setting, however, the rule was municipal rather than royal.

In passing, it is instructive to observe that sixteenth-century political conceptions and policies strikingly paralleled important features of Marxist-Leninist rule in the Soviet Union today, the atheism of the latter notwithstanding. Marxist-Leninists, Soviet-style, perhaps in part as heirs of the Byzantine tradition, at least until recently could no more conceive of civic and political unity, and hence stability, without ideological uniformity than could the sixteenth-century reformers. In the Soviet system the party and its dogma occupy a place similar to that held by the church and its creed prior to the October Revolution (1917). Doubtless this displacement of the church by the party accounts at least in part for the severity of the pressure on the churches during the period since 1917.

Radical Reformation: The First Free Church
H. S. Bender's "Anabaptist Vision" (1944), and revisionist reinterpretations meanwhile, have provided a fruitful point of orientation in sixteenth-

century Radical Reformation studies in recent decades. Outstanding disagreements in those studies need not distract us here. However turbulent and confusing that now distant era may have been, a distinct movement, surviving into our own time, crystallized around the seven articles drawn up by a group of "radicals" in 1527 in Schleitheim, a village on the Swiss-German border.[7] Not only did this statement shape the original ethos of that movement, the Mennonites, the Amish, and originally the Hutterites, but it offers classic formulas on the issues before us here, namely, those arising from the two-track mode of divine action in human history. These articles, of course, are the source of Bender's "vision."

These articles, compiled under the leadership of Michael Sattler, a former Benedictine subprior, were written under great stress. Felix Mantz, the first martyr of the new movement, had just been executed in his native Zurich. Decrees had been passed prohibiting the activities of the radicals, who later were to be dubbed Anabaptist. The issues they raised now suddenly took on life-and-death significance. Focusing on issues in dispute, the Schleitheim Articles deftly laid bare the fallacies that underlay the medieval synthesis of Christianity as civilization. On the other hand, these formulations clearly presupposed a common body of Christian tradition and understanding that did not need to be spelled out. In no way, then, did the Schleitheim Articles presume to offer a complete theology. In fact, their fragmentary nature was to haunt, in subsequent times, the communities gathered around them.

Schleitheim radically redefined salvation, church, and the fallen created order. Though order and symbolic observances remain, sacrament and hierarchy disappear. The church, now a voluntary assembly, consists of believers, prepared to submit to the disciplines of the gospel. Understood as the dialogical assembly of believers, the church is defined in this document in radically congregational terms. Structures beyond that are simply not contemplated. In a remarkably pregnant yet succinct phrase, the "sword" (magistracy) is viewed as "divinely ordained, outside the perfection of Christ." Overall, the articles are important, not only as an incisive and coherent paradigm in its own right, but also because of their paradigmatic power in the perpetuation of the communities formed around them.[8]

Though the statement appears sharply dichotomous, church against world, ambiguities remain. For example, how does this dualism compare with Luther's famous "two-kingdom" doctrine? Further, as has often been observed, the "sect" is a first-generation phenomenon. The children of parents who have left the host society to form the new community reach maturity under very different circumstances. This fact, of course, the Schleitheim Articles do not address. Nor do they address the problems of wider church polity: How is life beyond the congregation to be structured? In fact, while momentarily reopening the two-track dualism addressed at the beginning of this essay, the articles hardly sense the full consequences of what they are about.

Remarkably enough, until the Amish schism a century and a half later, the communities gathered around the Schleitheim Articles, at least in the Swiss-Upper German region, survived with a merely informal congregational polity. Visits and informal gatherings of leaders sufficed to nurture the common vision. Withdrawal from the surrounding society and persecution by it, however, abetted the ethnicizing impulses that inhered. Once encysted subculturally within the surrounding society, this faith community tended to mutate into an ethnicity.

Those impulses, everywhere incipient among Mennonites, reached full bloom under the unusual conditions offered in 18th/19th-century czarist Russia. Catherine the Great, in the second half of the eighteenth-century, included Mennonites in the extensive colonization by Germans which she undertook to develop her vast lands. Meanwhile, Mennonites living under privileged military exemption in Prussian lands, found their privilege jeopardized for other reasons. As a result many were responsive to the czarina's overtures. The charter given to Mennonites in Russia made them a self-governing colony under the crown, responsible for their own civic as well as religious affairs. Under these circumstances, in less than a century, Mennonites in Russia evolved into a new, albeit miniature, Christendom. Baptism, for those who failed to embrace it by choice, became a compulsory, hence civic, ceremony. Because of the accompanying--and resulting--spiritual laxity, a revival broke out, which, like the sixteenth century before it, led to schism and persecution (1860 ff.).[9] The original Mennonite community had effectively become a state church. Its response to revival in its midst was similar to the responses of the established churches, Catholic and Protestants, to the sixteenth-century radicals. This revival was triggered by the preaching of a German pietist evangelist, who also happened to be an immersionist in his view of baptism. Baptized Mennonites, born again in the revival, were now rebaptized, this time by immersion, an irony, indeed!

Modern Free Churches

If the sixteenth-century radicals were the first free church, other free movements were to follow independently in other lands in subsequent centuries. These, such as Baptists and Congregationalists, championed freedom in the minimal sense stipulated above--religious liberty, separation of church and state, and typically, believer's baptism. Most, however, did not embrace the maximal severity included in the Schleitheim paradigm. The distinction between the minimalist and maximalist free church paradigms, though important, need not detain us here.

With minor exceptions, free churches in the Western world won toleration only with the eighteenth-century Enlightenment and political revolutions. Meanwhile, many establishment conceptions and practices persisted well into the twentieth century even when minimalist freedoms were introduced. In some countries, England and Sweden in the West, for example, and Hungary and the German Democratic Republic in the East, institutional vestiges of establishment remain today. Churches once established have been slow to yield their privileges, or to tolerate, much less to recognize, free churches within their domains.

Many immigrants to the New World came in search of religious liberty.

Nonetheless several of the colonies originally had established churches. When it came to American independence, however, and the new constitution, diversity of traditions and churches in the various colonies precluded the favoring of one denomination over others. Hence the famous First Amendment clause: "Congress shall make no law respecting an establishment of religion, or prohibiting the free exercise thereof." The grounding for this solution was chiefly practical and political. There was little theological preparation for this revolutionary step.

Theological justification was to come only gradually, in Protestant thought earlier, in Roman Catholic thought, only since Vatican II. Today religious liberty and separation of church and state are defended, no longer merely on pragmatic grounds, but fundamentally. But do we have a full-blown conception of the "free church" in Christianity in America? In fact, do we possess an adequate ecclesiology at all? I will discuss this question briefly in the final section below. Here, by way of illustration with reference to these questions, I shall note only the denominational problem.

"Free churches," including Mennonites, while repudiating the Roman hierarchy, assiduously construct "denominations," vague replicas of what they ostensibly left behind in the break with Rome. Protestants built denominations after the breakup of Christendom in the same way that kings built ostensibly sovereign realms with the breakup of the "Holy Roman Empire." The medieval Catholic claim enjoyed a degree of plausibility that is lacking in any Protestant case (here I use the term "Protestant" in its loose modern, rather than its technical sixteenth-century, sense). Catholic appeal to historical continuity and universality possesses a certain logic. These claims, coupled with a conception of organic growth that permits the articulation of new doctrine from mere hints in the gospel text, make of the Roman formula a formidable force. Yet the premises themselves, to any but the devout, are implausible.

But what about other "churches," i.e., denominations? To be sure, many can appeal to the renewal movements out of which they arose, and thus, in effect, to the self-authenticating presence of Christ among the two or three gathered in his name. But if that, rather than historic succession, is the basis, whence the mandate for denominational empires? To sense the problem, one need only recall the verdict when the first hint of the denomination arose in New Testament times (1 Cor. 3). *Sola scriptura* was an early, and abiding, Protestant principle; but on those grounds precisely, denominations are ecclesiological nonentities.

In recent years "mainline" churches, denominations all, have declined numerically, while "Bible" and other "independent" churches have burgeoned. No single "cause," of course, can be identified. Some significance attaches nonetheless to the distance between denominational and congregational structures and the primary level of religious experience. If "Jesus saves," why all the other baggage? If we receive salvation *sola fidei*, does it help, or does it rather hinder, when one comes to faith, to be expected at the same time to buy into a particular historical tradition? How does one biblically justify the need to become a Lutheran, a Calvinist, or a Mennonite in order to be a Christian? In practice, to be sure, "Jesus saves" turns readily into a reductionist slogan. Responsible denominational witness is likely to present a fuller and more robust message than do many freewheeling gospel hucksters. But does that fact of itself constitute a foundation for a denominational ecclesiology? Protestants object to doctrinal accretions by papal fiat, but how does the erection of denominations by non-Catholics differ?

What Time Is This?

It was in retrospect that Blanke described the Anabaptist "free church" as a premature proposal for the sixteenth century. Conventional wisdom today regards it as self-evident that church and state should be separate, and that religious commitments are intrinsically free. At least to the people whose views prevailed in sixteenth-century Europe, these notions were anything but self-evident. The change in perception, meanwhile, does not necessarily mean that people today have grown better or wiser--that is not ours to judge, in any case--but that historical circumstances have changed. Now that other bases of social cohesion have emerged, churches can be independent, and religion can be free, without threat to the public order. Thus one can argue that the "free church" is an idea whose time has come.

Before finally assessing that claim, we must take note of several features of the modern free church environment. What specifically has transpired that makes conceptions viewed as seditious in the sixteenth century, axiomatically self-evident today? Events and developments during this period of history, and the records and literature about them, of course, are far too vast for any meaningful summary here. Two broad generalizations only, and their consequences, will be noted. First, social systems (groups, associations, organizations, and the like) have grown too vast, too complex, and too diverse to be forced into homogeneous and centrally controlled configurations. Modern societies are "active,"[10] participatory, and pluralistic. They comprise numerous actors, interests, and values. Only crushing totalitarian force could achieve religious uniformity, and that only in superficial, external terms.

Second, and by the same token, the stabilities sought in the sixteenth century by enforced symbolic consensus are being achieved far more effectively by other means. Specialization, exchange, communication, and hence realized interdependence among vast and diverse population aggregates, are proving to be far more effective as social stabilizers than was compulsory religious uniformity in earlier centuries. In a word, modern societies have outgrown the need for religion as political legitimation and integration. This is but a special case of a general evolution in the course of which science and a variety of empirical disciplines, by virtue of their greater practical effectiveness, supplant appeal to religion and the supernatural.

Yet, contrary to the conclusion that many people mistakenly draw, the religious dimensions of human existence do not disappear. Nor is "human nature" altered fundamentally by these social transformations. Quite to the contrary, the age-old question of the meaning of existence appears in heightened intensity. For the transformations in complexity and scale just noted entail the attenuation of the primordial solidarities of blood and soil that in the early epochs of our race hemmed in and determined our existence. Modernization means the pluralization, at times almost the atomization, of our communal solidarities. From these emerge, on the one side, the modern "autonomous" individual, on the other, the organization and the vast, role-based systems of contractual exchange. As a result we experience unprecedented freedom and at least potential rootlessness.[11]

A Time Whose Idea Has Not Come

I began with a dual question, posed by four millennia of Hebrew and Christian salvation history: How are the sociabilities of "nature" and those of "grace" related among the people of the covenant; and how are the covenantly chosen people related to the rest of humankind? In effect, how is the theologically posited tension between the centripetal ("come ye apart") and the centrifugal ("go ye into all the world") to be worked out historically? The faith community, suprahistorically grounded, enters history, as it were, only to succumb to the forces of nature. This occurred, as we saw, in the rise of the Hebrew monarchy(s), of European Christendom, and of the miniature Mennonite Christendom in Russia.

Is such sedimentation inevitable, *or are we missing something in the way we handle our sources, the biblical materials?* The reformation upheavals of the sixteenth century remain a fruitful context for reflection on these questions. In this respect, important Radical Reformation research has yet to be undertaken. Retrospectively we can say that the Reformation generally signaled the beginning of the end of Christendom, and was thus analogous to the end of the Hebrew monarchies in Old Testament times, and to the split among Mennonites in Russia in 1860. The break of the Reformers with Rome raised the above question acutely, not merely theologically, but above all existentially and historically. Where, and what, is "the church"? These questions were debated in the sixteenth century intensively, extensively, instructively--and inconclusively.[12]

The notion that the "free church" is an idea whose time has come has a bracing ring to it. History appears to have vindicated, at least in some measure, the courageous act of the little band in an obscure village (Schleitheim) in 1527. Those who consequently gave their lives, rightly join the "cloud of witnesses" (Heb. 11) who spur us onward. Yet as our era engages its inherited battery of ecclesiastical idioms, serious misgivings arise. Instead of an idea whose time has come, we confront *a time whose idea has not come.* Prevailing churchdom repels many people in our time, and leaves many who still hang on, dissatisfied. If with this history as background we turn attentively and critically to our biblical sources, our anxiety can only mount. We can find there no grounding for much of today's "churchianity." And I refer, not to the absence of proof texts, but rather to the "tenor of Scripture," to the entire narrative.

A claim as sweeping as this must be carefully qualified. It neither implies nor presupposes judgments of church or denominational programs nor of persons who serve in denominational or other ecclesiastical posts. Likewise it is not directed against the faithful in denominationally united congregations. One of the liberating aspects of our faith is the relative indifference of the Spirit to "earthen vessels" (2 Cor. 4:7) in which the waters of salvation are conveyed; "the word of God is not fettered" (2 Tim. 2:9). In any case, the denominational forest is not about to disappear, perhaps least of all the mighty oaks of Rome, Constantinople, or Antioch. From what we can see, church life tomorrow will closely resemble the church life of yesterday. But none of these qualifications relieves us of the responsibility to confront the profound obsolescence and errors of our ecclesiastical ways. The prevailing forms of church life are neither faithful to the gospel, nor do they engage the social configuration of our age. Sinful consequences, to be sure, calling for repentance, may flow in specific instances, and these will need to be dealt with accordingly. But those do not directly concern us here.

No, the problem lies far deeper. The ecclesiological idioms that shape the corporate experience of Christians today still hail largely from establishment times. Church bodies, both Catholic and Protestant, with establishment pasts, largely maintain the traditional establishment-engendered institutional and liturgical modalities. Free church denominations, if and when their sectarian fervor cools, gravitate toward "mainline" liturgical modes. Institutionally neither group, established or free, is responding directly enough to either the new situation or the biblical materials. Past ecclesiological idioms, whether formed to integrate populations and to legitimate power, or in defiance of such adaptations, are little-suited to the psychic needs of modern autonomous but fragmented and rootless individuals. At best, the reification of these earlier idioms distorts our perception of both texts and events.

Looking for the Tender Shoots

Given the sweep of this claim, it would be presumptuous to propose *the* or even *a* solution in one short essay. Indeed, our problem is profoundly human and spiritual, hence inaccessible to external blueprints. But it would be irresponsible to offer this critique without some clues as to the kinds of responses needed. I shall first note several vital signs among Christians today, and in scholarly inquiry, and then list several areas that call for critical reflection and action.

Despite our ecclesiological helplessness, many tender shoots of new growth are evident. Throughout this century there has been a growing "ecumenical" awareness in the churches, expressed concretely in developments such as the World Council of Churches (founded in 1948), consisting of "communions" other than Roman Catholics, and in initiatives from the Roman Catholics as well. These developments are accompanied by conciliar movements in many lands and at lower levels as well. More important than organizational advances, however, is the fact that many earlier barriers among Christians are softening. Though conflict and schism still inflict the Christian community, Christians are joining hands across boundaries that once seemed insurmountable. Admittedly, the critique offered here questions whether merger is panacea for the denominational malady. Summing illegitimacies will not legitimize. But this critique also entails, as already indicated, a responsiveness to the freedom of the Spirit whenever and wherever, and the Spirit is not bound by or to denominations.

Paralleling these "from above" stirrings is the ferment "from below"--"base communities," "house churches," and the like, in many lands and forms. Generically these have much in common with the sixteenth-century "free church" movements, though they possess their own dynamics. Some of these occur within existing churches, others at greater remove. Beyond this, creative energy continues to burst forth in existing churches and denominational agencies. Thus it must be emphasized: initiatives seeking "end runs" around existing churches, even with their troubled history, must be treated with utmost suspicion. Much of the brokenness in the history of the church stems from separatist attempts to reestablish the "pure church." No, we must stay together, within our broken heritage, but with bags packed for the new trek.

Ernst Troeltsch, in 1911, published a monumental work, eventually translated as *The Social Teaching of the Christian Churches*.[13] The work was monumental because it shaped or influenced the ways that scholars approached such questions as those raised in the present essay. Spanning the centuries of Christian history, his work identified three social embodiments of the Christian faith, the *Kirche* or church, the *Sekte* or sect, and mysticism (sometimes spiritualism). Against the prevailing view that made the *Kirche* (the folk- or state-church) of Christendom normative, and the other two expressions, especially the sect, mere deformations, Troeltsch argued that all three motifs appear side by side in the New Testament. "It has become clear," he wrote, "how little the Gospel and the Primitive Church shaped the religious community from a uniform point of view."[14]

Troeltsch's project took him through the eighteenth century, following which Christian history entered "a new phase of existence." The "unity of civilization controlled by a State Church" has disintegrated. Modern, scientifically reinforced individualism is fusing with the individualism of the older mystics to become "a refuge for the religious life of the cultured classes."[15] As other writers were to point out later, Christian values had become institutionalized and, in this manner, secularized. These values, now culturally embodied, live on, as it were, without necessary reference to their Christian origin.

This work is cited both because of its fecundity and because of its influence on modern scholarship. It has led the way, for example, in the rehabilitation of the sixteenth-century radicals. One of the promising developments in our own time is the reencounter of the *Kirche* traditions with the *Sekte* legacy of the pre-Constantinian era. This is seen dramatically in relegitimation of the pacifist option (World Council of Churches, 1948; Vatican II), and numerous corresponding actions by various church bodies meanwhile. The importance of these developments becomes evident when we consider that as recently as World War II, pacifists in many churches received no "official" or even pastoral support in the stand they took. Here, however, I am concerned with the ecclesiological rather than the ethical import of these breakthroughs.

Recognizing the disestablishment of the churches generally, George Lindbeck, a Luther scholar, anticipates "a sociological sectarian future in which the exclusivist claims of the orthodox mainstream of the Christian tradition are maintained, even if reinterpreted." Lindbeck follows Rahner[16] in distinguishing the "sociological" from the "ecclesiological" concept of the sectarian. "The mainstream of early Christianity was sectarian," he continues, "in the sense in which we use the term. It consisted of a small, strongly deviant minority, unsupported by cultural convention and prestige, within the larger society. This was true even though it was also 'catholic' in the ecclesiological sense of embracing a wide variety of classes, races, theologies, liturgies and styles of life, and of being unified, rather than splintered into competing groups."[17]

What of reencounters in the opposite direction, free churches with the "catholic" of the *Kirche* traditions? This will mean something more than the reassimilation which sets in among many sects as they cool off. And what of Troeltsch's third category, the spiritualist "refuge for the religious life of the cultured classes"? Was Troeltsch right in emphasizing "how little the Gospel and the Primitive Church shaped the religious community itself from a uniform point of view?" Or are these themes unified at a deeper level, ever available when we are able to respond at that level?

As Karl Ludwig Schmidt observes, the New Testament distinguishes the local *ecclesia* (we translate "congregation") from the total *ecclesia* (we translate "church"). He notes also the scholarly uncertainty as to whether the generic reference is to the totality, locally manifested, or to the totality of all those dispersed.[18] There is, of course, no doubt concerning the central significance of the *ecclesia* in the Christian scenario. But it is also of signal importance that numerous other metaphors for the covenant people appear in the New Testament. Indeed 1 Peter, perhaps the most important ecclesiological treatise in the New Testament, does not even use the term *ecclesia*.[19] Even in the Gospel of Matthew, where the term does occur, as a recent study emphasizes, the Christian assembly is household-based. This fact adds to the poignancy and urgency of the hard sayings of Jesus in the same Gospel concerning the challenge of kingdom loyalties to the ties of nature (e.g., Matt. 12:46-50).

When these teachings are properly read against the backdrop of the developmental thrust of Hebrew prophecy, climaxing as it did in the ministry of Jesus, it is evident at once that we move far too quickly and glibly from the biblical materials to our own religious institutions. We must take far more seriously the "iconoclastic" ecclesiology of the primordial New Testament materials--the Gospels, 1 Corinthians, 1 Peter. In the context of Reformation studies, the debate concerning the "invisibility" of the church will have to be readdressed. In New Testament terms, obviously the Christian person and the assembly of Christians are "visible" and "real." Both, however, exist in and by faith. But is this reality subject to social organization--bureaucracy, legal personality, real estate ownership, professional careers and ambitions, and the like? Can the Presence who appears where two or three are gathered (Matt. 18) be thus organized? What, in fact, is the object to which the term *ecclesia* refers? Have we extended, enriched, or promoted it when we build tabernacles to trap the transcendent (Matt. 17)?

Modernization, as I noted above, disengages us from the ascriptive solidarities of kinship and place, and both permits and compels us to achieve our own identity and place in the world. This development, though in part a fruit of the gospel, when responsible communally anchored selves are absent, degenerates into acquisitive self-interest. In the gospel the emancipated and autonomous person is a communal being, self-giving rather than self-promoting. The burden of our detached subjectivity may well be the most acute of our personal problems today. Contemporary modes of "church," however, are little-suited to respond to these needs. The machinery runs, whether or not people believe.

Michael Crosby (1988) regards the acquisitive consumerism of our society as "addictive," addictive in the sense that we are powerless to cope with it individually.[20] Hence he concludes that "only by turning over our lives to a greater power (through the religious experience of God's presence in *exousia*) and by creating alternative, house-type communities will we be able to provide the necessary environment for a new order of justice in our lives and that of society."[21] The epistle of 1 Peter[22] makes the same point, by means of the Diaspora metaphor. The faith community, as transforming reality, shines through all the configurations of nature, but can never be incorporated by them. That is the good news.

NOTES

1. See Joachim Wach, *Sociology of Religion* (Chicago: University of Chicago Press, 1944).

2. Roland H. Bainton, *Christendom: A Short History of Christianity and Its Impact on Western Civilization*, I (New York: Harper Torchbooks, 1964), 147.

3. George Mendenhall, *The Tenth Generation: The Origins of the Biblical Tradition* (Baltimore: Johns Hopkins University Press, 1973), 16f. Cf. Paul Peachey, "Europe as a Mission-field? Some Socio-historical Reflections," *Mission Focus* 16 (Sept. 1988), 43-47.

4. See D. W. Hamlyn, "The Concept of Social Reality," in *Explaining Behaviour, Consciousness, Human Action and Social Structure*, ed. Paul F. Secord (Beverly Hills: Sage, 1982), 198-209.

5. George H. Williams, *The Radical Reformation* (Philadelphia: Westminster Press, 1957).

6. "The German Mass and Order of Service, 1526," in *Selected Writings of Martin Luther 1523-1526*, ed. T. G. Tappert (Philadelphia: Fortress Press, 1967), 387-426.

7. John H. Yoder, trans. and ed., *The Legacy of Michael Sattler* (Scottdale, Pa.: Herald Press, 1973), 28-54.

8. For example, Beulah Hostetler, *American Mennonites and Protestant Movements: A Community Paradigm* (Scottdale, Pa.: Herald Press, 1987).

9. E. K. Francis, *In Search of Utopia: The Mennonites of Manitoba* (Altona, Man.: D. W. Friesen, 1955).

10. Amitai Etzioni, *The Active Society* (New York: Free Press, 1968).

11. Cf. Robert Bellah, et al., *Habits of the Heart* (New York: Harper and Row, 1985).

12. For the Anabaptists, the classic contemporary study is F. H. Littell, *The Anabaptist View of the Church* (Boston: Beacon Press, 1964). For a recent comparative study of Luther, Calvin, and Menno Simons, see John R. Loescher, *The Divine Community: Trinity, Church and Ethics in Reformation Theologians* (Kirksville, Mo.: Sixteenth Century Journal Publishers, 1981).

13. Ernst Troeltsch, *The Social Teachings of the Christian Churches* (New York: Harper Torchbooks, 1960; original German, 1911).

14. *Ibid.*, II, 993.

15. *Ibid.*

16. Karl Rahner, *The Christian of the Future* (New York: Herder and Herder, 1967).

17. George Lindbeck, "The Sectarian Future of the Church," in *The God Experience*, ed. Joseph P. Whalen (New York: Newman Press, 1971).

18. Karl Ludwig Schmidt, "Ekklesia," *Theological Dictionary of the New Testament*, ed. Gerhard Kittel, IV (Grand Rapids, Mich.: Eerdmans, 1967), 501-536.

19. Cf. John H. Elliot, *A Home for the Homeless* (Philadelphia: Fortress Press, 1981).

20. Michael H. Crosby, *House of Disciples: Church, Economics and Justice in Matthew* (Maryknoll, N.Y.: Orbis Books, 1988).

21. *Ibid.*, 212.

22. Cf. Elliot, *A Home for the Homeless.*

Cornelius J. Dyck: Biographical Vignettes

Robert Kreider

Cornelius J. Dyck was thirty-eight years old in 1959 when he began his career teaching historical theology at the Associated Mennonite Biblical Seminaries, Elkhart, Indiana. He came to the profession of seminary teaching a circuitous way, along the servant's path in distant lands, a road less traveled by.

Born in 1921 in the village of Lysanderhoeh in the Soviet Union just beyond the Volga River, C. J. was the eighth of nine children born to John J. and Renate Mathies Dyck. He was born into a world of drought, hunger, epidemics, revolutionary disturbances, and anxiety, but more important, enveloped in the security of a loving home. The family of eleven immigrated to Canada in 1927.

C. J.'s story continues with a boyhood on farms on the Saskatchewan prairie, survival through the Great Depression, the warm fellowship of the Tiefengrund Mennonite Church, study at Rosthern Junior College, the war years farming in lieu of military service, followed by six years of service with the Mennonite Central Committee in England, the Netherlands, Germany, and Paraguay. After his marriage to Wilma Regier, he received a baccalaureate degree from Bethel College and a master's from Wichita State University, meanwhile pastoring four years at the rural Zion Mennonite Church of Elbing, Kans. He went on to doctoral studies at the University of Chicago, living in an urban neighborhood in the throes of a rapid transition, serving on the side as business manager of Mennonite Biblical Seminary, and in 1959 joining the faculty of the newly established Associated Mennonite Biblical Seminaries of Elkhart, Indiana. A road less traveled by.

For the past thirty-one years C. J. Dyck has lived a full and creative life as church statesman, distinguished teacher, administrator, editor, speaker, writer, and keeper of his people's memory. Following are excerpts from his reflections along the road that led to Elkhart and beyond. These are drawn from the transcripts of three interviews, April 28, 29, and May 2, 1988.[1] Here are his responses to a series of questions about influences which shaped his person and vocation. To preserve the flow of conversation, the record has been freely edited.

For thirty-five years C. J., Wilma, and their children--Mary, Jennifer, and Suzanne--have made almost annual trips to Saskatchewan "to meet our own emotional needs, and partly, to help our girls grow roots of family and identity."

In 1987 Wilma and C. J. compiled and edited a 176-page narrative and pictorial story of their extended family, *A Pilgrim People*. It includes a genealogical chart which traces the family back to 1495 and to a forebear who fled for his life as an Anabaptist in 1532. In 1647 a C. J. van Dyck was received as a member in the Haarlem (Netherlands) Mennonite Church, thus C. J.'s comment, "Was I predestined to be a Mennonite?" C. J.'s identity and faith clearly are woven of the fabric of family.

C. J. speaks appreciatively of his sisters and brothers: Of Elise, the eldest, "a model of piety and self-denial, the one who wanted to go to the mission field but was needed at home, the one whose back was broken in a tractor accident that shook the family for all time, the one who went every summer to teach Bible schools all over northern Saskatchewan. She represented faith at its best. To her I owe that I can read the Gothic script fluently."

He speaks of Anna, cheerful, vibrant, and outgoing, who died early, leaving a lovely family. Of Irma, with a great sense of humor. "She has all kinds of gifts and is a very caring person." Of John, who "was the anchor man, especially after Dad died in 1948. After early financial success he and his wife, Paula, were able to spend most of the rest of their lives in voluntary projects: seventeen years as a business manager at Rosthern Junior College without pay, starting the General Conference bookstore in Canada, establishing the Mennonite Foundation in Western Canada, helping to start the Foodbank, closing out MCC work in Paraguay, then in Korea and later in Jordan. Peter and I have had more headlines over the years [than John], but I really believe that he deserves more than Peter and I together in terms of what he achieved and stood for--not least his vigorous and very painful tax resistance stand during the last decade. I had a great deal of respect for his financial ability, his business 'sixth sense,' his love for Christ, and his gentleness with people. He died of cancer, May 14, 1988."

"Peter had a part in my going into MCC, because he was already in it, but I don't think he was the primary factor. I think it was Alvin Penner, my good friend from high school days, who was shot down over Germany. I felt this sacrifice needed somehow to find a visible response in me. For many Mennos, Peter is *Mr. MCC* today. As one reflects on his leadership and charisma, one is led to ask the old question about whether history (the nexus of events) makes a man or whether a man (or woman) makes history? Would Churchill have been great if there had not been a war? It is probably something of both with Peter."

C. J. speaks of his sister Helene: "She is an artist. She paints a great deal and has won significant citations. We are so grateful to her, and husband Abe, for standing by our parents when I left for MCC. Their son Ray is presently a member of Parliament in Ottawa (NDP)." And Clara: "A nurse for many years. Then earned two M.A.'s, one in German and one in English at the University of Manitoba, taught briefly at CMBC, and is now serving as voluntary chaplain in the Winnipeg hospitals on a regular basis." And, finally, Renata: "We call her Rena; creative teacher, librarian, mother of four stalwart sons. She and her husband, George, instead of retiring, just returned from two years in China with the China Educational Exchange program."

These remarkable nine children had remarkable parents. C. J. speaks with admiration of his father:

Dad never was a farmer at heart, though he did an excellent job of it. He traveled in Germany as a young man, then went back to Russia and humored his father by taking the farm. He apparently subscribed regularly to half a dozen German and Russian journals. When in Moscow he would attend the opera and the theater. He was active politically after the Revolution when Kerensky tried to establish his new democracy. He was surprised that he was able to escape from Russia; he was a marked man. Though he was not a preacher, he brought home the high-profile speakers we had in church, like C. F. Klassen, David Toews, and others. In those draft years when I stayed on the farm, those long winter evenings lent themselves well to discussions with him. I remember reading Tolstoy's *War and Peace*, which he had read earlier in Russian, and dialoguing with him about it. It was almost like an independent study course. He introduced me to a wide range of classical Russian literature. Dad was the keeper of the springs of our peoplehood. I am amazed how he wrote this thick autobiography when he wasn't well, and at his remarkable memory for detail. I was in Europe when he died in 1948.

C. J. felt particular affection for his mother who had unique gifts:

She was gentle, cheerful, usually sang quietly to herself when she worked. She carried a very heavy load. To me she was a kind of saint. She understood Dad, and when he died--the way she patiently and graciously lived alone in her retirement home, content, happy, reading and crocheting--she was a real inspiration to us.

When the Dyck family arrived in Saskatchewan in 1927, they settled on a farm near Hanley, seventy miles south of Saskatoon. C. J. remembers how in that community at a distance from established Mennonite congregations, several families gathered in the Dyck home and other homes for Sunday worship services, often with a visiting minister. His sister Elise would round up the children for Sunday school. In 1933 the family moved to the Laird community, fifty miles north of Saskatoon, where the family became a part of the Tiefengrund congregation. C. J. describes their new church home:

We had two lay ministers. Both were patient, kind, gentle, and understanding. Both preached in German. The sermons were simple, without many illustrations, but very sincere. They must have had a deep impact upon many, because somehow these two men got more people into Christian service than many others. There was a kind of piety in the congregation that was not Pietism. Sometimes we knelt for prayer, or else we stood. We never sat. We did much singing, and I remember the hymns to this day. J. J. Nickel came every winter for Bible Study Week, often on Ephesians or Philippians. Elder Regier usually wore a swallow tail coat, always for communion, and would usually stop at the door on entering and say in German, "The peace of God be with you." We did not have revival meetings like Laird. Itinerant preachers would occasionally come and preach in our church, and, while they were more fluent, we were usually glad that they were not our preachers.

C. J. cannot remember when he did not read: "I have run across little German booklets that I got when I was five, so I must have been reading by then." He speaks of his early love for the British poets, as also for Goethe, Schiller, and, not least, Shakespeare, whom he later studied under the guidance of Honora Becker at Bethel College. He remembers his first six years of school near Hanley as good years, but acknowledges a slump in interest after the family's move to Laird. He has his grade nine report card with the notation, "Cornelius could do so much better if he wanted to."

His academic ardor revived in grade ten. "I'll never forget Clarence Palmer," he declares, "a young fellow with curly hair fresh out of the university. My grades went way up and I enjoyed school. I don't know what his field was. Neither do I know what he did to turn me on, but I was obviously highly motivated."

C. J.'s interest in history was ignited in the home and during his year at Rosthern Junior College. He attributes his interest to Peter P. Rempel:

"P. Square" we used to call him. He also taught literature, but what I remember is history. He would sit on his desk, no lectern, few notes, dangling his legs, and talk about things historical in a way that, as I reflect on it now, I became hooked on it for life. It probably started with my dad and his reminiscing and reflecting and analyzing such questions as to what might have prevented the Bolshevik Revolution if the [orthodox] church had been different. It was either history or literature, and I was convinced that it ought to be history.

Eventually Peter P. Rempel was asked to resign from the school because "he was considered not orthodox enough." C. J. observes: "Maybe that's what I liked about him. He was a revisionist, fresh and creative and not always 'safe'-- some of the older people thought. We liked that."

With World War II and six years of postwar service, C. J.'s formal studies were interrupted for ten years. First the draft service, 1941-45, and from the summer of 1945 to 1951 with Mennonite Central Committee, "the best school the Mennonites have." Through MCC he "became aware of the world in a new way":

I saw all kinds of exploitation which I did not like, but also saw Mennonites participating in it. I found that the stories of the poor were not written, or if they were, they were written by those who didn't really understand. I met people and MCC workers who raised my horizons and made me ask questions I'd never thought of before. My first real university education was to mix with the students and professors of Kiel University, where we had a feeding program. I became increasingly modest about our achievements when I realized that we were part of the victors and that I was speaking to the vanquished. It increased my pacifist stance and added a strong concern for the economic dimension. It was also in those early MCC years that I used late nights to read (in German) Karl Barth's commentary on Romans and other works new to me.

In 1948 he planned to conclude his MCC service and continue studies in Basel. At this point MCC asked him to go to Paraguay to head up their programs in lower South America. He demurred, but then agreed.

> I spent nearly three very intense years down under. Helping to settle the refugees in Paraguay and Uruguay, starting the leper hospital at Kilometer 81, getting the first bulldozer there for road building (with funds from the Northern District Mennonite Men), raising funds in North America for their first mental health facility, and making so many friends for life were more than reward enough for my going. But I never did get irrigation water or a spinning-weaving industry to the Chaco. I tried.

In the course of his MCC service C. J. learned Dutch, French, and Spanish, which further equipped him for his life of scholarship.

In the fall of 1951 he resumed his studies at Bethel College, North Newton, Kans., where he spent much time in the Mennonite Library and Archives. He graduated in 1953. He speaks appreciatively of his studies in history and philosophy at Wichita State University with John Rydjord as his adviser.

Arriving on the campus of the University of Chicago in 1955, C. J. found a stimulating academic climate. The Lutherans, Reformed, and Baptists had taken control of the erstwhile citadel of liberalism in the Divinity School. He was especially delighted with Jaroslav Pelikan, who became his doctoral adviser. He speaks of others: Dean Jarold Brauer, Paul Tillich, Marcus Barth, Mircea Eliade, Charles Long, James H. Nichols, Robert Grant in early church history, R. Pearce Beaver in missions, Sidney Mead in American church history, Walter Harrelson in Old Testament, and James Luther Adams. Of Adams, C. J. says, "I really enjoyed his ethics classes.... It was what Don [Smucker] also represents, a synthesis of theology, sociology, ethics, and history all in one." He speaks appreciatively of classmates Vincent Harding and Martin Marty, the latter writing his dissertation when C. J. arrived on campus.

When asked which theologians or schools of thought he identified with particularly, C. J. replied:

> Oh my, that requires time and careful thought! All I can do on this is identify a few person and movements. I mentioned James Luther Adams and Don Smucker, and earlier the global economic injustice I had found. So, it won't come as a surprise when I mention Walter Rauschenbusch and the Social Gospel. In Canada the Mennos who came out of the USSR have often been suspicious of the Social Gospel as sort of Communist. Yet most of the work of MCC stands in its own social gospel tradition. The mother of J. S. Woodsworth, founder of the Cooperative Commonwealth Federation, now the New Democratic Party in Canada, was of Mennonite background. In Saskatchewan, my home province, the CCR was the first socialist government elected in North America. It was they who first had the vision for a Canada-wide health care and pension plan. Rauschenbusch's *A Theology for the Social Gospel*, while idealistic, has been a very important book to me as has Don Smucker's Chicago dissertation on him.

You can quickly see how this influenced my concern to go beyond the historic Anabaptist love emphasis to include justice, both in theory and practice, including the local level. Food baskets for the needy were not enough; during the civil rights era I found myself on the street talking to merchants about hiring minorities. M. L. King became a powerful inspiration for me and pushed me beyond nonresistance to nonviolent options. This tied in with my reading Paul Tillich, especially his *Love, Power and Justice*, as well as hearing his lectures and seminars at the University.

You asked which writings, to use George Fox's phrase, "spoke [speak] to my condition?" Tillich's *The Courage To Be* certainly did at that time, but even more, much more, Martin Buber and Kierkegaard. I taught a seminar on Buber and SK at AMBS sometimes. There is the mystic in me, the importance of I-Thou relationships, a willingness to live with unanswered questions, like the meaning of the resurrection, which I consider central to my faith. And SK? I have difficulty with authoritariansm and dogmatism and bureaucracy in the church and in church institutions. I see my ordination as functional, not as "office." I consider Vernard Eller's *Kierkegaard and Radical Discipleship* an important book.

Shall I continue? Okay, perhaps just a bit more.

It will not surprise you, after what I said about Buber, that Thomas Merton's writings have meant a great deal to me. I think I began with his *Seven Story Mountain* and then *No Man Is An Island*, and then others. His view of life is liberating; asceticism, or discipleship, does not appear as a burden when seen through his eyes. He was a man of hope. With my background of work being next to Godliness he helped me a great deal to center down, to see that being is of at least as much value as doing, to wait for the burning bush, to find theophany in silence or in community.

One other context. You know of my involvement with Mennonite World Conference during the sixties and early seventies. My MCC involvement had encouraged my ecumenical interests, but only modestly. I could have driven to Amsterdam for the 1948 WCC Assembly, for example, but didn't. In the fall of 1965 I was able to attend Vatican Council II for a time. I had hoped that MWC might authorize me as the Mennonite representative, which would have given me official observer status, but Mennos weren't ready to send anyone to Rome, so I went on my own. I had press credentials. I was received most royally, especialy by Thomas Stransky of the Secretariat for Christian Unity, later head of the Paulist Order. Of all my growth experiences that was certainly one of them. I won't forget the reception where guests were asked to introduce themselves and after giving my name added, "I'm a Mennonite." After seeing mostly puzzled faces I added, "You know, Anabaptist." Then they knew.

What a kairos moment! Dialog continued for many days whenever one of those present met me, the "Anabaptist."

A few years later I was able to spend a sabbatical at the Ecumenical Institute in Collegeville, Minn., and a few years after that, during a fall semester at Tübingen University, I enjoyed an evening seminar with Hans Küng. We discussed his book *Christ Sein*. I recall one evening when I asked how one could discuss being a Christian in a thick volume without once mentioning nonliturgical, personal prayer. "Can't cover everything in one book!" Right. The dialog continued.

After reflecting on his comments C. J. said, "We're both historians, yet in my comments on people and books which have influenced me, I made no reference to important historians and their writings, especially on methodology--persons like Pieter Geyl, Collingwood, Butterfield, von Ranke, Danielou, Shinn, Cullmann, and others. Is that significant?" And he continued, "Like Küng said, I can't say it all in a few minutes or a few paragraphs." But then he added:

I have been thinking in a larger than historical frame and yet more personal in terms of identity. I did not think I could here get into historical issues per se, or methodology. It has been my good fortune to have had many excellent mentors--Pelikan, Bainton, George Williams, Bender, Brauer, Nichols, others. With them I hold scrupulous objectivity as an ideal for my work, but I also need to acknowledge, even confess, my bias.

This does not mean I am a relativist. However important context may be, it does not exhaust the meaning of an event. Positivism and historicism are illusions of infallibility. The historian, perhaps even more than others, is called to conserve a heritage, not through apologetics but by telling the story to every new generation with humility and courage and faith.

We must move on to your other questions.

Erland Waltner, speaking for the board, invited C. J. to join the faculty of Mennonite Biblical Seminary (MBS), which in the fall of 1958 was affiliating with Goshen Biblical Seminary to form the new Associated Mennonite Biblical Seminaries (AMBS), located on a new campus at Elkhart, Indiana. He remembers conversations with R. L. Hartzler and A. E. Kreider about this vocational decision. He accepted because "it seemed natural and congenial. It fitted into my long-range hopes for myself." His association with MBS had begun earlier in 1955 when he and Wilma were invited to serve as host and hostess at the campus on South Woodlawn in Chicago. When soon thereafter John Neufeld suffered a heart attack, C. J. served as part-time business manager of the seminary.

In the entire history of Mennonite publication no one has edited and facilitated the publication of more volumes on Anabaptist and Mennonite sub-

jects than C. J. Dyck. In his role as director of the Institute of Mennonite
Studies (IMS), 1958-1979, as well as editor for a decade for the Mennonite
Historical Society, he has nursed through to publication about sixty volumes.
He speaks highly of the staff at Herald Press and Faith and Life Press. His
monumental efforts have profoundly enriched the quality and diversity of
Anabaptist-Mennonite studies. However, the price paid has been the defer-
ment of his own writing. He describes several of his experiences as an editor-
publisher-entrepreneur of scholarship:

> Through IMS I convened conferences which often generated manuscripts.
> When, for example, the Mennonite Missionary Study Fellowship (MMSF)
> received good manuscripts, I began publication of an MMSF series with
> the help of Wilbert Shenk. I saw John H. Yoder had a manuscript on
> capital punishment, which led IMS to begin a pamphlet series. The first
> one in that series was Yoder's on capital punishment, later another by
> Gordon Kaufman, and others. Yoder's met an immediate need on Parlia-
> ment Hill in Ottawa, where they were debating capital punishment.
>
> John H. Yoder had written and lectured a great deal but published very
> little. People were asking for his writings. In talking with him and John
> A. Lapp, then secretary of the MCC Peace Section, we went to the
> Schowalter Foundation and asked for a substantial grant. With the grant
> we bought three years half-time of John Yoder's time from Goshen Bibli-
> cal Seminary. It turned out to be four years. Given this time and the
> editorial-logistical support, John and IMS were able to send to the press
> the *Legacy of Michael Sattler, The Original Revolution, Nevertheless,* and
> the *Politics of Jesus* in relatively short order. I began to see that this kind
> of service had great potential for good.
>
> One more illustration among others. Jacob Enz once asked me
> whether I'd ever read Millard Lind's dissertation, adding, "It's a good
> one." I read it and agreed. I asked Millard, who was to go on sabbatical,
> whether he would be interested in revising this twenty-year-old disserta-
> tion. He said he would. So we sent copies of the volume to key Anabap-
> tist and Old Testament scholars and convened a conference with Millard
> to discuss what it would take to bring the book up to date. Then he went
> off to Israel and began researching and writing further. That was the
> genesis of *Yahweh Is a Warrior.*

In addition to all the manuscripts he had edited and published, C. J. has read
many of which have not been accepted and were returned to the authors with
friendly, helpful counsel. C. J. has developed criteria for his work of editing:

> First I ask whether the manuscript contributes anything new that is not
> already known. Then, are the theses advanced tenable, can they be
> sustained? If it is an historical contribution it ought to be based on pri-
> mary documents and then interpretation, not on secondary material.
> There is a considerable difference between a dissertation and a book. It's
> more than just footnotes. It's refocusing your audience from the faculty
> to the general reader. We publish books, not dissertations.
>
> I concern myself with the general structure of a manuscript. Is it con-

ceived broadly or narrowly enough? Does it have adequate context? Are the sources adequate and do they bear out the conclusions? I go back to the sources to verify whether the interpretation has been faithful to the source. Then, of course, there is style, readability, fluency, and good English. I usually read a manuscript very quickly first to get a feel of the language and style and focus. Then I go back and begin work. I leave copy-editing to the copy editors. If you want it rewritten then you send it back for rewriting. Copy editors sometimes set the plow too deeply and then run into trouble because they get into a rewrite job. While there are accepted rules, including Webster's and *The Chicago Manual of Style*, editing is also a question of taste. It may be your way of saying things, and it's as legitimate as my way of saying things.

C. J. considers himself a revisionist historian. He explains: "I don't know of any historian really who isn't. I think a good historian ought to be a revisionist, not deliberately, but simply by doing his/her job well she/he takes a critical look and is bound to come out different than predecessors, or else why write the article or book?" He sees his revisionism illustrated in Anabaptism, for example, as follows:

I see more revolutionary dynamic in Swiss Anabaptism than the Bender school did and see the Grebel group, and Hubmaier, as nonseparatist, actually thinking of forming an Anabaptist state church. I am indebted to the work of Stayer, Snyder, Packull, and others in this, of course, as well as my own. I see a strong dualism in Schleitheim article IV, light and darkness, good and evil, over against Menno's much more modified dualism, cosmic yes, but ethical dualism, much less. Menno had a place for a magistrate being a Christian and a Christian being a magistrate. Early on, Menno even advocated capital punishment. These revisions are based on new documents and research. I would surely be a revisionist in the way I talk about nonviolence in this post-Ghandi and M. L. King era. I would be a revisionist in talking about justice, which is "in" today but which was a bad word for Mennos not long ago.

The three books which C. J. has written for the general reader have sold well: *They Gave Themselves*, an elective quarterly for the Sunday school on stewardship; *Twelve Becoming*, a book of biographies for youth; and "the most rewarding," *An Introduction to Mennonite History*. He conceived of the latter as a book for an inter-Mennonite readership:

I had wanted to do that volume when I first came to Elkhart, but Harold Bender felt we were not ready to write our history together. I picked it up a few years after his death. It became clear to me that if it was to be used by all the different Mennonite groups it should not be written by myself alone. So I drafted the outline and met with key Mennonite historians to critique it. They then were kind enough to "rough in" chapters, and I wrote some. They knew I would be rewriting most of the text for the sake of uniformity and gave me permission to do that. It was published in 1967 and has met a real need in schools and congregations. I revised it in 1981.

As he approaches retirement from teaching, C. J. continues to facilitate the scholarly production of others. He edited volume V of the *Mennonite Encyclopedia* and with others translated and edited the works of Dirk Philips, a volume in The Classics of the Radical Reformation (CRR) series which he edits. In process is a volume which may become his most significant work to date, one which grows out of his popular class on Anabaptist history and theology. Other projects are on the "back burner." And then there is that dissertation written "on the side" during his first years of teaching. "What I really want to do," he says, "is to continue my study of second-generation Dutch Anabaptism. There is a lot of electricity in it: the charisma of the leaders, their teaching devices, their confessions, their catechisms, their hymnody, their martyrologies, their debates both within and without the community." He adds, "This would be paradigmatic for the transmission of faith from any one generation to another. Is there such a thing as a second-generation believers' church?"

His thoughts on the unfinished tasks of Anabaptist-Mennonite studies have been shaped in part by his years of MCC service and his twelve years as executive secretary of the Mennonite World Conference, 1961-1973. His travels to Mennonite centers in South America, Africa, India, Europe, and North America and his meetings with Mennonite leaders from all over the world, he says, "enlarged my worldview immensely." He adds, "The whole story of modern Mennonites globally has been told well in small snatches in the *Mennonite World Handbook*, but it needs to be told fully, including the stories of twentieth-century martyrs in Zaire, Central America, and many other places." He also sees an unfinished agenda in the sixteenth century:

> In the sixteenth century there is a lot of biography that needs doing. Also a lot of theology, like Voolstra in his dissertation on the heavenly-flesh Christology of Menno and Dirk, and John Rempels' on the Lord's Supper. No one has done a sociology of Dutch Anabaptism. That means going from village to village, city to city, and finding the tax rolls, Reformation era records, etc. Very little has been done on worship or economics. The field of Anabaptist studies has not been exhausted. People who are willing to do their linguistic homework beginning with Latin and other languages, like German, French, Dutch and/or Czech, Hungarian, or Polish, have a great opportunity to do further work; it will enlarge and deepen our studies and bring Anabaptism much more into a contextual rather than parochial relationship. Anabaptism is, after all, as fully and legitimately a part of the history of the church as any group is, including Roman Catholicism. It has too often been taken out of that *una sancta* context.

Since 1980, when he took the Anabaptist and Sixteenth Century portfolio on the AMBS faculty, C. J.'s most widely acclaimed course has been Anabaptist History and Theology. It has drawn large enrollments. Of this course he says, "I enjoy doing that course." He explains:

> In part because that is where I am theologically and existentially. That's also where I can potentially help our churches by helping students in their understanding. I have the assignment of time to work more intensely on

this course and offer it annually, even twice a year sometimes. When I approach a large lecture class I don't care much whether they take notes or just sit and listen. What I want to see happen is a kind of "a-hah" experience, a "that's for me" insight. I try to give them what they can't read in any book. This means drawing from a dozen books for any given lecture. Not all of them are in Anabaptism. Last night I drew from the book *The Road Less Traveled* by Scott Peck. It has nothing directly to do with Anabaptism, but with psychiatry. Maybe I never really want to be "pure historian." I guess I'm fairly person-oriented and community- and church- and theology-oriented.

He teaches as he likes to write: "I see the congregation looking over my shoulder. So what does he mean by this statement of Christology, this interpretation of discipleship and nonviolence?" Teaching and writing in the context of congregational awareness and commitment has placed him in great demand as a speaker in the churches. Few seminary professors have been a guest in more congregations than C. J.

These are glimpses, fragments of the C. J. Dyck story, intimations of the complexity and extensiveness, richness and depth, of his life. There is much more fascinating detail to draw from the record. Neither one article nor an entire book could contain the whole of it. One senses that after his early years of wanderings to and fro, C. J. Dyck--a person of many and distinguished gifts-- was led providentially to be a member of that first faculty of the new Associated Mennonite Biblical Seminaries. Indeed, he came to the kingdom for such a time as this.

NOTES

1 The author conducted interviews with Cornelius J. Dyck in his office at Associated Mennonite Biblical Seminaries, Elkhart, Indiana, in three sessions, April 28, 29, and May 2, 1988. The transcripts of the interviews on which this article is based were edited both by the interviewer and interviewee. The complete transcripts may be found in the papers of C. J. Dyck, Associated Mennonite Biblical Seminaries, and Robert Kreider, North Newton, Kans.

Bibliography of the Works of C. J. Dyck

Prepared and edited by Henry Poettcker

When in 1979 C. J. Dyck was being honored for giving leadership to the Institute of Mennonite Studies for twenty-one years, he had prepared a list of fifty publications which he had helped to birth. Some of them he wrote, some of them he edited, and for some of them he served as catalyst and facilitator.

In the intervening ten years that list has grown. In 1979 there was no attempt to be exhaustive. The list was focused on the IMS-related publications. The bibliography which is here presented is much fuller but is also not complete. Thus book reviews, which total four score and more, will not be included. The titles of those may be found in the *Index to Book Reviews in Religion*. These reviews have appeared in such periodicals as *Church History, Dialog, Historische Zeitschrift, Mennonite Quarterly Review, Review of Religious Research, Mennonite Life, Journal of Church and State, The Mennonite*, etc.

Similarly, numerous forewords or introductions written for many books for which C. J. served as mentor or adviser will also not be included here.

Basically there will be eight categories: books written, books edited, articles and chapters in books and periodicals, IMS Faith and Life Pamphlet Series (editor to 1979), IMS Missionary Study Fellowship Series (editor to 1979), IMS Classics of the Radical Reformation Series (CRR) (editor), Studies in Anabaptist and Mennonite History Series (SAMH) (editor to 1988), and Sunday school lesson quarterlies.

C. J.'s pen, typewriter, and now computer, have rarely been idle!

This word about abbreviations: Many of the titles, when listed for the first time, will be spelled out, followed in parentheses by the abbreviations. These abbreviations will then be used in subsequent entries in this bibliography. Further, the two publishing companies Herald Press and Faith and Life Press, after the first listing, will be designated simply by Scottdale and Newton, respectively.

I. Books Written

"Kansas Promotional Activities with Particular Reference to Mennonites." Master's thesis, University of Wichita, 1955.

Mutual Aid in a Changing Economy. Bluffton, Ohio: Association of Mennonite Aid Societies, 1963.

They Gave Themselves. Newton, Kans.: Faith and Life Press, 1964.

An Introduction to Mennonite History. Writer, ed., Scottdale, Pa.: Herald Press, 1967, 1981.

Twelve Becoming: Biographies of Mennonite Disciples. Newton, 1973.

II. Books Edited
A Legacy of Faith. Ed., Newton, 1962.

The Lordship of Christ. Ed., trans., contributor. Elkhart, Ind.: Mennonite World Conference (MWC), 1962.

The Witness of the Holy Spirit. Ed., trans., contributor. Elkhart, Ind.: MWC, 1967.

The Witness of the Holy Spirit: A Study Guide. Ed. Elkhart, Ind.: MWC, 1967.

Jesus Christ Reconciles. Ed., trans., contributor. Elkhart, Ind.: MWC, 1972.

E. G. Kaufman. *General Conference Mennonite Pioneers*. North Newton, Kans.: Bethel College, 1973.

The Mennonite Central Committee Story. Ed., compl.
    Vol. 1. *From the Files of MCC*. Scottdale, 1980.
    Vol. 2. *Responding to Worldwide Needs*. Scottdale, 1980.
    Vol. 3. *Witness and Service in North America*. Scottdale, 1980.
    Vol. 4. *Something Meaningful for God*. Scottdale, 1981.

Willard M. Swartley and Cornelius J. Dyck, eds., *Annotated Bibliography of Mennonite Writings on War and Peace: 1930-1980*. Scottdale, 1987.

Cornelius J. and Wilma L. Dyck, eds., *A Pilgrim People*. Saskatoon, 1987.

Mennonite Encyclopedia, vol. V. Edited by Cornelius J. Dyck with the assistance of Dennis D. Martin. Scottdale, 1990.

III. Articles and Chapters in Books and Periodicals

"Wir besuchen den Chaco." *Mennonitische Rundschau*, July 6, 1949, pp. 1, 4; July 13, 1949, p. 1.

"Unsere mennonitischen Kolonien im Chaco-Paraguay." *Unser Blatt*, Feb. 15,

1950, pp. 2-4.

"The Paraguayan Water Situation." Appendix 4 in *U.S. Operations Mission in Paraguay: The Paraguayan Chaco*, prepared by Wm. E. Bradford et al. Asunción, Paraguay, 1955.

"The Concept of Vocation as Seen through Scriptures and the Anabaptist Tradition." In "The Christian in Business," a report of the General Conference Study Conference held at First Mennonite Church, Hillsboro, Kans., Apr. 15-16, 1955.

"Discipline in the General Conference." In *Proceedings of the Study Conference on the Believers' Church*, held at Mennonite Biblical Seminary, Chicago, Ill., Aug. 23-25, 1955. Newton, Kans.: General Conference Mennonite Church, 1955.

"The Concept of Vocation as Seen through Scriptures and the Anabaptist Tradition." *Mennonite Weekly Review*, June 23, 1955, pp. 10-11.

Biography of Johannes D. Dyck. *Mennnonite Life (ML)*, 11 (1956), 25-28, 80-81.

"The Challenge of Christian Stewardship." *The Mennonite*, Oct. 23, 1956, 672-673.

"Fernheim Colony." In vol. II (1956), 323-325, of the *Mennonite Encyclopedia (ME)*, edited by C. Henry Smith and Harold S. Bender. 4 vols. Scottdale, Pa.: Mennonite Publishing House, 1955-59.

"Menno Colony." *ME* III (1957), 575-576.

"Gemeindezucht in der Allgemeinen Konferenz." *Der Bote*, July 3, 1957, 1; July 10, 1957, 1; July 17, 1957, 1; July 24, 1957, 1; July 31, 1957, 3-4.

"The Christology of Dirk Philips." *Mennonite Quarterly Review (MQR)* 31 (1957), 147-155.

"Love Working Through People" and "Early Ideas of Authority." In *Studies in Church Discipline*, edited by Maynard Shelly. Newton, Kans.: Mennonite Publication Office, 1958.

"Puerto Casado." *ME* IV (1959), 230.

"What Is the Mennonite World Conference?" *Mennonite Observer*, Nov. 10, 1961, 1, 10.

"The Role of Preaching in Anabaptist Tradition." *ML* 17 (1962), 21-26.

"The First Waterlandian Confession of Faith." *MQR* 36 (1962), 5-13.

"The Middelburg Confession of Hans de Ries, 1578." *MQR* 36 (1962), 147-154.

"Harold S. Bender, July 19, 1897 - September 21, 1962." *Brethren Life and Thought* 8 (1963), 9-18.

"Harold S. Bender: The Church Historian." *MQR* 38 (1964), 130-137.

"A Short Confession of Faith...." *MQR* 38 (1964), 5-19.

"From Ignatius to Wyclif." *ML* 19 (1964), 79-83.

"Vatican Council II (1962-65): A Review Article." *MQR* 41 (1967), 167-173.

"The Mennonite World Conference: A Brief Introduction." *MQR* 41 (1967), 277-287.

"The Literature of Vatican Council II: A Bibliographical Commentary." In *American Theological Library Association: Summary of Proceedings*, 1967. Also in *Anglican Theological Review* 49 (1967), 263-280; and *Encounter* 30 (1969), 148-160.

"Bibliography." In *The Concept of the Believers' Church*, edited by James Leo Garrett, Jr. Scottdale, 1968.

"Anabaptism and the Social Order." In *The Impact of the Church Upon Its Culture*, edited by Jerald C. Brauer. Chicago: University of Chicago Press, 1968.

"Angeeignetes Täufertum." *Mennonitische Geschichtsblätter* 28, n.s. 23 (1971), 5-18.

"Die Mennonitenkolonien in Südamerika." In *Die Mennoniten*, edited by Hans-Jürgen Goertz. Stuttgart: Evangelisches Verlagswerk, 1971.

"The Anabaptist Understanding of the Good News." In *Offical Report of the First Asia Mennonite Conference*. Dhamtari, M.P.: Mennonite Church in India, 1972. Also in *Anabaptism and Mission*, edited by Wilbert R. Shenk. Scottdale, 1984.

"The Life of the Spirit in Anabaptism." *MQR* 47 (1973), 309-326.

"Concept of Mission: An Unfinished Task." In *Call to Faithfulness*, edited by

Henry Poettcker and Rudy A. Regehr. Winnipeg: Canadian Mennonite Bible College, 1973.

"Menno Simons" and "Mennonites." *Encyclopedia Britannica,* 1978 ed., XI, 904-907.

"The Place of Tradition in Dutch Anabaptism." *Church History,* 43 (1974), 34-49.

"An Anabaptist Scholar Evaluates John Wesley." In *A Wesleyan-Anabaptist Dialogue on the Nature of the Christian Life,* held at Messiah College, Nov. 11, 1974 (a supplement to the *Evangelical Visitor,* Feb. 10, 1976, pp. 15-20).

"The Scholarly Pilgrimage of Cornelius Krahn." *ML* 32, no. 3 (1977), 11-17.

"1525 Revisited? A Comparison of Anabaptist and Mennonite Brethren Origins." In *Pilgrims and Strangers: Essays in Mennonite Brethren History,* edited by Paul Toews. Fresno: Center for Mennonite Brethren Studies, 1977.

"Hermeneutics and Discipleship." In *De Geest in het Geding,* edited by I. B. Horst et al. Alphen a. d. Rijn: H. D. Tjeenk Willink, 1978. Also in *Essays on Biblical Interpretation,* edited by Willard M. Swartley. Elkhart, Ind.: Institute of Mennonite Studies (IMS), 1984.

"Mennonite World Conference in Review--A Photographic Essay," by Cornelius J. Dyck and Robert S. Kreider. *ML* 33, no. 2 (1978), 4-23.

"History of the Mennonite World Conference." In *Mennonite World Handbook,* edited by Paul N. Kraybill. Lombard, Ill.: MWC, 1978.

"The Believers' Church in Canada: Past." In *The Believers' Church in Canada,* edited by Jarold K. Zeman and Walter Klaassen. Brantford, Ont.: The Baptist Federation of Canada; Winnipeg: Mennonite Central Committee (Canada), 1979.

"Teaching Church History from a Missional Perspective." In *Occasional Papers of the Council of Mennonite Seminaries and Institute of Mennonite Studies,* No. 2, edited by Willard M. Swartley. Elkhart, Ind.: IMS, 1981.

"Hans de Ries (d. 1638) and Socinianism." In *Socinianism and Its Role in the Culture of XVIth to XVIIIth Centuries,* edited by Lech Szczucki. Warsaw: Polish Academy of Sciences, 1983. Also in *Doopsgezinde Bijdragen,* n.s. 8 (1982), 18-32.

"Anabaptist-Mennonite Perspectives." In *Perspectives on the Nurturing of Faith*, edited by Leland harder. Occasional Papers, No. 6. Elkhart, Ind.: IMS, 1983.

"European Mennonite Motivation for Emigration, 1650-1750." *Pennsylvania Mennonite Heritage*, 6 (1983), 2-13.

"Die Anfänge von Germantown in Pennsylvanien." *Mennonitisches Jahrbuch*, 83 (1983), 71-75.

The Brethren Encyclopedia (3 vols.; Philadelphia and Oak Brook, Ill.: The Brethren Encyclopedia, Inc., 1983-84): "Anabaptism," I, 28-29; "Bender, Harold Stauffer," I, 116; "Braght, Tieleman Jansz van," I, 171; "Fast, Henry A.," I, 480; "General Conference Mennonite Church," I, 536; "Menno Simons," "Mennonite Central Committee," "Mennonite Church," "Mennonites," II, 814-16; "Miller, Orie O.," II, 841.

"The Suffering Church in Anabaptism." *MQR* 59 (1985), 5-23.

"Who Are the Mennonites Today?" In *Mennonites and Reformed in Dialogue*, edited by Hans Georg vom Berg et al. Studies from the World Alliance of Reformed Churches, No. 7. Geneva: World Alliance of Reformed Churches; Lombard, Ill.: MWC, 1986.

"Hans de Ries en het erfgoed van Menno Simons." *Doopsgezinde Bijdragen*, n.s. 12-13 (1986-87), 266-283. Also in *MQR* 62 (1988), 401-416.

Encyclopedia of Religion (16 vols.; New York: Macmillan, 1987): "Anabaptism," I, 247-249; "Mennonites," IX, 376-378; "Menno Simons," XIII, 324-325.

Mennonite Encyclopedia V (1990): "Association of Evangelical Mennonites," "Church, Nature of," "Frontier," "Historical Writing," "Liberalism," "Martyrdom, Theology of (bibliography)," "Menno Simons," "Nonconformity," "Pietism," "Social Gospel," "Kenneth G. Bauman," "H. J. Dyck," "John R. Dyck," "C. L. Graber," C. J. Ramer," "Menno Schrag," "In the Name of Christ (feature)," "Joe Walks Along (feature)," "Menno Simons (feature)," "Ngongo David (feature)."

IV. IMS Faith and Life Pamphlet Series (Editor to 1979)

No. 1. John H. Yoder. *The Christian and Capital Punishment*. Newton, 1961.

No. 2. Paul Peachey. *The Church in the City*. Newton, 1963.

No. 3. John H. Yoder. *The Christian Witness to the State*. Newton, 1964.

No. 4. Paul Peachey. *Who Is My Neighbor?* Newton, 1964.

No. 5. Gordon D. Kaufman. *Nonresistance and Responsibility and Other Mennonite Essays*. Newton, 1979.

V. IMS Mennonite Missionary Study Fellowship Series (Editor to 1979)

No. 1. Wilbert R. Shenk, ed. *The Challenge of Church Growth*. Scottdale, 1973.

No. 2. Gottfried Oosterwal. *Modern Messianic Movements*. Scottdale, 1973.

No. 3. Edwin and Irene Weaver. *From Kuku Hill: Among Indigenous Churches in West Africa*. Elkhart, Ind.: IMS, 1975.

No. 4. Wilbert R. Shenk. *Bibliography of Henry Venn's Printed Writings With Index*. Elkhart, Ind.: IMS, 1975.

No. 5. Samuel Escobar and John Driver. *Christian Mission and Social Justice*. Scottdale, 1978.

No. 6. David J. Bosch. *A Spirituality of the Road*. Scottdale, 1979.

No. 7. Robert L. Ramseyer. *Mission and the Peace Witness: The Gospel and Christian Discipleship*. Scottdale, 1979.

VI. IMS Classics of the Radical Reformation Series (CRR) (Editor to 1989)

No. 1. John H. Yoder, ed. and trans. *The Legacy of Michael Sattler*. Scottdale, 1973.

No. 2. William Klassen and Walter Klaassen, eds. and trans. *The Writings of Pilgram Marpeck*. Scottdale, 1978.

No. 3. Walter Klaassen, ed. and trans. *Anabaptism in Outline*. Scottdale, 1981.

No. 4. Leland Harder, ed. *The Sources of Swiss Anabaptism*. Scottdale, 1985.

No. 5. H. Wayne Pipkin and John H. Yoder, eds. and trans. *Balthasar Hubmaier: Theologian of Anabaptism*. Scottdale, 1989.

VII. Studies in Anabaptist and Mennonite History Series (SAMH) (Editor)

Vol. 18. Fred R. Belk. *The Great Trek of the Russian Mennonites to Central Asia, 1880-1884*. Scottdale, 1976.

Vol. 19. Werner O. Packull. *Mysticism and the Early South German-Austrian Anabaptist Movement*. Scottdale, 1977.

Vol. 20. Richard K. MacMaster et al. *Conscience in Crisis: Mennonites and Other Peace Churches in America, 1739-1789: Interpretation and Documents*. Scottdale, 1979.

Vol. 21. Theron F. Schlabach. *Gospel versus Gospel: Mission and the Mennonite Church, 1863-1944*. Scottdale, 1980.

Vol. 22. Calvin Redekop. *Strangers Become Neighbors: Mennonite and Indigenous Relations in the Paraguayan Chaco*. Scottdale, 1980.

Vol. 23. Leonard Gross. *The Golden Years of the Hutterites*. Scottdale, 1980.

Vol. 25. Murray L. Wagner. *Petr Chelcicky: A Radical Separatist in Hussite Bohemia*. Scottdale, 1983.

Vol. 27. C. Arnold Snyder. *The Life and Thought of Michael Sattler*. Scottdale, 1984.

Vol. 29. Daniel Liechty. *Andreas Fischer and the Sabbatarian Anabaptists: An Early Reformation Episode in East Central Europe*. Scottdale, 1988.

VIII. Adult Bible Study Guides
(These were prepared as Sunday school lesson quarterlies, published in Newton by the Board of Education and Publication, General Conference Mennonite Church.)

Mark and *Inspiration from the Psalms*. 2:1963.

The Christian Faces His World. 2:1964.

They Gave Themselves. (Faith and Life Press, 1964)

A Nation United. 2:1965.

The Kingdoms of Israel and Judah. 2:1966.

Acts of the Apostles. 3:1967.

The Story of God and His People. 3:1969.

Studies in Genesis. 3:1970.

The Bible and Church History. 3:1976.

(Published jointly with the Mennonite Church, Scottdale.)

LIST OF CONTRIBUTORS

Stephen B. Boyd, associate professor of religion, Wake Forest University, Winston-Salem, NC 27109.

John Friesen, professor of church history, Canadian Mennonite Bible College, 600 Shaftesbury Blvd., Winnipeg, Man. R3P OM4.

Walter Klaassen, research professor, Conrad Grebel College, The University of Waterloo, Site 12A, C23, R.R. 7, Vernon, B.C. V1T 7Z3.

Robert Kreider, former professor of history, Bluffton and Bethel Colleges, Box 365, North Newton, KS 67117.

Werner O. Packull, associate professor of history, Conrad Grebel College, The University of Waterloo, Waterloo, Ont. N2L 3G6.

Paul Peachey, director, Rolling Ridge Retreat Community, Harpers Ferry, WV 25425.

H. Wayne Pipkin, professor of Anabaptist and sixteenth-century studies, Associated Mennonite Biblical Seminaries, Elkhart, IN 46517-1999.

Henry Poettcker, former president of Mennonite Biblical Seminary, Elkhart, IN 46517-1999.

Edmund Pries, Ph.D. cand., Department of History, The University of Waterloo, Waterloo, Ont. N2L 3G1.

Rodney J. Sawatsky, president, Conrad Grebel College, associate professor of religious studies, Conrad Grebel College, The University of Waterloo, Waterloo, Ont. N2L 3G6.

C. Arnold Synder, associate professor of history, Conrad Grebel College, The University of Waterloo, Waterloo, Ont. N2L 3G6.

Paul Toews, professor of history, Fresno Pacific College, 1717 S. Chestnut Ave., Fresno, CA 93702.

Sjouke Voolstra, professor of theology and Anabaptist-Mennonite studies, The University of Amsterdam. 't Plankenpad 18, 1121 JL Landsmeer, The Netherlands.